CLODIA
of
ROME

CLODIA

of

ROME

CHAMPION
of
THE REPUBLIC

Douglas Boin

W. W. NORTON & COMPANY

Independent Publishers Since 1923

For information about permission to reproduce selections from this book, write to
Permissions, W. W. Norton & Company, Inc., 500 Fifth Avenue, New York, NY 10110

For information about special discounts for bulk purchases, please contact
W. W. Norton Special Sales at specialsales@wwnorton.com or 800-233-4830

Manufacturing by Lakeside Book Company
Production manager: Lauren Abbate

ISBN 978-1-324-03567-1

W. W. Norton & Company, Inc.
500 Fifth Avenue, New York, NY 10110
www.wwnorton.com

W. W. Norton & Company Ltd.
15 Carlisle Street, London W1D 3BS

10 9 8 7 6 5 4 3 2 1

CONTENTS

PREFACE

Sometime during the afternoon of April 4, 56 B.C., after hearing two days of testimony and courtroom arguments, a jury of fifty-one Roman men convened in the center of their ancient capital to deliberate the guilt or innocence of a handsome but inscrutable twenty-six-year-old man, Marcus Caelius Rufus, accused of murder. The trial, which involved the assassination of a visiting foreign dignitary on Italian soil, exposed Rufus's financial troubles and his shady political dealings and became the spring's most notorious court case. As evidence in the trial mounted and the public grew more convinced of the defendant's guilt, Rufus's lawyers, led by the ruthless Cicero, devised a novel defense. Instead of disputing the problematic facts, they launched a personal attack on the prosecution's star witness—a wealthy activist, widow, and the defendant's former lover, named Clodia—gambling that an all-male jury would likely exonerate their client if presented with a more compelling villain: an outspoken woman.

Clodia's decision to deliver the trial's key testimony set her reputation on a collision course with history. Twenty-one centuries later, it has scarcely recovered. Daughter, granddaughter, great-granddaughter of heads of state, widow of an ambitious politician, voice of reason to a quick-tempered sibling, and single mother, Clodia played numerous roles over her four decades in the public eye. But none was more fraught than her performance that April in the murder case against her one-time romantic partner. This book tells Clodia's side of the story.

The extraordinary life of Clodia of Rome offers a fresh perspective on the final years of the Roman Republic, a period of perennial interest to historians and modern political prognosticators. The exploits of Cicero, Caesar, and countless other Roman men hold a stubborn place in accounts of that time, when astronomical levels of new wealth flooded into the city as a result of the republic's many decisive conquests in Asia Minor. Imported silk from the Greek island of Cos, delicate cameo-cut stone tableware from Egypt, private oyster ponds on the Bay of Naples—by the middle of the first century B.C., the republic's elite enjoyed an unparalleled quality of life. New urban investment and neighborhood development lifted the livelihoods of many families.

Behind Clodia's four-decade journey to the center of the story in an ancient courthouse lies an overlooked history about women and power and the radical hope for social change that Clodia's generation saw within their reach. In this age famed for its builders, Clodia dismantled many of her culture's stereotypes about women. In a republic that not only prohibited women from voting or holding elected office but also suppressed the votes of its own progressive citizens, she fought alongside others to expand the rights of like-minded but disenfranchised Italian men. Her moral sensitivity to the existence of the republic's strugglers and strivers, a radical stance for any affluent Roman, left the establishment incensed. Had she lived under the Roman Empire, when empresses were worshipped as gods, her charisma might have earned her the status of a *diva*, the Romans' term for an immortal. Nothing in Rome annoyed a toga-wearing man more than the simple confidence of Clodia's authority.

Born in or around 95 B.C., Clodia came of age surrounded by inescapable signs of privilege. In the days of the Roman Republic, her family's pedigree came as close to the heights of Mount Olympus as any mortal could expect to ascend. Her father was an Appius, descended from an impressive line of senators, statesmen, architects, mathematicians, engineers, and rhetoricians.

Businessmen in Clodia's day still traveled the Via Appia, a highly trafficked road crossing the Italian peninsula named for her fourth-great-grandfather, Appius Claudius. Twenty meters beneath Rome's hills, an aqueduct, the Aqua Appia, engineered by that same distant ancestor, channeled fresh water into the capital. Just as deep in Clodia's veins coursed her own unflagging commitment to justice, economic decency, and increased civic participation. Above all, the family held a steadfast belief in personal agency, as reflected in a saying of Clodia's fourth-great-grandfather Appius that became a popular Latin aphorism: "Everyone crafts his own future."

The gross inequalities of the Roman world tested Clodia early. In what was likely a calculated fit of adolescent rebellion against her father, she changed the spelling of her given name from Claudia. Members of the Roman upper class preferred the lengthier nasal intonation. Clodia's preference lent her name a folksier, more rural sensibility, at least to the ear of Rome's urban sophisticates. With the declaration of her new identity, she asserted her own burgeoning populist ideals. In her youth she saw tyranny descend on the republic in the guise of a constitutional anomaly, the dictator Sulla, then watched as people suffered from his arbitrary application and willful disregard of the rule of law. Spartacus's revolt, an uprising of enslaved people in 73 B.C. that ended with more than six thousand dead, shook the Italian peninsula when she was in her early twenties—an event that would prove to be as destabilizing to her world as any volcanic eruption. Many of these episodes left a mark on her moral character. Decades later, the memory of Spartacus's rebellion lurked behind Clodia's decision to manumit her own slaves.

Clodia's radicalism never quite aligned with her parents' expectations of her. They envisioned their aristocratic daughter as the docile spouse of a future politician. Even when she became a bride, her frankness never fit her culture's image of a demure wife. Well educated, she and her husband, Metellus, kept an address in one of Rome's most exclusive neighborhoods. The couple had a daughter, Metella. When her husband won election as consul—one of the two annually elected magistrates with the authority to call assemblies, set their legislative agendas, and act as the republic's commanders-in-chief—Clodia used her proximity to power to advocate for her own ideals. One year later, aged forty-two or forty-three, he died, almost certainly by natural causes though the circumstances were not recorded.

Due to changing marriage laws in Rome, which permitted a first-century widow to repossess the balance of her dowry, Metellus's death left Clodia with a stable future. Through a technicality in inheritance law, she also likely inherited a substantial portion, if not the entirety, of her husband's estate. To infer from Clodia's accustomed luxuries, the sums must have been staggering. Without any fanfare she had fulfilled the two preconditions that feminist Virginia Woolf would identify as a requirement for a modern woman's emancipation: Along with a "room of one's own," Clodia now had "the right to possess what money [she] earned." Freedom followed.

Eager to forge a new direction for the republic, Clodia used her time, as well as her money, to back her brother Clodius in his successful campaign to become one of the year's ten tribunes, or Protectors of the People. Invested with the authority to reject any legislation adverse to popular interests—a powerful constitutional tool that even the consuls lacked—the tribunes regularly irritated the political establishment. Their ability to halt the legislative process, expressed in the Latin word *veto*, meaning "I forbid it," curtailed the worst of the Senate's clubby decision-making. Together, the siblings, both of whom adopted the unconventional spelling of their names, launched a two-pronged assault against the political and economic inequities of their day. Clodia's profile skyrocketed. During the twelve months leading up to election day, her influence became a topic of gossip. In the twenty-two pieces of surviving Latin correspondence traded that year between two dear friends, Cicero and Atticus, the men consume almost one-quarter of their prose discussing Clodia. Atticus, a wildly successful entrepreneur, cultural ambassador to Greece, and bon vivant famed for his soirées, counted her among his closest connections.

Within two years of her husband's death, Clodia had disregarded all her society's unwritten expectations for wealthy widows. She refrained from rushing into another politically convenient marriage, and she showed no enthusiasm for embracing the role of subservient Roman wife. Her magnetism drew artists, poets, and sizable contingents of men and women into her orbit, where they were graced with her unexpected generosity: luxury vacations to the Bay of Naples, extended stays in the tranquility of her country villa, weekends strolling her gardens on the bank of the Tiber. When romance did strike, it came in the guise of the eager provincial lawyer Marcus Caelius Rufus, thirteen years her junior. Almost overnight, and largely because of her age and gender, the visibility of her surprising new relationship turned Clodia into a political lightning rod. If Helen's face launched a thousand ships, Clodia's "penetrating eyes"—the lone contemporary physical description of her—inflamed a thousand letters: lyrics, love poems, chants from the crowd in the Forum, courthouse speeches, and reams of personal correspondence, none of which unfortunately survives in her hand or even bears her signature. With few exceptions has one individual's visage so loomed, like a silent omniscient character, over the history of a decade, as Clodia's does over Rome during the roaring 60s B.C.

In April 56 B.C., the republic's forces of misogyny and patriarchy took their revenge when the day's preeminent legal mind, Cicero—a rival and sworn enemy of Clodia's brother—used the closing arguments in the spring's most anticipated trial to defame her. The first of his family to be elected to Rome's highest office, a man who had risen from "mouse to millionaire," as the Romans would have phrased it, Cicero had won early acclaim for the integrity of his moral compass, having successfully prosecuted a case of government corruption in Sicily. By 56 B.C., however, a panicked instinct for self-preservation had transformed Rome's formerly beloved rhetorical maestro into a bitter orator, intent on revenge. His desire to protect the status quo led him to oppose any economic and political reformer, like Clodia and her brother, who threatened the authority of the establishment.

Cicero dragged Clodia into a court case against her former lover, who was accused of murdering an Egyptian diplomat. In his defense of his client, he questioned her motivations, impugned her morals, and castigated her for aspiring to an oversized role in Roman political life. In one colorful moment, he and his client branded her a "knockoff Clytemnestra," insinuating that Clodia had killed her husband—an outrageous claim employed to distract the jury from considering the accused man's guilt.

In betting on misogyny, Cicero prevailed. Due largely to his efforts, Clodia became infamous among ancients and moderns alike as a heartbreaker, a home-wrecker, and a high-class harlot, unsubstantiated claims that have been repeated on the thinnest possible evidence. This book rescues Clodia's reputation from the damage it suffered at Cicero's hands.

The premise that an iconic woman occupies a pivotal place in the events that precipitated the fall of the Roman Republic might surprise the modern age, that has come to expect the classical world's starring roles to conform to a predictable set of gendered stereotypes: the heroic general, the visionary statesman, the dashing leading man. Of Plutarch's surviving fifty-two *Lives*, those entertaining profiles of antiquity's preeminent figures which fired Shakespeare's imagination and informed the plots of countless toga-and-sandals dramas, not one foregrounds a woman's experiences. When women appear in ancient historical accounts, they figure obliquely—as goddesses, mythical creatures, or fictional characters—their roles limited to nurturing mothers, loyal wives, or irrational, theatrical monsters, the Clytemnestras and Medeas. When women are bold enough to speak their mind, they are usually described as ahead of their time.

Women throughout history have played the parts of both "originators and inheritors," Virginia Woolf once wrote. Clodia's life illustrates that double role. The beneficiary of centuries of classical progress in women's education and civic engagement, Clodia found her own voice in the middle of the first century B.C., braved the criticism of men, and—despite being excluded from elected office on account of her gender—pressed for urgent reforms to address the fortunes of Rome's most disadvantaged. The humiliation she endured and the silencing she suffered were symbolic of the extreme misogyny that awaited any first-century woman who aspired to public life. But Clodia's radical contributions to history, undertaken in an age when antiquated notions about a woman's role in society looked within reach of being overturned, continue to inspire.

The fifty-one-year-old Clodia, a widow and devoted single mother, died sometime around 44 B.C., largely forgotten by Rome's historians, preoccupied as they were with the rise of a dictator, the collapse of constitutional norms, and the death of their republic. But Clodia's legacy of assertiveness and persistence in the face of men's power remains indisputable. For generations of women, her story would loom as a cautionary tale about the hostility women faced and the resilience they required to overturn the prejudices of their world. A smart, perceptive girl in Rome at the time of the infamous trial, the young and unknown Cleopatra, may have been the first to make the connection. But she would not be the last to carry forward Clodia's example.

PART I

Privilege

CHAPTER ONE

Clodia's Moment

The woman you're reading about possessed an undeniable gift.

—FROM A ROMAN TOMBSTONE

Among the many artworks that populated the ancient city of Rome, one bronze commission attracted attention among the grizzled statesmen and stoic divinities. The incongruity of the statue's placement, not to mention its unexpected subject matter, earned it an impressive thousand years of commentary. It depicted a young Roman girl named Cloelia triumphantly riding on horseback through the city streets. Equestrian monuments in the classical age always turned heads. Generals erected them to commemorate their battlefield valor. Citizens saw, reflected in their polished surfaces, models of selfless civic behavior. Athletic, brave, and crafty, Cloelia's example bested them all.

Kidnapped in a nighttime raid by neighboring Etruscans around the birth of the Roman Republic in 509 B.C., she escaped her captors, dodged enemy javelins, and swam safely south home. As the details of her flight circulated, they set Cloelia's reputation as one of the early republic's most fearless patriots. For ten centuries, almost every Roman found some lesson in Cloelia's "unconventional spirit." For almost the same span of time, her statue stood in the valley that held the city's legal, commercial, and religious center, the Roman Forum, where it stared down the city's stony ring of hills until the backward-looking priorities of a later day toppled it, melted its bronze, and erased every physical trace of her story.

In that same Roman Forum on April 3, 56 B.C., Marcus Caelius Rufus stood trial. Twenty-six, of modest means and notable ambitions, hailing from the unpretentious Italian town of Interamnia, Rufus had come to Rome two years earlier to advance his political career. The trial, which involved charges of sedition and a salacious plot to cover up the crime, was scheduled to feature two days of testimony about Rufus's financial troubles and his shady conspiracies. That spring, it was Rome's most notorious court case. If you liked your public entertainment packed with rhetorical flair and a touch of intellectual panache, few places in the ancient world entertained as well as Rome's Forum.

Notwithstanding the city's otherwise underwhelming appearance—a grimy town of slipshod roads, where scrums of cart and carriage traffic mixed with disorganized masses of pedestrians—Rome in those years had witnessed stunning population growth. During the past decade, the city's census office registered 500,000 new citizens. By the middle of the first century B.C., according to census records, 910,000 citizens of every social class and economic level called the republic's capital their home. A stream of voices and noises filled its streets: carpenters, fish-mongers, stonemasons, cattle wranglers, and every variety of vendors. On any given day, dockworkers offloaded crates and ceramics at the Tiber quay. The majority of the city's workers lived in cramped four- and five-story tenements.

In a city that lacked any stately piazzas, where the use of marble for public or private construction was a rarity, the open pavements of the Forum functioned as the republic's most hallowed political gathering space. Groups of protesting Phrygians from Asia Minor or members of Rome's Jewish community might march outside the courthouses and public buildings while politicians consulted with their concerned constituents on the steps of imposing brick-and-terra-cotta temples. Crowds of commoners, eager for the latest happenings, congregated daily beneath the Forum's central speaker's platform, the rostrum.

"As long as our republic lasts," Romans said, "trials will take place." Every day, the Forum featured a new, intriguing case. Tales of these lurid crimes held Romans enrapt: inheritance disputes, embezzlements of public funds, stolen property, family murder plots. What repeatedly drew Romans to the courthouse, though, was the prospect of an outstanding oratorical performance. Romans set a high value on writing and rhetoric in all aspects of their public life. An important political speech or courthouse presentation might last anywhere from forty minutes to two hours. A dry recitation of facts swayed few listeners. A speaker's worst nightmare was an audience who drifted away.

The best performers conducted symphonies of emotion, a carefully calibrated arrangement of feeling and fact. In the Forum's more packed courthouses, dynamic public speakers composed their opening and closing arguments with colorful characters, sympathetic protagonists, and easily understandable plots to hold their audience's attention. There was little need for heady legal theories or abstract argument when jurors could identify with a victim's plight or associate a name and face with an obvious wrong. Everyone in Rome knew that it took more than a strict adherence to the facts to win a favorable verdict. Yet elocution— a complex recipe of images, vocabulary, delivery, pacing, and the occasional snappy turn of phrase—although widely taught in schools, was rarely mastered.

Incompetence bestowed its own form of entertainment. Amateur speakers did not modulate the volume or the pitch of their voices, arrogance compelling them to pontificate rather than to explore different tonal registers. (In a culture that put a premium on elegance, mere "shouting," Roman critics said, "was for those who refused to speak.") Sloppy lawyers belabored their arguments and, like lazy riders shuffling between two hitching posts, meandered from point A to point B.

Critics published reviews of these disastrous deliveries. Teachers assigned them to students as case studies and warnings. The dim-witted and inept were encouraged to pursue a less pressured line of work than public speaking. Had the aspiring attorney considered the more leisurely life of a poet? Ineptitude produced moments of unintended comedy. Never announce a list of three items, the rhetorical manuals instructed, unless you can remember your third point. The worst speakers in the Forum regularly failed to complete their own trains of thought.

The most eagerly anticipated trial of April 56 B.C. featured a steamy romance, international intrigue, poisoning, multiple murders, and a surprising twist: The prosecution's star witness was a woman.

For most of her adult life, the forty-one-year-old Clodia had been known as Clodia Metelli, "Clodia of Metellus." An elementary construction of the Latin language by which grammarians denoted the concept of possession, the formula rendered a wife dependent on her husband's identity, set expectations for her submission, and served as a reminder of the presumption of a Roman woman's invisibility.

Sexism pervaded the ancient world, although many women found creative ways to circumvent it. The city of Rome was still in its infancy in the seventh century B.C. when the Greek writer Sappho voiced one of the first radical expressions of women's agency in antiquity. "I desire, and I endeavor," she wrote in one surviving scrap of poetry. Rigid social rules separated the Greek house into men's and women's quarters, where wives spun linen and wool fiber into valuable yarn to weave garments for themselves and their husbands. Much of Greek women's work was done quietly, without recognition, and out of the sight of men. Nonetheless, there were exceptions. Three hundred years after Sappho, one Athenian, Nicarete, found a moment of self-expression by echoing Sappho's words. "I worked with my hands. I was a thrifty woman," she declared to those who passed her modest tombstone—one of a sorority of ancient women who, on their graves, boasted of the personal fulfillment they had found in their work as painters, sesame seed vendors, perfume sellers, shoemakers, barbers, and seamstresses. Much later, the Jewish writer Maria authored a highly technical treatise in Greek in which she provided instructions to alchemists for safely bringing chemicals to a boil. The modern laboratory technique Maria described, submerging glass tubes into a hot-water bath, still bears her name: the *bain-marie*.

Like their Roman counterparts, Greek women faced prejudice, discrimination, and misogyny in artistic, philosophical, and political pursuits. "It does women credit to keep quiet," Sophocles's Tecmessa told the audience in a line of dialogue from the play *Ajax*. Set during the bygone era of the Trojan War, the play expressed the pervasive ideology of the playwright's own day. In the stultifying milieu of classical Greece, it was not surprising that even respected intellectuals like Aristotle formulated arguments about women's inferiority, drawn from superficial observations of the animal kingdom. "Except [for] the bear and the leopard, all females are less spirited than the males," Aristotle observed. "Even in the case of cephalopods, when the cuttlefish is struck with [a fisherman's] trident, the male stands by to help the female; but when the male is struck, the female runs away." Pericles, the much-admired Greek statesman who stewarded Athens through its meteoric rise in the fifth century B.C., believed that an Athenian woman's greatest glory was to be "least talked about by men." Yet his own second wife, Aspasia, was the kind of firebrand Clodia would have admired.

Aspasia had come to Athens from Miletus, a cosmopolitan port on the coast of Asia Minor. With a sharp intellect, Aspasia distinguished herself in academic circles, an impressive feat in a Greek city that boasted two prestigious philosophical schools, the Academy and the Lyceum. After Pericles divorced his first wife, he and Aspasia lived together in a civil union approximating marriage. Everything Athenian men were taught to loathe in women, Aspasia embodied. Clever, informed, and engaged, she offered frank opinions about economic inequality and gender inequity and stunned Pericles's peers into silence. With a discerning logic, she rendered the blusterers speechless. Socrates admired her authority. Asked to explain how women might describe the institution of marriage, he deferred to Aspasia's expertise. Adoring students composed their own dialogues, now lost, that featured Aspasia as their central interlocutor. These intellectual exchanges, modeled after Plato's, likely conveyed Aspasia's inimitable and intimidating style of inquiry.

What truly impressed contemporaries, though, was the honest affection between Pericles and Aspasia. Every day before he departed for work in the Athenian agora, Pericles kissed Aspasia goodbye. When he returned at day's end, she greeted him with another kiss. Cynics doubted the authenticity of such love. One of Athens's leading comedic writers, Cratinus, lampooned Aspasia on the stage as a "prostitute past shaming."

Four centuries after Sophocles and Pericles, a similar prudish patriarchy governed Clodia's Rome. The names of men invariably held prominence in myth, history, and law. Under Rome's monarchy, whose founding in 753 B.C. the Romans credited to their legendary first king, Romulus, husband of Rome's first queen, Hersilia, men alone had filled the city's essential civic tasks. They deliberated bills, drafted laws, and advised the king. From the basic noun for father, *pater*, those first Romans derived related verbs—to control, to command, to assert power, to conclude a war, to ratify a treaty. These terms wove the paternalistic ideology of the Roman home into powerful assumptions about who was qualified to lead in public life. Reflections on "virtuous" behavior, in Latin, required claiming one's identity of its root word: *vir*, meaning "a man."

After Rome's leading families expelled the last of the city's kings and established representative government in 509 B.C., the founders of the Republic excluded women from positions of authority. The earliest generation of political leaders saw themselves as their society's "Chosen Fathers"—*Patres Conscripti*, as the men referred to themselves in meetings of the senate and in addresses to the Roman people. Gendered morality was strictly enforced.

A Roman woman in these early years of the republic could find herself subject to divorce if she attended the games without her husband's approval or left home with her head uncovered. Centuries before Clodia's time, a censorious bureaucrat expelled a Roman senator, Manilius, from office on the charge that he had kissed his wife "while their daughter was watching." Among the republic's elite, marriages often lasted only as long as a husband could profit from the arrangement. A wife's infertility or the waning clout of her in-laws was sufficient legal grounds to dissolve a union. A woman was told to relinquish her household keys,

A Roman father dotes on his young toga-wearing son as the boy practices his speaking skills. Roman daughters, relegated to the margins of public life, rarely received attention from artists, biographers, or even their own fathers.

take what remained of her dowry, and return to her father's supervision until her family could identify another groom. (Roman divorcées, especially those from wealthy families, rarely remained unwed.) Divorce gave Roman men an easy exit from their discontent. Death, in a macabre way, offered another. Romans joked about a farmer who mourned each of his seven wives by burying them on his estate: "Nobody gets a better return from his land than you."

Only freeborn male citizens were deemed fit by the constitution to govern the Roman Republic. Since military service, from which women were barred, was a prerequisite for public office, women had no path to elected power. All Roman women were denied the franchise. From an early age, sons and daughters recognized their differing social rules. Parents showered attention on the republic's future "Chosen Fathers."

At birth, every son received a moniker, or *cognomen*, which bestowed on him the personality quirks of his elders: Blind, Handsome, Stutterer, Warty, Cross-Eyed. (The popular Roman name Brutus means "Dim-witted.") The majority of these nicknames, scholars think, were intentionally unflattering. Young men who owned their moral or physical failings developed strong character. The practice, which predominated among elite families, paid dividends in a republic where name recognition increased one's chances at the ballot urn. By one estimate, 70 percent of Rome's elected politicians hailed from households with one previous officeholder. By Clodia's day, sons and grandsons of politicians won election 80 percent of the time. In this context many young men learned to see the charm behind their sobriquets. Storytelling imbued social engagements, business dinners, and gatherings with a boys' club jocularity, which subtly drew attention to their lineage and confirmed their self-perception as the republic's handpicked voices of authority.

Daughters received minimal attention. A Roman girl was usually given a modified version of her father's name; if she had sisters, the addition of a colorless adjective sufficed to distinguish them: First, Second, or Third. Mothers entertained daughters with anodyne dreams of domesticity. The lives of historical figures furnished powerful examples. The biography of Gaia Caecilia, for instance, was a favorite. The wife and mother of well-known politicians and a respected matriarch, Gaia devoted her married life to perfecting the craft of weaving and wool-working while her husband served in public office. After Gaia's death, several of her personal effects—including the dusty distaff and spindle she used at the loom and a worn pair of leather sandals—became precious objects of national lore and were put on display in a temple on Rome's Quirinal Hill. Every woman in Clodia's day could relate some version of her first visit, accompanied by her family, to admire Gaia's treasured relics. The trip to Quirinal Hill taught young girls to aspire to their own life of "domestic tranquility" and to respect the "values of good housekeeping." Or so traditional parents hoped.

A repertoire of similar stories circulated widely in the first century

B.C. and reinforced Rome's conservative values. In one, Lucretia, the wife of a respected politician, is sexually violated by a neighbor and, after painful deliberation, takes her own life so that her husband's reputation remains unblemished. In another, a wealthy Roman's daughter, Virginia, is kidnapped by a lustful suitor before her father can complete the arrangements for her wedding. Virginia submits to death by her father's hand, so that his mastery of the house can remain unquestioned. Preached chastity as a girl and modesty and fidelity as a wife, rarely did a young woman escape constraints on her autonomy. By the time she married, a Roman woman was widely assumed to be untrustworthy when left alone and dangerous should she—like diabolical witches and shady alchemists were said to do—ever congregate with other women behind closed doors.

Only rarely did Rome's women express their disapproval of the inequitable system under which they lived. At the end of the third century B.C., in response to the invasion by Hannibal of Carthage—which was bloodying the southern Italian fields of Apulia and the Tuscan and Umbrian hills, with hundreds of thousands of Roman casualties mounting—the Senate passed Oppius's Law. Sponsored by the eponymous senator, the legislation required Rome's wealthiest women to forfeit most of their savings, minus half an ounce of gold, for the war effort. At a time when wives could supplement their dowries by owning property or investing in a business, the financial penalty was harsh. The law also forbade women to wear expensive clothes or to use a horse and carriage within one mile of the city. After the Second Carthaginian War ended in a treaty, in 202 B.C., women descended on the Senate to demand the law's repeal. They "blockaded every street in the city and every entrance to the Forum," according to Livy's account of the historic episode. Many fathers and sons, he reports, stood supportively beside their wives and mothers.

Alarmed though they were by this manifestation of "female fury" and "womanly rebellion," the Fathers dismissed the women's postwar protestations as a nuisance. The senator and statesman Marcus

Cato, one of that year's two consuls, a man with unassailable conservative credentials and a ferocious defender of the republic's paternalistic ideology, reminded lawmakers that men were not required to listen whenever women marched. He met the moment with derision. "Our ancestors, who required that women conduct all business, public and private, under the supervision of a legal guardian, decreed that they be placed under the authority of their parents, brothers, and husbands," he said. "By clogging our streets, they are persuading us to support their interests. If these women succeed, what will future women attempt? As soon as women become the equals of men, they will have become our masters." The senators took no further action.

Incensed by Cato's response, the protests increased in size and ferocity. Daily, Livy reports, their numbers grew as the city's noblest wives and women from surrounding Italian towns poured into the capital to join the demonstrations outside the Senate building. When the demonstrators took their grievances to the neighborhoods of leading politicians, the majority of the Chosen Fathers relented, much to Cato's chagrin. In 195 B.C., the senate abrogated the law's wartime-era prohibitions. Through the power of their collective voice, women regained their economic freedom—despite being denied the franchise, despite being ineligible for office.

A century and a half later, as Clodia prepared to deliver her testimony, many women of the Roman Republic saw themselves as the inheritors of this multigenerational legacy of activism, civic engagement, and public leadership. The decades following the repeal of Oppius's Law inaugurated a period of important cultural change. These years also brought new freedoms to women.

After the military's annihilation of Carthage in 146 B.C., Rome's generals turned their war machines eastward. Less than a century later, a series of victories in Syria, Asia Minor, and along the southern shore of the Black Sea in the regions of Pontus, Bithynia, and Cilicia brought five new provinces into the republic's possession. A windfall of tax revenue squeezed from the inhabitants of the conquered lands filled the republic's depleted coffers. Long-overdue relief for Rome's poor, destitute, and debt-ridden seemed possible to the day's most ardent economic reformers, men like Clodia's uncles—the fiery Tiberius Gracchus and his equally charismatic brother, Gaius. The brothers fought to improve the fortunes of ordinary Romans before both were killed in the last decades of the second century B.C.: Tiberius by an assassin, Gaius by suicide to avoid an angry mob.

The republic's conquests challenged the parochial worldview of its citizens. In the eastern Mediterranean, elite and non-elite women alike had long enjoyed higher levels of autonomy and greater access to political power than they had in Rome. The lands of ancient Africa, in particular, possessed an impressive legacy of strong womanhood. Fifteen centuries before Clodia, in Egypt, Queen Hatshepsut, regent for an infant Thutmose the Third, adopted a false beard, donned a man's robes, and reigned as pharaoh for twenty years. "My heart turns to and fro, in thinking what will the people say, / They who shall see my monument after years, / And shall speak of what I've done," Hatshepsut reminisced in a text that still decorates the base of one of her obelisks. To Egypt's south, in Nubia, seven generations of women were crowned queen, ruling their land six hundred years before Clodia was born.

Over time, eccentric Greek-speaking royals, who had inherited their kingdoms from Alexander the Great, populated these eastern Mediterranean lands. Like the Macedonian-born Alexander, these new monarchs valued hunting, fighting, and displays of military prowess, pastimes in which women were expected to participate. In Macedonia, young women were often reared to become battlefield mercenaries.

After Alexander's death, this egalitarian sensibility spread throughout his colonial conquests. In Greek-speaking Egypt, women of every social class and economic status began to lend and borrow money. Throughout the kingdom women held sizable farms as investments, leasing their land in exchange for a flow of capital to reinvest. Many women during the third and second centuries B.C. worked alongside men in trades such as Egypt's lucrative textile industry, although, as tax records indicate, women were paid a lower wage. Fathers gave daughters profitable tracts of vines, olives, sycamore trees, vegetables, and grain as wedding gifts. One woman, according to a letter on papyrus unearthed in Philadelphia, Egypt, jointly owned and managed a brewery with her daughter.

Royal women set their own names on Egypt's currency. To benefit the residents of cities wrecked by earthquakes, they often distributed their own largesse. On multiple occasions Greek-speaking queens established and contributed to endowments for marriageable girls who could otherwise not afford dowries. One owned a lucrative shipping line. Another sponsored a racehorse at the popular games; well-trained and well-financed, her team celebrated by taking first prize. Women throughout Greek-speaking Asia Minor enjoyed a similar range of freedoms.

For women of Clodia's grandmother's generation, familiarity with the cultures, customs, and histories of Rome's conquered lands prompted candid discussions about the pace of women's emancipation at home. As more Greek-speaking territories fell into Rome's orbit, it hardly seemed fair that such high levels of personal and economic independence were practiced overseas but not at home. By the second and first centuries B.C., Rome began to loosen its conservative customs. With a change to Roman marriage law, a bride was no longer required to forfeit her dowry to her father after a divorce. In an age when the most expensive bridal gifts reached over a million Roman sesterces, a sum sufficient to purchase a pleasant seaside villa, Roman women achieved greater levels of financial security.

By Clodia's mother's generation, women exercised greater financial influence. If a husband or brother lacked the money needed to launch a political campaign, his wife or sister could provide the funds. A generous wife might use her savings to cover her husband's reckless business speculations or extravagant expenses, rescuing their household from the embarrassment of financial ruin. Socially, women threw open the doors of their homes, hosted salons, and sponsored literary performances. The wealthiest endowed their estates to civic causes.

Yet stubborn prejudices persisted. "For Hercules's sake, never let a woman read any history books," wrote the later poet Juvenal, a master of comedic sexism. "There ought to at least be a few things she doesn't understand." Wordsmithing women who, after consulting the eminent reference work Palaemon's *Grammar*, dared to correct men's sloppy understanding of its rules, were grudgingly recognized by the dons as "good *female* scholars." From wardrobe assistants to bath attendants to teachers, no Roman ever confused an *ornator* with an *ornatrix*, an *unctor* with an *unctrix*, or an *educator* with an *educatrix*. The scrupulous grammatical rules of Latin generated these and other sly insults by assigning gender to every actor and agent.

By Clodia's day, however, women's newfound self-confidence was everywhere, including the Forum, where Roman women not only pressed charges but gave depositions and testified as witnesses. By the first century B.C., it was not unusual to hear a Roman woman arguing a case before a magistrate. The republic never required its litigators to pass a course of accreditation or show proof of professional licensing, the only prerequisite for an appearance in court being the time and financial means to do so. For her own displays of elocution in court, one such litigator, Maesia, earned especially high praise.

Maesia had drawn the Roman public's attention after falling afoul of a mercurial politician. Served with a spiteful lawsuit, she successfully dispensed with the frivolous charges, then built a career by pleading cases on behalf of others. Self-assured and formidable, a woman in an overwhelmingly male-dominated profession, she would address "the great concourse of people" in the Forum and patiently elucidate the details of her clients' cases. Her steely resolve baffled Rome's more bombastic prosecutors. Her quick wit silenced others. An expert advocate, she was nicknamed Androgyny by court-watchers, a paternalistic pat-on-the-back meant to acknowledge, as one Roman writer explained, that "a woman could possess the same intellect as a man." But the notion that a Roman woman might command the regard of a male judge and jury remained a perennial gag. From Titinius's largely lost comedy *The Lady Lawyer*, which scholars have reassembled from a collection of surviving fragments, comes a telling exchange between the unnamed title character and a chaotic courthouse: "Will I never be allowed to speak?"

As Clodia awaited her own highly charged case, she and other women of her generation might have reflected on their many forebears in and outside Rome who had made her own appearance in court possible. Equal standing before the bar, participation in the city's judicial proceedings, and the opportunity for the earnest debate of her own ideas augured well for women's fortunes. Four decades as a champion of progressive values had led her and the republic to this moment. What Clodia likely never predicted was how tragically the course of so much progress would be forestalled one April day.

CHAPTER TWO

Clodia's Roots

How tender her look,
so similar in every way to her mother.

—NOSSIS, DAUGHTER, GRANDDAUGHTER, POET

Everything you needed to know about Clodia's childhood you could gather from her parents' address. The Palatine Hill neighborhood afforded a young girl every possible social and economic advantage. Shaded by soaring cypresses and stone pines, it was as exclusive an abode as any father could hope to provide. Amid these atmospheric surroundings, the hill's brick townhouses offered residents a rare combination of privacy, charm, and an incomparable quality of life.

Row after row of residences belonged to the republic's most well-heeled families: the Aemilii Scaurii, the Fulvii Flacci, the Licini Crassi, the Livii Drusii. Aspiring politicians like Clodia's father, Appius Claudius Pulcher, appreciated the neighborhood's proximity to the Forum, the seat of the Senate and the assemblies and a pleasant stroll down from the family's house. A single square meter of land on Palatine Hill in Appius's day was valued at 1,550 Roman sesterces, the equivalent of eighteen months' wages for an average laborer. The prices for properties ran upward of tens of millions of sesterces.

Inside, Appius surrounded his three sons and three daughters with all the usual trappings of a prosperous Roman family. Only the finest furnishings filled their rooms. On Palatine Hill, imported bronze candelabra, citrus-wood desks, and colorful paintings decorated a master's study and reception hall. Open-air skylights flooded spacious atriums with light, where wives passed their hours at the loom. Slaves fueled the hearths, changed the dishwater, and did the laundry.

Rosters of specialized laborers tended to every master and mistress's pressing need. Water-carriers, goldsmiths, shoemakers, handymen, physicians, caterers, secretaries, scribes, accountants, seamstresses, doormen, bakers, and a masseuse are attested on the grounds of a single Palatine Hill property. The staff included a *tonsor* for the gentleman when he needed a trim and a *tonstrix* for madame. Verdant gardens and private porticos gave children a protected place to run and play. Silversmiths designed and crafted a family's prized dinnerware. Slaves polished it.

In a cramped, crowded, and cacophonous capital devoid of any noticeable mark of urban planning, Palatine Hill offered security, stability, and routine. That, at least, is what Appius and his wife envisioned when their second child and first daughter, Claudia, later Clodia, was born in or around 95 B.C.

Four years later, in 91 B.C., Clodia was not yet five when the murder of Livius Drusus shocked the neighborhood. A patriot, statesman, and vocal proponent of populist causes, Drusus first riled Palatine Hill's conservative sensibilities when he acquired a highly visible plot of land on the hill's northern slope and announced the construction of an unusual mansion. While most Romans opted for dark, cozy, candlelit spaces and tall public rooms awash with natural light, Drusus wanted to expose his new home's interior to passersby. "Whatever I do," he instructed his architects, "should be on view to everyone in the neighborhood"—no small challenge in an age before floor-to-ceiling windows and cantilevered construction. An engineer was required to study the feasibility of erecting a building on the site.

The audaciously egalitarian design fit Drusus's personality. Shortly after his house was completed, perhaps no more than a few years later, Drusus was elected as a tribune, which endeared him to his middle- and lower-class constituents, whose livelihood often depended on policies steered toward economic populism. Drusus began his term with a bold gambit, introducing a bill to extend Roman citizenship to residents of other cities on the Italian peninsula.

Politically, the peninsula looked vastly different during those years, notwithstanding its iconic shape. Geographical, linguistic, and ethnic borders had, centuries before Clodia, created hundreds of local communities: Oscans, Etruscans, Sabines, Umbrians, Ligurians, and more. Not everyone spoke Latin, a language used only in the central region of Latium, where the city of Rome was located. Many populations valued their independence, including the Bretti and the Enotri, who dwelled opposite the island of Sicily, at the peninsula's southernmost point.

The republic's northern border terminated not at the Alps, where it is drawn today, but some 100 to 200 miles to the south, in the valley of the river Po. The longest waterway on the peninsula, flowing west to east, the Po functioned as a vital artery for the cities situated on its banks or along its network of tributaries. It irrigated the agricultural heartland, allowing the cultivation of rice and grains, before disgorging into the Adriatic Sea. Because the course of the river set a useful dividing line, the Roman Republic classified the people who lived north of it—including inhabitants of the cities now known as Milan, Brescia, Modena, and Turin—as foreigners, residents of Cisalpine Gaul, or "Gaul on the near Alps." They held neither Roman citizenship nor the right to vote in the republic's elections.

Drusus's plan to extend citizenship throughout the Italian peninsula represented a stunning but long-overdue act of political generosity. For hundreds of years, many men from these "foreign" regions had fought on the front lines, shoulder to shoulder with Roman soldiers, to defend the peninsula from invasion. In Rome, many believed they deserved the right to participate in assemblies and to vote on legislation.

At the end of the Forum's business day one fall evening in 91 B.C., Livius Drusus was found murdered in the atrium of his eccentric mansion. A shoemaker's knife left at the scene suggested a lower-class assailant and ensured that Drusus's citizenship bill would go nowhere. The shocking act of violence shattered the picture-perfect serenity in which Appius and his wife had hoped to rear their children.

Clodia was still too young to comprehend the ramifications of Drusus's murder, but within days war erupted. The epicenter of the uprising was the village of Ascoli in eastern central Italy, a three-day journey from Rome by horse. Though Ascoli was located south of the river Po, its residents also lacked citizenship and were demanding enfranchisement. In the following weeks, they assembled a confederacy of other aggrieved cities across the peninsula and spearheaded an armed conflict against Rome's patchwork of interests. As more and more individuals picked up swords to fight for the cause of claiming Roman rights, the republic's senators remained intransigent. Days of siege of Roman outposts became months of relentless guerrilla attacks, dragging into three years of conflict and decimating whole regions of the peninsula. An estimated 300,000 soldiers and civilians, both citizens and noncitizen residents of the peninsula, perished during the hostilities, the most deadly civil war then known on Italian soil.

Appius, Gaius, Claudia, Claudia, Claudius, and Claudia came of age just as the Roman Republic almost came to ruin. In 88 B.C., the senators relented and agreed to a truce. The assemblies ratified a version of Drusus's law and awarded citizenship with the franchise to every freeborn male born south of the river Po. Our Clodia turned seven at the war's end.

The colorful pictures on the walls of her parents' home taught Clodia her first civic lessons. Every day, she walked past a portrait gallery of her distinguished ancestors, each of whom had contributed to the rise of the Roman Republic. The walls in Rome's most affluent homes showcased similar displays. Delicately drawn vermilion lines joined impassive, stoic portraits, making it easy to read the names and recognize the faces. The arrangement, Romans said, resembled a tree. Clodia traced hers back to Rome's founding.

Long ago, before the existence of the republic, before the founding

of Rome sometime in the eighth century B.C., the house of Appius's legendary founder, Attius Clausus, dwelled in the bucolic hills northeast
of Rome in the territory of Sabina. Eight hundred years later, no one
in Clodia's day could claim to know for certain how many generations
removed Attius Clausus's time was from their own. But family lore pictured Attius enjoying his uneventful life amid Sabina's rolling fields,
awash with a rippling shimmer of olive trees. Back then, Rome was a
modest city whose origins were clouded in myth. The Romans believed
a fratricidal brother, Romulus, had founded it in 753 B.C. and declared
himself king.

According to later stories, when a dearth of marriageable women
in Rome threatened the survival of its thinning population, Romulus
raided the nearby region of Sabina, kidnapping wives and daughters and
forcing them to submit to new Roman husbands. The Sabines did not
forgive or forget that abduction. Centuries of poets, playwrights, novel-
ists, and artists, from Dante to Rubens to Picasso, would reference and
depict "the rape of the Sabines."

As word trickled up the valley of the Tiber in the sixth century
B.C., 245 years later, that Rome had expelled its last monarch and was
embarking on an experiment in representative, republican government, Attius Clausus packed his belongings onto a cart and traded farm
life in the Sabine hamlet of Regillum—or Inregillum, the sources are
conflicting—for the rapidly growing city. Under its last kings, the former
hamlet on the Tiber had seen an impressive new range of public works.
Monumental temples of extraordinary craftsmanship rose across its
hills. A complex sewer system, which engineers had tunneled beneath
the city, prevented the valleys from flooding. Though suspicious of
Sabine names, Romans received Attius warmly.

In the new republic, a two-tiered legal framework sorted Roman
households by income level into either the plebeian or the patrician class.
By law, only men from the wealthier patrician families were eligible to
hold higher office. In recognition of their public service, these men were
guaranteed a lifetime appointment to the city's chief legislative body,

Whereas most societies in ancient Italy traced lineage through the father's side, Rome's neighbors, the Etruscans, charted family trees through the mother's ancestry, which may explain the prestige afforded to women's burials, like that of Seianti Hanunia Tlesnasa.

the Senate, where they were expected to safeguard the establishment's social, political, and financial interests. The Fathers, duly impressed by Attius's resources, enrolled him among the patricians. Attius increased the return on his landed investments, ingratiated himself into Rome's noble circles, and started a family. During the next decades, the ethnic spelling of Attius's name disappears from historical sources. The household of Appius Claudius, as Clodia's family's distant patriarch came to be known in her Latin tongue, rose to civic prominence.

More than an inspiring origin story, the painting of her family tree inculcated young Clodia with surprising examples of her ancestors' anti-establishment leanings. Attius's own encounters in Rome as an outsider and immigrant contributed at least in part to his family's legacy of unorthodox political views. After his death, as Rome emerged as a hub for Italian trade and with new overseas opportunities abounding for its merchants, plebeians quickly attained income levels equal to or surpassing their patrician peers. Yet the republic's rigid two-tiered system of laws disqualified them from holding office. Decades of reformist wrangling followed until, in the fourth century B.C., senators agreed to implement a series of democratic changes. First, the establishment of a board of elected officials from plebeian stock, the tribunes, redistributed the balance of legislative power between the patricians and the people. Second, a new constitutional mandate stipulated that one of the republic's two annually elected chief executives, the consuls, should hail from a historically disadvantaged background.

Clodia's family participated in the implementation of many of these and subsequent reforms, although, as scholars caution, democratic idealism was not their primary concern, at least not in the family's earliest generations. Pride, self-interest, and a delightful irreverence for authority drove much of their decision-making, rather than a coherent liberal platform. In a republic where relevance equated to power, the Appius family valued the prominence of its own name. These were the years when Clodia's fourth-great-grandfather, Appius Claudius Caecus—his portrait placed near the crown of the family tree—emerged as a leading reformist voice.

If ever there was a moment in young Clodia's childhood when she first understood the weight of her family's activism, it was the day she learned the story of her fourth-great-grandfather. Self-educated in a range of subjects, from engineering to literature to the rudimentary principles of finance, Appius left behind the records of a full and varied life. As an intellectual, he penned a scathing essay, *De Usurpationibus,* in which he chastised rapacious moneylenders who preyed on foreclosures and profited from the financial hardship of ordinary citizens. He balanced the strength of his moral convictions with the occasional light aside, such as when he famously expressed his contempt for the letter z. This novel addition to the Latin alphabet, borrowed from the Greeks, required Romans to bare their teeth in a macabre imitation of "a corpse's smile," a joker-like rictus that Appius found grotesque. His belief that diligence and hard work brought personal satisfaction became the family's unofficial motto.

Outspoken and opinionated, Appius was as civically engaged as his ideas were intellectually quirky. When he announced, in the last decades of the fourth century B.C., that he and a fellow explorer would undertake a search of the Roman countryside to locate a more salubrious source for the city's water supply, most Romans scoffed. Despite their proximity to the Alban Hills, with their rain-fed springs and crystal-clear mountain reserves, Rome's residents happily drew their water from the river Tiber. (Latin poets perennially described it as turbid, colored brownish-yellow by silt.) Few expected Appius's quixotic escapade to succeed.

Appius's geological sleuthing not only identified a source, it culminated in the construction of Rome's first aqueduct, financed and engineered by Appius himself. When it was completed, around 312 B.C., two million gallons of water flowed daily to the city's fountains, basins, cisterns, bathing pools, and bathhouses. To acknowledge his role as co-discoverer, the senate awarded Appius's partner, Gaius Plautius, the *cognomen* Venox, "the Hunter." For his own ingenuity, financial patronage, and scientific contributions, Appius received naming rights to the new monument, the Aqua Appia, in perpetuity. Centuries later, young Clodia and her friends still drank from the waters that her fourth-great-grandfather had supplied for the city.

The episodes in Clodia's family tree touched upon every aspect of Rome's history, geography, and culture. They also guaranteed her an unusually precocious childhood. She learned the names of famous generals and the dates of important battles before beginning her formal education. Years before other children encountered civics lessons in a classroom, Clodia could animate dry, otherwise impersonal chapters of the republic's history by recalling her ancestors' participation in them. Much of the history she and other children learned promoted the self-aggrandizing mythology that was characteristic of the Roman Republic.

The story of fourth-great-grandfather Appius's pivotal role in the war against King Pyrrhus of Epirus illustrated the family's bona fides. Pyrrhus was a formidable warrior who ruled the Greek-speaking lands on the east coast of the Adriatic Sea, opposite the Italian peninsula's southern heel, and he fancied himself the equal of Alexander the Great. When a series of circumstances compelled him to invade the peninsula in the early third century B.C., his act of territorial aggression sparked immediate consternation in Rome.

For centuries a mix of indigenous Lucanians and Samnites, as well as foreign traders including Greeks from Epirus, had lived along the peninsula's southeastern coastline. A strong sense of community pervaded the terrain of Apulia, whose broad plains, prosperous harbors, and sleepy towns overlooked the Adriatic. From Apulia's main port, Brundisium (now known as Brindisi), Italian sailors charted the shortest nautical path across the Adriatic to Epirus. Over time, native traditions and Greek ways, including the use of the Greek alphabet, merged. The Apulian people formed tight-knit communities with a distinct regional patois, suspicious of outsiders, including the Romans. Hostilities erupted in 280 B.C. when disgruntled residents of Tarentum, resentful of the heavy presence of Rome's military, destroyed the Roman fleet.

Pyrrhus, who had long dreamed of possessing Apulia's fertile fields, capitalized on Tarentum's discontent by announcing that he would defend the villagers against any retaliation from Rome. When word of Pyrrhus's intentions reached the Senate, it ignited a partisan debate over the proper level of response. If the king succeeded in annexing Apulia, the move would threaten Rome's interests in the southern part of the peninsula, not to mention adversely affect the quality of life for residents of the region, some of whom held Roman citizenship and were expecting the republic's aid. While Rome dithered, Pyrrhus, gambling that the Romans would not wage war to defend interests so deep in the south, attacked.

Towns were already besieged and crucial ports taken when Appius rose in the Senate and rallied the republic to the defense of the peninsula. No second-rate Macedonian monarch, Appius insinuated, should be permitted to invade without a punishing response. It was the republic's destiny, Appius said, to control the entire peninsula. This rousing speech convinced the Senate to deploy troops. Battles raged for months across the plains of Apulia, with heavy loss of life. Though he had bested the Romans in a series of campaigns, Pyrrhus withdrew after five years due to unsustainable levels of casualties—thus begetting the phrase "a Pyrrhic victory." With Pyrrhus's departure, the republic realized Appius's vision of domination: Its territory now stretched from Etruria, north of Rome, to the southernmost shores of the Italian peninsula.

Clodia's fourth-great-grandfather, the preeminent statesman of his day, whose aqueduct had already made him a household name, would forever be associated with fortitude in the face of Pyrrhus's aggression and resilience in a time of crisis. Schoolchildren in Clodia's day were instructed to memorize the text of his memorable address, which was included in the standard Latin grammar books. Later, the first Latin epic poet, Ennius, who chose as his subject Rome's unexpected rise from obscure beginnings, reworked Appius's speech into a musical performance.

> APPIUS: Minds that once did stand strong and straight,
>   What madness bends them from wonted ways?

By the time teachers assigned it to boys at school, Clodia could likely recite it from memory.

The chapter in her fourth-great-grandfather's biography that likely left the most powerful impression on young Clodia, though, was his vision for a vast new highway that would cut across central and southern Italy, easing travel from and to the capital. For all his accomplishments as a statesman and orator, this was arguably Appius's greatest legacy, as radical in its intent as it was practical in its application.

Appius never had the satisfaction of seeing the final volcanic paver set in the 364-mile road stretching from Rome to Brundisium. Ground was broken on the ambitious project during the last decades of the fourth century B.C.; it involved untold numbers of laborers, huge costs, and took about 120 years to complete. But a good-sized segment—Rome to Capua, one-third of the total distance—opened in Appius's lifetime. Capua was a major stopping point for travelers to and from the Bay of Naples. Appius lived to see the project dedicated to him: Via Appia, the Appian Way. The "Queen of Roads," as the Romans later styled it, sent pleasure-seeking Romans to the welcome sun and leisurely tempo of life on the Neapolitan shore and onward to its nearby islands—such as Ischia, well regarded for its thermal springs—and brought to Rome new citizens and eager voters. Their presence incensed the political establishment.

Every year, multiple political vacancies had to be filled to ensure the basic functioning of the Roman Republic. By the time of Clodia's childhood, in the first decades of the first century B.C., some forty-odd of these open positions were filled by election. Roman law barred incumbents from serving successive terms; outgoing officeholders were required to wait ten years before declaring their next electoral campaign. These term limits ensured that every year, the republic saw a new and capable crop of city managers, judges, treasurers, and tribunes, not to mention the republic's two consuls. With no public financing of elections available, however, victors usually came from the same select group. Men who could afford the weeks and months of self-financed campaigning, including politicking, dining, and travel, usually won.

Voting was of paramount importance in the Roman Republic but came with significant limitations on any one individual's ballot preference. In place of classical Athens's democratic principle of one person, one vote (restricted to freeborn men), Rome's Fathers instituted a system of representative democracy, directing civic participation toward assemblies of electors—one term for "assembly," in Latin, being *collegium*, or "college." With the creation of an electoral college, the Fathers aspired to build a firewall against the spread of popular sentiment. Should any policy or candidate prove especially favorable to the people's interests or be manifestly opposed by the elite, the electoral college system would render the popular will impossible to implement.

The mathematical formula that guided Rome's voting rules tilted the result of every election in the establishment's favor. In the republic's two main assemblies, the Comitia Curiata and the Comitia Tributa,

A formidable intellectual authority among her peers in 1950s Italy, the American historian Lily Ross Taylor (right) produced scholarship that exposed the dark history of disenfranchisement in the ancient Roman republic's voting practices.

electors gathered to deliberate bills and to elect the next year's office-holders. In the Comitia Curiata, 193 voting blocs, each corresponding to subtle grades of financial status, determined the proportional strength of a male citizen's vote. Measures only moved forward if they received a majority of the assembly's electoral votes.

By design, the republic operated on the dubious moral principle that the most financially privileged should be heard first. Seventy of these blocs represented citizens of the highest income level. Lower-income electors cast their ballots last, after the outcome of the election had already been decided. Just as at the racetrack, where a runner might obtain a competitive advantage by sneaking a foot over the starting line, the patricians' head-start in the assembly ensured that their interests prevailed.

A slightly different scheme to manipulate the democratic process operated in the Comitia Tributa. Here, citizens also voted on bills and candidates standing for election to second-tier city services, such as city manager or treasurer, or to the board of tribunes. Voting blocs were arranged according to place of residency in electoral districts, which the Romans called "tribes." If modern politics has earned a reputation for being "tribal," the blame lies with ancient Rome. As essential to civic identity as one's legal name, one's voting district was assigned at birth, followed one into adulthood, and remained with one's family in perpetuity. A Roman's electoral district determined when he might be summoned for jury duty, as well as how and where he paid taxes. Freeborn citizens with the right to vote included their electoral district after their signatures in a handy three-letter abbreviation, which was required on all legal documents and official transactions.

When the republic was founded, the city of Rome was divided into four electoral districts. Two held residents of conspicuously high income levels: Clodia's own Palatine neighborhood, PAL., and Collina, COL. The two remaining were traditionally categorized as representing the poorer folk: Esquilina, ESQ., and Suburbana, SUB. Over time, as the republic's territorial reach expanded, the number of districts in this electoral college increased. In one half century alone, twelve new voting districts were added to the electoral map, six within a frenzied period of thirty-three years of conquest. By the time of the citizenship war, the republic boasted thirty-five districts, each carrying a single electoral vote. Victory in the electoral college required a simple majority: eighteen.

At the outbreak of the citizenship war, in 91 B.C., the system was riddled with inequities. For decades, as the republic grew, the Fathers drew new electoral districts in contorted shapes to ensure that like-minded constituencies voted in unison. The broader aim was to draw districts so that they contained a large number of one's supporters and relegated the political opposition to less competitive ones. By Clodia's day, the republic's electoral map resembled nothing so much as a haphazardly arranged, vermiculated mosaic floor. To a Latin speaker, for whom *ver-*

mis meant "worm," the maps looked "worm-eaten." Today, this process is called gerrymandering.

If a new citizen aspired to hold office, the census director would assign him a primary residence in the countryside so that his vote would align with the interests of his neighbors, powerful men with landed wealth. Having a voting residence within the city became unappealing and déclassé. The partitioning of the peninsula's hills and valleys into this patchwork of highly irregular shapes remained an effective practice of voter suppression throughout the early republic until fourth-great-grandfather Appius's radical proposal to build a road.

Appius had witnessed firsthand how conservatives used the ancient equivalent of gerrymandering to stifle the electoral power of Rome's freed slaves. Well provisioned with gifts from their masters, many formerly enslaved men possessed sizable fortunes. The entrepreneurial ones launched lucrative careers, amassing even more wealth in trades that Rome's elite considered vulgar: shipping, trading, and importing and exporting sundry goods such as ivory, silk, and spices. Those who were politically engaged expected to participate in the electoral process. Since no source of wealth rankled the Fathers more than new money and no political agenda frightened them more than that of a former slave, the senators perennially ordered the census director to assign freed slaves to the four voting districts of the capital. There, the new voters were technically given a representative voice in the government while the thirty-one rural districts remained in genteel hands.

Enraged that the lopsided interests of the countryside set the policy agenda for the city, Appius strove to address the electoral logjam. As census director, he implemented a voting rights package that registered the newly freed slaves among the republic's rural voting districts. Then, because Roman law required voters to cast their ballots in person, Appius announced investment in the Via Appia, the road project, that would literally pave the way for Rome's expanded electorate.

The backlash was swift. According to gossip, Appius entered and exited theatrical shows through the actors' curtains to avoid heckling from his conservative peers. Upon his retirement, his reforms were canceled. Freed slaves were removed from the rural districts and their votes reapportioned to the urban ones, where the republic's fuzzy electoral accounting could diminish their collective voice. Appius died before his expansive vision for civic participation could change the balance of the political landscape in the republic.

These issues remained stubbornly unresolved at the time of Clodia's childhood, right down to the outbreak of the civil war that concluded when she was seven. The conflict, in hindsight, must have seemed inevitable to every Roman adult. Nearly every generation in Clodia's family tree, since the time of her fourth-great-grandfather, had tried and failed to implement a similar set of electoral reforms that would have expanded rights across the peninsula and increased the political power of new voters in Rome. Yet time and again, as reformers shepherded a new voting rights bill through the assemblies, the forces of the establishment would watch, wait, and prevail in repealing it. Clodia's great-grandfather Gaius Claudius, feeling the constant whiplash of these partisan duels, marshaled his family's history of eloquence when, in the second century B.C., he memorably addressed the Senate. His speech, recorded by Livy, offered a dire prediction:

> If a census director can arbitrarily change a Roman citizen's voting district, what's to stop our government from removing a man from the census records entirely—in effect, stripping a citizen and a free person of his right to exercise the power of his vote? We are approaching a frightening scenario, my fellow Romans, where I can foresee the public conversation will be not where certain men should register to vote but whether certain men should be allowed to vote.

Little wonder, two generations later, that the residents of the town of Ascoli assembled a coalition to wage war in pursuit of the franchise.

The Senate's practice, dating back multiple generations by then, was to refuse these rights until violence became the only tactic left.

Whether seven-year-old Clodia grasped every detail of this history, the portraits on the walls of her childhood home reinforced a powerful story: of a republic beset from its beginning by glaring injustices that Clodia's ancestors had fought to correct—until circumstances abruptly compelled her father to steer the family's legacy in a radical new direction.

CHAPTER THREE

Clodia's Education

Into the deep wave
from madcap-bound white horses, you leapt.
"I'll catch you," I cried, "my friend."

—ERINNA, *THE YARN*

S ometime on or around November 3, 82 B.C., the year Clodia celebrated her thirteenth birthday, the text of a chilling announcement was disseminated throughout Rome on wooden placards and papyrus handbills.

TO BE SOLD AT PUBLIC AUCTION!

THE PROPERTY OF ALL POLITICAL ENEMIES—

BOTH

THOSE WHO HAVE RECENTLY BEEN PROSCRIBED

AND

THOSE PREVIOUSLY APPREHENDED IN ENEMY ITALIAN TOWNS

WHO HAVE ALREADY BEEN PUT TO DEATH.

Along with its ominous tone, the notice contained one Latin vocabulary word, *proscriptus*, "proscribed," which would have tested the comprehension of even advanced students in Clodia's grammar classes. A legal term, it was synonymous with "public enemy."

For those who lacked basic literacy, ancient Rome was a confusing cityscape of unreadable placards, unintelligible abbreviations, and miles of meaningless gravestones. That number has been estimated at 90 percent of the population in Clodia's day. Boys and girls from Rome's wealthier homes started their lessons early. Wax tablets, a stylus, and fine sets of ivory plaques painted with the twenty-three characters of the Latin alphabet afforded young girls like Clodia invaluable practice with their ABCs. It was a proud moment when a well-to-do Roman matron could boast to family, friends, and neighbors that their child "knew her letters."

Clodia's education sheltered her during these tumultuous years, as signs and flyers throughout the republic announced the hunt for political outlaws. The rigorous assignments and voluminous exercises that constituted her early education in reading and composition occupied most of her adolescence. Regular lessons also set her intellectually miles ahead of the average Roman thirteen-year-old. And her experience departed radically from the conservative classical curriculum.

As recently as Clodia's grandfather's day, classrooms were informal gatherings that served an exclusively male student body. Charismatic male teachers delivered their lessons in the shade of the city's sycamores. Studious boys listened attentively while mischievous ones rubbed olive oil in their eyes to blur their vision and escape the demands of having to read aloud. By Clodia's adolescence, there were upward of twenty private schools in the city and, more importantly, a revolutionary educational spirit in the air. For wealthy parents of this later day, reading, writing, and arithmetic were nonnegotiable foundations, regardless of a child's gender.

The open-minded approach to education at the time of Clodia's youth shines through the published writings of the intellectual Musonius Rufus. Writer, philosopher, and pacesetter in ancient educational theory, Musonius rose to prominence with radical ideas about pedagogy, which he disseminated from his classroom podium. Admirers transcribed his lectures and preserved some of their surprising titles: "Why Roman Daughters Should Receive the Same Education as Sons" and "Why Roman Women Should Also Study Philosophy." Each class critiqued the Romans' uncritical assumptions about the supposedly different abilities of boys and girls.

Whereas classroom curmudgeons had once restricted Greek language lessons to boys—a knowledge of Homer's Greek, the language of international diplomacy, was widely seen as a useful tongue for galli-vanting Romans, while its grammatical complexities were considered to be wasted on girls—Musonius pushed for broader, more equitable access to foreign languages. Young girls could no longer be expected to thrive on the consumption of childish romances and saccharine love poetry. Musonius encouraged a new generation of teachers to expand their reading lists. His essays, bringing a strong tonic to the academy's stuffy ways, challenged the sensibilities of Roman parents, too.

Musonius observed that both young men and women under his tute-lage demonstrated significant personal and emotional growth when exposed to a course of exacting intellectual work. The fields of Latin and Greek philosophy and rhetoric, in particular, he argued, equipped students' minds with the tools of critical thinking. Languages and lit-erature nudged students toward maturity into thoughtful, engaged citi-zens. They taught young minds to be more confident and self-aware, to value reason and evidence-based arguments, and to seek justice in their civic engagements, the sine qua non of classical education for the devel-opment of responsible adults.

What distinguished Musonius among educators was his belief that both boys and girls would benefit from an early investment in a human-istic education—especially, Musonius underscored, "if we are finally to move beyond the idea that Roman women are inferior to chickens and other birds since it is well known that even birds fight beasts larger than themselves to defend their nestlings." A love of reading empowered girls to trust in the courage of their convictions, which meant they would "never be intimidated by a man simply because he might boast a noble birth or hail from a politically powerful family or possess extraordinary wealth, not even if he swaggers through the city acting like a tyrant."

Unevenly adopted by later Roman society, Musonius's manifestos injected a much-needed dose of radical thinking into the staid world of classical education. Convention can hardly capture the general feel of this milieu. Primary and secondary school, in antiquity—which is to say, grammar lessons followed by rhetorical instruction—was the exclusive

purview of families who could afford to pay the tens of thousands of sesterces that private teachers demanded. Yet even in the first century B.C.,
the core of Musonius's ideas about equity in gender, if not yet extended to
economic class, was taking root in the Palatine Hill neighborhood, where
it was not uncommon to hear women boasting of descent from three generations of educated foremothers. Grandmothers, wives, and aunts were
unabashed lovers "of literature and extensive learning," the "attainments"
of which were "not hard to come by" in families of financial means who
lived in such a privileged enclave. On Palatine Hill, already before Clodia's time, a young girl might greet her father, returning from war, with a
warm embrace and an impromptu recitation from Homer's *Iliad*.

Conservative responses to these changing trends in women's education were derogatory and patronizing. In the mind of a conservative
father, a well-educated daughter represented a dead-end investment.
Only if a wife could balance a family's finances during her husband's
absences might there be a genuine benefit to a woman's learning. A
daughter's personal fulfillment or intellectual satisfaction rarely crossed
most Roman fathers' minds.

For more broad-minded parents, like Clodia's, the challenge was how
to navigate, if not circumvent, the biases that young girls still encountered in the Roman curriculum.

Originally designed exclusively to prepare young men for careers in
public service, the two-sequence Roman educational system featured
a set of canonical texts and was organized into lessons intended to
ensure that students learned to act, sound, and comport themselves in
one manner, namely, as men. Students were expected to write mono-
logues in which they impersonated widely regarded historical figures, the great generals and revered statesmen of the past. Divergent
traits in rebellious or nonconforming boys were identified by teachers,
quickly shamed, and publicly demeaned. Boys who spoke in "musical
voices" were encouraged to tone down their "higher vocal pitch"; traits
and behaviors deemed too effeminate for the Fathers' sensibilities were
repeatedly suppressed.

Harsh, humiliating evaluations relied on two-dimensional views of gendered behavior. "If you're auditioning for musical theater," one instructor told his male pupil during a disappointing poetry recitation, "you show a lack of talent. But if that's your voice and you are honestly trying to read the text I assigned you, and not sing it, there's no need to go any further. I've heard enough." Critiques and notes that the modern era would condemn as bigoted and discriminatory passed in the Roman classroom for acceptable pedagogy and were thought to produce morally excellent young men. Textbooks underlined this pervasive ideology:

> When a young man should breathe, at what point he should introduce a pause into his delivery, where the sense ends or begins, at what point his voice should be raised or lowered, where he should increase or slacken the pace of his delivery or when to speak with greater or lesser energy: To accomplish all these things effectively, a young man must first understand what he is reading. But to do that, he must first learn how to make his voice sound virile.

Only a style deemed *virilis* communicated "dignity and charm." What was pleasing in the classroom, in effect, came down to a judgment about a student's masculinity. From this stultifying milieu, even the most sensitive acquired the beginnings of a lifelong casual misogyny. To receive adequate recognition for one's work, only manliness would do.

Women's experiences were not only omitted from classrooms but disparaged in the standard curriculum. Misogynistic plots, characters, and themes that alienated young girls were common. The first four books of Homer's *Odyssey*—the earliest piece of ancient Greek literature and a perennial favorite among classical audiences, who enjoyed its artfully composed epic lines—describe the directionless adolescence of Odysseus's son, Telemachus, whose emotional maturity as the young man of the home has been stunted by his father's unexplained ten-year absence. When his mother, Penelope, requests the household's musicians to strum a less painful tune than the usual one, telling of the fall of Troy, her son erupts, indignant at his mother's unjustified assertion of domestic authority. "Go to your chamber, and busy yourself with your woman's tasks, the loom and the yarn," Telemachus says. "Speech will be for men." Homer's contemporary Hesiod voiced a similar judgment in his moralizing tale about Pandora's Jar. With a "bitch's mind and thieving heart," women wove "lies and tricky speeches"—no wonder, he continued, articulating a popular worldview, that the primordial origins of evil lay with women. Every boy and girl internalized that myth from an early age.

By Clodia's adolescence, however, there was no shortage of women who were willing to read with a young girl and to introduce her to more positive literary role models. The only trick was getting one's hands on suitable scrolls. The works of the "Tenth Muse," Homer and Hesiod's contemporary Sappho, the much-heralded, mysterious pioneer of women's love poetry, were widely popular. So, too, were Sappho's many overlooked, unsung successors. By one count, the texts of fifty-five Greek and Latin women authors have been identified in the corpus of writings from the ancient world, their works spanning a thousand years. Pythagorean philosophers, early practitioners of the scientific method, scholars devoted to historical inquiry, love poets, composers of bawdy lyrics: The range of women's literary work dazzles. Time has given much of it the unfortunate appearance of Sappho's own poetry: An isolated word survives here, an elliptical line of verse there.

Yet women figured among classical antiquity's most impressive literary stylists. They delighted in unusual combinations of genre, toyed with their audience's expectations of simple metrical poetic expression, and dabbled in the sort of formal experimentalism that, two thousand years later, would have outpaced even the most zealous postmodern artist. Their exuberance gave rise to identifiable schools and clever techniques that bore their names, such as the jazzy dactylic line the Praxilleion, named for the fifth-century B.C. Praxilla's distinctive beats. Men scoffed and claimed there was nothing new in this work, but women writers continued to innovate. To the perennially exhausted topics of war and seafaring, they brought original, daring points of view. "Rest here, my murderous spear, and no longer / From your bronze claw drip the dark blood of enemies," the fourth-century B.C. Anyte wrote in her direct address to the equipment of battle. She achieved lasting fame with an avant-garde collection, *The Lilies*, comprising occasional verses delivered by personified animals (a goat), insects (a locust), and an abandoned fishing vessel beached on a lonely sandbar ("No longer exulting in the swimming sea / Will I toss up my neck, rising from the depths"). Little more than a handful of these verses survive, but luck, matched with dogged scholarship, sometimes still hits treasure.

In 1928, Egyptian laborers, working with a team of foreign academics, lifted a scrap of papyrus from the desert sands, holding on its reedy surface fifty-four previously unknown lines of poetry by the fourth-century B.C. poet Erinna. Written in hexameter, Homer's meter, the Greek verses were attributed to Erinna's widely acclaimed masterwork *The Distaff*. (The metaphor of the poem's title, which refers to a wool-worker's spindle, might be better translated as *The Yarn*.) A touching vignette about the zigzagging path that the friendship of two young girls takes over the course of two decades, *The Yarn* was justly celebrated among ancient audiences for having disrupted stereotypical images of the daily drudge of a woman's life—full of domestic chores, with hours spent at the loom. In their place it offered a powerful narrative about the milestones in a one girl's adolescence, the importance of her friendships, and the prospect of a marriage that loomed as an end to the pleasant independence of her youth.

Erinna's poem begins with the memory of how she and her childhood friend Bauchis filled their afternoons with the popular game of Tortoise in the atriums of their families' homes. "When you were Tortoise / out you ran leaping through the yard of the great court." The game required its young participants to sit patiently in a circle until the chosen leader selected one at random ("Tortoise!") and a chase ensued, rewarding the players with an excuse to howl and scream. After these carefree years of youth comes Erinna's lament to lost time: the recollections of innocent and occasionally not-so-innocent hours spent in the company of Bauchis's family until "towards dawn your / Mother who allotted wool to her attendant work-women came / and called you to help with the salted meat." The two young girls evinced, at least to their parents, little concern for the complexities of adulthood, telling bedtime stories about a four-legged beast, "the monster Mormo," with "massive ears," whose face disrupted both their dreams. "We clung to our dolls in our chambers when we were girls, playing Young Wives, without a care."

At the climax of the narrative, nineteen-year-old Erinna realizes she is about to lose the joyful presence of her friend to the institution of marriage. The separation not only overwhelms her but prompts an honest reflection on the twists and turns of the girls' friendship over the years, one that refuses to suppress any notes of bitterness, abandonment, or accusation. "Aphrodite filled your thoughts with forgetting," Erinna says, deeply wounded by the path that has pulled the two friends in separate directions. What follows is the real tragedy of the poem: Bauchis's untimely passing.

An evocative portrait of two girls' dear friendship and the agonizing transition of adolescence—requiring these young women to leave behind the freedoms of horseback riding and foolish pranks and grabbing each other's horses by the reins—*The Yarn* is ultimately the heartfelt cry of a girl struggling to hold onto the life of her lost friend.

In 82 B.C., when Clodia reached thirteen and the disturbing handbills calling for the arrest of public outlaws were papered across her city, she, too, had to leave behind the freedoms of an untroubled childhood and face the complications of adulthood. A series of events that unleashed a political maelstrom also poisoned Clodia's relationship with her father.

⋙

The author of the handbills was Lucius Cornelius Sulla, a politician senior to Clodia's father by about eight years. During the civil war, he had fought as a soldier to impose Rome's law and order across the peninsula and to deny the disenfranchised Italians' demands for justice. Elected consul at the war's end, he sought to repeal the law granting voting rights to the republic's newest citizens—the linchpin of the truce. Uncompromising politics spawned Sulla's authoritarian ambitions. In the 80s B.C. he embraced political violence.

No politician in these years could boast a record untarnished by brutality. By the century's turn, Romans had seen political assassination and vengeful public killings become all too common. Even the most well-regarded reformers had complicated histories, a predictable outcome of the day's growing partisan rancor. Yet Sulla stunned Romans with his uniquely fiery brand of strongman politics. Among the city's religious leaders, talk was already circulating about the coming of "a man of exceptional moral disposition, of rare courage and surpassing appearance, who would take the government in hand and free Rome from its present troubles." Many Romans expected a messiah-like figure to liberate their republic from the tyranny of its perennially dysfunctional assemblies and its year-in, year-out bickering. This prophecy, purposefully vague but also expressive of the flights of fancy that were a hallmark of the Romans' paganism, drew upon the widespread belief that there was a fixed number of cycles in the history of the world—eight ages of humankind, by one popular count—whose beginnings and ends were secretly known to the gods. A government-appointed board of priests, called the Board of Fifteen, was charged with determining the rhythm of these cycles. For "whenever the circuit of a former age concludes," Romans explained, "some marvelous sign will appear, on earth or in the heavens, so that it instantly becomes apparent to the initiated that a new order of the ages has dawned." Devout believers identified Sulla with this long-heralded savior, an unusual role for a boy from troubled beginnings who had shown little interest in politics.

After losing his father in his teens, Sulla and his mother faced years of financial want and emotional distress. Forced to sell her deceased husband's villa, she moved her son into a rental property where space was cramped, the lighting poor, and amenities nonexistent—kitchenette, yes;

running water, no. It was here that a fatherless Sulla learned firsthand the Roman stigma associated with poverty. In ancient Rome, wealth was interpreted as a measure of one's accomplishments and a pledge of one's moral fitness to participate in civic life. The lack of it earned the establishment's scorn.

To escape the hardship, young Sulla fashioned a new persona. He struck his father from memory and invented his own origin story. He downplayed, forgot, or outright omitted names that had once decorated his family tree and spent days and nights, Plutarch later said, cavorting with "actors and buffoons." It's not difficult to hear, behind Plutarch's account, the men of Sulla's father's generation lamenting the wayward youth's squandered potential. Sulla's fortunes changed overnight upon the death of his father's affluent first wife, Sulla's mysterious step-mother. After her funeral, the woman's estate lawyers contacted Sulla and informed him that, because she had loved Sulla "as her own son," he stood to receive a substantial inheritance.

Sulla knew, from the hard-luck years of his youth, that Rome's repub-lic rarely amplified the voices, let alone the savings accounts, of its aver-age citizens. Sulla put his newfound money to immediate use. Speaking to impoverished butchers, bakers, and barmen, Sulla built a constitu-ency of the aggrieved. The ranks of his supporters swelled when he promised members of the establishment that he, too, opposed any plan to offer Roman citizenship to the residents of cities and towns across the Italian peninsula. Any increase in the number of voters threatened native Romans' hold on their own republic, or so it was believed.

Sulla stormed the city's public forums, delivered tirades that preyed on anti-immigrant sentiment, and whipped up a xenophobia that lurks behind the off-color humor of so much first-century B.C. Latin poetry. "Stingy Umbrians," "stout Tuscans," and "saw-toothed Lanuvians" were its regular punchlines. Preying on a fear of immigrants likely helped win Sulla election to consul. He was joined in office that year by a docile colleague, a relative by marriage.

None of the sources for this period of history offer a straightforward picture of what happened next. A scholar from Alexandria in Egypt, Appian, writing a century and a half after Sulla's death, spun vivid narratives of the 80s B.C. as a bloody prelude to the end of the republic. Only some of his details are verifiable. Moralizing and tongue-clucking over Sulla's behavior shaped both Plutarch's later biography and the narrative of Cassius Dio, who wrote in the third century A.D., when Sulla's name already counted as ancient history.

As Sulla's term of office opened, the most urgent task was to draw a new electoral map and to distribute the newly enfranchised Romans among the republic's thirty-five districts. In a painstakingly bureaucratic effort, municipality by municipality, family name by family name, the city's census officers would be required to review each new citizen's property qualifications and confirm their primary residence. Then, census officers would assign them to the appropriate voting bloc in the upper assembly and to one of the thirty-five electoral districts in the lower assembly. Since Sulla's archconservative coalition opposed an equitable distribution of the voters—an arrangement that would upset their domination of the electoral college—they announced a plan to assign all the newly enfranchised to the four urban districts, diluting their voting power so that they would be citizens in name only and stripping from them any ability to speak with one voice.

To circumvent the approaching political disaster, one of the year's tribunes, Sulpicius, devised a compromise package. An unflagging populist and suffragist, Sulpicius enlisted one of the republic's most respected statesmen, the seventy-year-old general and éminence grise Gaius Marius, to endorse the plan for full enfranchisement for the Italians. If Marius would shepherd the law's passage through the Senate and the assemblies, Sulpicius promised to use his authority to appoint Marius supreme commander of the armed forces in the Black Sea against King Mithridates. Fantasies of conquering the eastern kingdom and returning to Rome with mounds of gold and silver counted among every soldier's wildest dreams.

By the middle of the year of Sulla's term, while Sulla was away from the capital in the south, Sulpicius brought this liberal voting rights package to debate. Marius marshaled his supporters, former soldiers and political allies, to pressure recalcitrant senators to support the bill. Sources report clashes outside the Senate House and violence in the streets. The voting rights measure carried. Sulpicius, true to his promise, appointed Marius supreme commander of the east.

The news stunned Sulla. Standard government protocol was that an outgoing chief executive would be awarded the next year's most lucrative military assignment. From his position in the south, Sulla summoned an armed band of loyalists, marched them toward Rome, and in 88 B.C. besieged the capital. The assault on Rome by a Roman citizen, to exact retribution for a vote that he had lost, represented a stunning breakdown of the civic order. With his loyalists' swords drawn, Sulla forced the senators to declare Sulpicius and Marius enemies of the state. Then, threatening further violence, Sulla canceled the new voting rights law and claimed the Black Sea assignment. Marius escaped to Africa. Sulpicius was murdered. For six years, shocked by Sulla's brazen repudiation of the law, all Rome stood on edge.

Public discourse devolved into a cycle of recrimination as Sulpicius's supporters clamored for justice, which never came. No doubt Clodia's parents wanted their daughter to spend these fraught years as involved in her studies as possible.

By 83 B.C., Clodia's father, Appius, was nearing his forty-second birthday, the age at which a free Roman man became eligible for the city's highest office, consul. But Sulla's return from the east that year portended frightening implications for domestic politics. The situation forced Appius to rethink his own ambitions and values. Romans knew they had to thwart Sulla's second act in order to protect their republic. Patriots assembled a makeshift militia to oppose Sulla's return. But on November 1, 82 B.C., they lost that battle. At Rome's eastern perimeter, the Colline Gate, Sulla and his soldiers met, then routed, the forces of the resistance. One of the year's two consuls, Marius the younger, son of the popular opposition leader of the same name and embodiment of his father's selfless civic ideals, fought bravely to defend the republic. ("Rest is impossible for one who fears the lion's return to his intended prey," the elder statesman had once remarked.) He took his own life after failing to halt Sulla's siege.

Two days later, November 3, Sulla's posters went up on the walls across the city, and Appius's political dreams went up in smoke.

By the end of the first week of November, eighty men were declared public outlaws. Among them was the second of the two consuls, Papirius Carbo, who was later arrested and murdered. The families of all outlaws, living and future, were banned from ever holding office. Daily, bounty hunters brought severed heads to the Forum to verify the faces of the deceased against Sulla's published lists. They murdered first and sought confirmation later.

After the first round of executions, two hundred more names were added as a second political purge. One man was shocked to find his name "proscribed" not because of his political views but because he owned coveted property in the Alban Hills. Euphemism sanitized the worst of the horrors. Those who went to meet their unjust deaths, Sulla said, "were receiving correction." Even Sulla's own cadre of murderers, Plutarch wrote, understood that "the size of a man's house, the luxuriousness of his gardens, or the exorbitant cost of his water installations signed the death warrant." From these years Sulla earned his reputation as Rome's "ill-omened Romulus." What Sulla achieved by the end of 82 B.C. he did, one scholar writes, with "unrestrained atrocities, brutal force, and sheer terror."

With his arbitrary application of the rule of law and his efforts to turn neighbors against one another for his own political and financial gain, Sulla brought the republic to an existential brink not seen in its first four centuries. Deploying a combination of arcane legal maneuvering and his own loyalists' enthusiasm for political change, Sulla had himself declared *Dictator Legibus Scribundis et Rei Publicae Constituendae*, Dictator for Drafting Legislation and Reorganizing the Constitution of the Republic. While Romans had always allowed the temporary appointment of an emergency executive during outbreaks of instability, Sulla's title broke all precedent. With its capacious powers, the office was to be held indefinitely. That so much anti-republican sentiment took hold in less than a decade suggests that greed, extreme self-interest, and a hostility to compromise were less exclusively Sulla's failings than they were symptoms of a widespread civic breakdown. Ordinary Romans, mid-level officials, and spineless senators played their part in this great unraveling.

Sulla changed the constitution to prevent legislation from being initiated in the popular assembly. No law could be ratified unless it originated in the upper assembly, whose electoral college, weighted toward the wealthy, would predetermine an outcome in Sulla's favor. "No legislative question," Appian reported of the time, "should ever again be brought before the people which the Senate has not previously considered first." The dictatorship gave Sulla's executive orders the force of law.

These were the months when restless children on Palatine Hill were hustled away from the adults' conversations. Nervous parents sent them to play in the secluded gardens behind their homes. Even among trusted friends, people spoke guardedly. Front doors were bolted shut. Neighbor turned against neighbor, loyalties were questioned, acquaintances scrutinized. Sulla's own family shamelessly profited from the revolution. His daughter, who purchased an elegant mansion in Naples from one of her father's enemies, acquired the property at the scandalously low price of 75,000 sesterces. When she sold it on to one of Sulla's associates, the price was 10 million sesterces, a 13,000 percent markup.

⋊⟴

Even the fanciest, most expensive education could not protect Appius, Clodia's father, from the pervasive moral rot. In 80 B.C., intent on being elected consul, Appius bowed to political pressure, condoned Sulla's autocratic behavior, and sought his endorsement.

It's hard to hear at a distance of twenty-one centuries the sound of a townhouse's cedarwood bedroom doors slamming shut during a family row. (Pliny knew that cedar, treated with a resin released during the production of olive oil, prevented mold and decay during the wet winter months, so it was likely the material of choice.) But from fifteen-year-old Clodia's perspective, her noble father's decision to countenance Sulla's violence must have constituted something of a seismic shock.

On January 1, 79 B.C., Clodia's father became the next man in the illustrious house of Appius to be inaugurated as one of Rome's two consuls. Sulla retired that same year to his mansion on the Bay of Naples, where he occupied himself with his memoirs and left others to clean up the remains of a tattered republic. Among the families he had outlawed, whose heirs had been declared ineligible for elected office, fierce resentment festered and brewed. Questions of how to enfranchise the new Italians remained, a decade later, unresolved.

Clodia's father's year in the consul's chair passed uneventfully. Sulla spent the next months focused on his writing by day and by night behaving in an undignified manner that "disgraced his years." Plutarch calls him a charlatan who had "dishonored his high office" and "neglected much that required attention." When Sulla died the year after Appius's consulship, six thousand sympathizers poured into the Forum to celebrate the onetime dictator's life and deeds. Awakening from this political nightmare, Clodia's family had, just barely, survived.

CHAPTER FOUR

Clodia's Path

Love the brave, and keep away from cowards
since from cowards the return is small.

—PRAXILLA, POET AND LYRICIST

For Clodia's three brothers, Appius Junior, Gaius, and Clodius, the end of adolescence meant the arrival of a required period of military service, followed by apprenticeships in the Forum to improve their oratory and rhetoric in the service of the law. With the right mix of timing and good fortune, they would see the beginnings of a promising public career, the kind every accomplished Roman father dreamed of for his son. For Clodia and her younger sisters, their teenage years came with the appointment of a conservator. An adult male guardian registered with the state, the conservator was authorized to make all personal, legal, and financial decisions for the young woman under his protectorship. Though similar requirements were lifted for Roman boys upon their fourteenth birthday, the law decreed that women have a conservator indefinitely because, according to the Fathers, they lacked the intellectual acuity and emotional judgment to make informed decisions on their own behalf.

At the root of the sexist law lay the Romans' purposeful ignorance of trends in Mediterranean science and biology, particularly as they pertained to matters of women's health. Sophisticated accounts of the physical and emotional changes that overcame young girls in their second decade eluded most of classical antiquity's leading medical minds. Starting in the fifth century B.C., the Greek physician Hippocrates of Athens and his students compiled a set of teachings based on the bizarre assumption that the onset of puberty in young women was a condition of imbalanced humors, unregulated body temperature, and wandering organs, like the womb, whose movements inside a girl's body were presumed to require immediate medical attention. The Hippocratic School's influential approach to medicine and physiology coalesced around their teacher's crude ideas. After the conquest of Greece in the second century B.C., practitioners of Hippocratic medicine flourished in Rome.

In more established cities—those with stronger library collections, more advanced research institutions, and well-funded academies, like the ancient world's intellectual epicenter, the library of Alexandria in Egypt—scholars pursued daring new scientific horizons. When, in the second and first centuries B.C., dissection of human cadavers emerged in Alexandria as the gold standard for anatomical investigation, the breakthrough demonstrated that the differing signs of puberty in boys and girls were a natural step in a human's process of biological maturation, not an ailment specific to the lives of young females.

In Clodia's Rome, a scientific backwater whose populace resisted the latest intellectual advances and whose politicians expressed open contempt for the highbrow ways of worldly Alexandria, many of these groundbreaking discoveries would remain inaccessible, unknown, or underappreciated for centuries. During that time, most of Rome's Fathers preferred to rely upon a combination of guesswork and their own ill-informed understanding of biology, physiology, and anatomy to make pronouncements about women's bodies. Conveniently, their misinformed opinions fit their paternalistic ideology. From Clodia's day into the Roman Empire and on to the Middle Ages, Rome's libraries brimmed with shelves of medical advice whose intellectual foundations were outdated even by the standards of the premodern world. Chief among the popular authorities were Rufus of Ephesus, author of a widely consulted treatise on diet and exercise, and the slightly later Soranus, author of *The Gynecology*, an encyclopedic survey of topics related to women's reproductive health.

The regimes that medical writers prescribed taught Roman parents to treat their adolescent daughters as little more than future child-bearing wives. Told to extract natural medicines from widely available plants, such as laurel leaves and the bulbs of the squill, a Mediterranean coastal lily, families taught young women to adopt highly unusual personal hygiene routines to prepare for childbirth—instructing them, for example, to fumigate their bodies using a range of therapeutic pastes, powders, and concoctions. Physical activity was encouraged during this important second decade of young women's lives since, as Hippocratic doctors believed, movement regulated a girl's fluctuating temperature and stabilized her internal organs. Doctors trained in the tenets of Hippocratic medicine diagnosed most of the ailments of ancient women as the result of a wandering womb. By Clodia's day, the ubiquity of such questionable scientific authorities exacerbated a belief that women suffered from a general "feebleness of the mind," what the Romans termed *imbecillitas*.

Not every health recommendation involved quackery. Rufus of Ephesus encouraged hikes, modest runs, and bouts of tumbling in the dust and dirt. Demanding activities like chorus work, which involved both dance and vocals, repaid "double the health benefit," he explained with unusual foresight. Young girls with an aptitude for athletics were encouraged to practice their throwing, provided that, as Rufus cautioned in *A Regimen for Young Girls*, the physical act did not appear strained or ungainly. For "while there is a demonstrated value in exercises that warm up the body, when a young woman exerts herself, she should always take care not to seem too manly." On more than one occasion, antiquity's gendered norms proved too intractable to break. The gradual consumption of wine properly diluted with water, an essential step in a young Roman man's social formation, was strictly forbidden to young Roman women.

Only one exception existed for a woman who aspired to reach adulthood without the assignation of a legal guardian. Young girls who entered the service of the goddess Vesta and completed a thirty-year term of virginity were, upon completion of their religious duties, released from the requirement of conservatorship. Every year, these

six celibate priestesses kindled the Eternal Flame, presided over circus races and games on religious holidays, and ground and mashed the
sacred cornmeal cakes that were a mainstay of Rome's many religious
rituals. The tight knit sorority of two novices, two junior priestesses,
and two seniors, each pair representing a distinct decade in a woman's
lifespan, lived in a shared house in the Forum.

Young girls who expressed interest in the religious order of the Vestal Virgins, or whose families encouraged their daughters to consider
it, were required to affirm that both their parents were alive, that there
was no record of divorce on either their mother's or father's side, and
that during their three-decade appointment they would renounce all
sexual activity. Women who were admitted into the prestigious order
earned a state-funded salary. Many important families believed it was
in their family's interests to encourage at least one of their daughters to
enlist, as Vestals held an omnipresent role in public affairs and developed social connections with leading government officials.

Former Vestals acquired not only the ability to inherit property but to
draft their own wills and to dispose of their financial holdings on their
own terms. Some former Vestals recalled their years of sisterhood with
such fondness that after leaving the order they made the unusual choice
to live as independent women, neither taking nor seeking a husband.

Clodia, by the time she reached seventeen, around 78 B.C., faced a
much more conventional future: a politically convenient marriage,
followed by multiple pregnancies and decades of motherhood. These
familiar milestones would arrive in quick succession, as recognizable as
Clodia's own reflection in the polished surface of a favorite hand mirror,
a cherished part of every noble woman's trousseau.*

Wool-working would occupy the remainder of Clodia's days. Occasions for self-fulfillment were rare and only modestly rewarding, but

* With etchings of the Muses, the Graces, the Gorgons, and other goddesses, the accessories often featured racy allusions to classical myth. Athena's innocent attempt to learn
the flute, in one story, for example, earns a knowing reprimand from a watchful satyr,
who judges the position of the goddess's unpracticed lips unbecoming to a divinity.

Ubiquitous in the bedrooms of a Roman home, mirrors counted among a wealthy Roman woman's treasured possessions. This elegant silver handheld Roman mirror is inscribed with the name of its otherwise unknown owner, Iris.

they did exist. Like Mrs. Dalloway, the fictional character who visits the florist and picks her centerpieces to claim a modicum of independence, in Roman society there were women like Pomponia, Clodia's contemporary and sister of Atticus, who made it known to her household on the eve of her husband's important business luncheon that she preferred to set the menu herself. Putting the finishing touches on the home and its décor was a Roman wife's prerogative.

Urbane, well connected, and exorbitantly rich, the twenty-three-year-old arch-conservative Quintus Caecilius Metellus Celer offered, to Appius's pragmatic sensibilities, an ideal husband for Clodia and a smart financial arrangement between their two families. Appius's future son-in-law boasted deep roots in the republic and a family tree with its own full canopy of illustrious ancestors. After a relative led a troop of elephants through the city in a memorable military parade in the third century B.C., the Metellus family had embraced the animal as an unofficial badge. They wove it into their clothing, painted it on the sides of their carriages, and in so doing anticipated the designs of later medieval heraldry. Powerful, intimidating, and combative, the elephant fixed the strength of the Metellus name in the mind of the electorate. Among Metellus's family there were six consuls, four appointments as census director, and numerous victory parades. Raised to run roughshod over their opponents, the young men who bore the Metellus name were eager defenders of the Fathers' most traditionalist ideals. A typical to-do list for a Metellus boy read like a world-conquering manifesto:

> [Be] a first-class warrior, the best public speaker, the bravest general, do the greatest deeds under [your] own command, hold the highest offices, be of outstanding wisdom, be considered the most distinguished senator, obtain great wealth in an honorable way, leave many children, and be the most preeminent man in the republic.

Winning became their family's birthright, dominance in every arena of Roman life the anticipated outcome for its prized sons, an egotistical creed unlikely to have been lost on a wary young Clodia. The antiquated men in Metellus's family publicly demeaned their wives as trifling "annoyances," burdensome appendages to their self-important husbands' careers.

An elite wedding in the city of Rome promised to be a storybook affair, a grand celebration in front of family and friends, especially when it united two households of such dignity and wealth. The bride's glowing orange-red veil, her crown of marjoram, an exquisitely woven fine white dress, and a self-assured groom are not hard to imagine. Less clear are the circumstances surrounding Clodia's engagement, which can be plausibly dated to around 76 B.C. On average, thirteen, not seventeen, marked the age at which a Roman father gave away his daughter's hand in marriage. In Clodia's case, the curious departure from standard practice has led to speculation. Might Appius have delayed her marriage because he lacked the wherewithal to offer an appropriate dowry? If it's true that Appius's funds were tight, this would have been a sudden reversal for a man who, with Sulla's imprimatur, had likely realized sizable gains during his time as consul, when real estate profiteering was rampant and brazen property confiscations widely condoned. And yet, given how Sulla's terror had filled the coffers of many up-and-coming families and augmented the reserves of well-established ones, it's also hard to imagine that, in such a shamelessly selfish age, Clodia's father's account books showed a deficit. The likelier explanation is that Appius, as penny-pinching parents were known to do, simply bemoaned the costs that were required to secure his daughter's marriage. Even affluent fathers insisted upon a payment plan for dowries, more so when they knew their future sons-in-law hailed from ungodly levels of wealth, as Metellus did.

Settling on an auspicious date for the wedding ceremony was many a Roman bride and groom's first quarrel. Entirely out of question were the months of February and May, when the Romans organized citywide picnics at the tombs of their departed family members. The month of March was largely eliminated, too, since the thought of celebrating a marriage during a season dedicated to the belligerent Mars, the god of war, sat uncomfortably with most Roman brides. The celebration of the foundation of the city of Rome occurred on April 21. A multiweek harvest festival occupied mid-August. The riotous Saturnalia holiday concluded the year in December. Almost by a process of elimination, the Roman consensus for wedding planning settled on June.

Relocation, a Roman woman's first change of address from her childhood bedroom, inaugurated a young bride's new life. An investment property on Palatine Hill, Clodia and Metellus's new home counted among Appius's most generous wedding presents. The land alone was estimated to be worth millions of sesterces, and it was held in Clodia's name. Instructed by their fathers to be fanatical stewards of their dowries and inheritances, Roman wives were expected to manage these real estate holdings in trust for sons and grandsons and pledge that any proceeds derived from their sale would remain within the family line. Ancient marriage contracts explicitly stipulated that any property or monies belonging to a Roman wife's family prior to marriage devolved, at her husband's death or divorce, to her. Parents, facing the sudden reality of empty homes, adapted in creative ways. Clodia's father, in the months prior to his daughter's wedding, had arranged for an extended government appointment in Macedonia. Appius's looming absence might have offered father and daughter an excuse to smooth out any of the lingering tensions arising from his betrayal of the family's long history of activism.

When the scions of two distinguished Roman families merged, cartloads of belongings accompanied their move. Rugs were unfurled to warm damp interiors and soften the herringbone brick or tiled floors. Crates of dishes needed unpacking, ceramic for everyday use and silver for special occasions. Wardrobes of nicely woven wool togas followed for him, cupboards of fine silk gowns for her. Old-fashioned newlyweds assembled a miniature bed in the front room of their house as a symbolic profession of their fidelity. The slog of examining their combined possessions, arranging their furniture, and ornamenting their rooms transformed the raw space into a comfortable home. Slaves tackled the more arduous labor.

No set of heirlooms was more priceless than Clodia and Metellus's collections of ancestral portraits. These waxen masks, the pressed faces of their deceased family members, figured among any newlywed couple's most meaningful possessions. Molded during the deceased's lifetime, the masks were costly, impossible to replace, and handed down from one generation to the next. Centuries of smoke and incense settled in their porous surfaces. Romans described them as exuding a ghostly glow, as if they were *vividus*, "animated." Time transformed them into relics. Some were hundreds of years old, invested with a household's history and memories. They were stored in protective cupboards and brought out during funerals.

Clodia and Metellus would need their ancestors' masks sooner than they expected.

Stationed on the Roman borderlands in Macedonia in 76 B.C., Clodia's father had accepted a senatorial assignment to train a class of counter-insurgent rebels to quell unrest among the local Thracian tribes. State-sponsored appointments like these usually lasted twelve months. The mandate and title varied according to the republic's needs: governor, field general, aide-de-camp. Ruthless ambition remained a constant, the task being "to impose the customs of peace" on local populations. Appius's predecessors had levied taxes, extorted from rich and poor, and filled their personal coffers with provincial excess. Some postings, like Thrace, northeast of the Greek peninsula, bounded to the east by the Black Sea, and south of the Danube River, were active theaters of war.

Roman writers depicted the region's inhabitants as bloodthirsty savages. Men and women, they said, drank from human skulls "still dripping with blood and covered with hair, whose inner cavities were bedaubed with brain matter badly scooped out." Thrace was notorious for raising defiant warriors. During the past decade, the territory, a mix of rugged mountains and invting plains, had witnessed a steady series of dangerous incursions from an aggressive Black Sea monarch, Mithridates. With his daring European military designs, not seen since the likes of bygone Persian kings, Mithridates hoped to stymie the Roman Republic's eastward military expansion. According to one scholar's reconstruction, a resourceful, largely unknown twenty-year-old Thracian warrior, Spartacus, may have been among Appius's most talented crop of local recruits. Clodia's father, fifty-three, never returned home. He died at the Thracian border. If the later sources are accurate, the cause of death was disease, a common malady on Rome's frontiers.

Word of their patriarch's passing sent Appius's six children scrambling. By custom, it would have fallen to Clodia to arrange a dignified funeral, worthy of the Appius name. In Rome, though an eldest son inherited the authority of the paterfamilias upon his father's death, an eldest daughter assumed the logistics for her father's memorial. Celebrating an eminent life required attention to extraordinary levels of detail. Not only would Clodia's father's body need to be washed, dressed, and laid out in his home, where it would be presented for extended family and clients in Appius's best clothes, custom dictated that the memorial of every Roman grandee include a funeral cortege and a public eulogy. Days of planning and collaboration were required to strike the appropriately somber tone. Hundreds would witness it in the Forum.

The weight of the moment left no room for improvisation. Many Roman households redoubled their family's good name by staging a respectful funeral. "By sharing memories of their dearly departed," the ancient writer Polybius explained to his Greek readers, "the Romans bestow an immortal quality on the reputations of their most high-accomplished family members. In this way, their own loved one's full and rich lives become lasting examples for other citizens." In Clodia's Rome, it was not uncommon for strangers to gather at the rostrum to listen to a young son's moving reflections on his father's life and, afterward, to accompany the mourners on their solemn procession to the family tomb. Unlike Rome's poorest, whose bodies were deposited in a common graveyard, an insalubrious place on the Esquiline Hill where corpses decomposed and formed loose mounds of "death-white bones," men of Appius's stature were interred in impressive, multigenerational mausoleums. A bystander's expression of sympathy at the tomb might spawn, weeks later, an unexpected business partnership with the heirs.

In her role as coordinator, it fell to nineteen-year-old Clodia, with her sisters' assistance, to plan the sequence of events for the day. Her father's memory, even as a recent partisan of Sulla, demanded an appropriate level of decorum. The funeral cortege, specifically—what the Romans called a *pompa*, a "theatrical parade"—was an opportunity to reintroduce to the wider public the most notable figures of the family tree. A wealthy family's beeswax masks were an essential prop in staging these performances of grief. Troupes of actors, suitable in height and weight to play the roles of Appius's many ancestors, had to be solicited, auditioned, and hired. Accompanying them would be professional musicians and vocalists, including women from Rome's local funeral society, who were skilled at singing dirges and marketed their services. At home, there would be costumes to sew and gowns to stitch for the participants of every age who would march in the ceremony. The siblings had to honor their father's legacy by projecting a persona of honesty and humility, rather than narcissism and hubris, in the eulogy that Clodia's youngest brother, sixteen-year-old Clodius, would deliver from the rostrum. (Eulogies were thought best delivered by adolescents because they could not yet run for office. Romans were contemptuous of those who exploited a solemn funeral for vulgar personal gain.) The speech had to be drafted, redrafted, and rehearsed if any of the Appius men aspired to have a political future.

Later in life, Clodia would earn a reputation as an "expert storyteller" and "author of compelling dramas." If that source can be trusted and its testimony applied to the year 76 B.C., there is reason to think that stage-managing Appius's funeral gave Clodia valuable experience as a communicator. To redeem the life of a complicated public figure, a father who had compromised generations of populist principles to remain relevant during an age of rising authoritarianism, required significant dexterity, emotional as well as intellectual. Appius's choices had ensured a future for his sons. The relief that Appius Junior is reported to have felt once the funeral expenses were settled was no doubt shared by Clodia when the last of her father's mourners offered their condolences and departed her father's grave. The stillness that followed, for Clodia, invited reflection on her own life's direction.

"What is the point of all these family trees, glutted with their masks?" the Latin poet Juvenal asked, in a later, scathing satire on the Romans' fixation on aristocratic status. An anonymous eulogist who lived closer to Clodia's time posed a similar question: "What can such precious relics possibly avail a man whose own life is crumbling to pieces?" Honor, nobility, dignity, and self-worth: The force of these ideals, the Romans understood, arose from the values one professed and the life one lived, not from the privilege one carried. For Clodia, both her father's death and the memory of a name from her father's past clarified her own path to adulthood.

In 73 B.C., a slave uprising shook the otherwise quietly industrious southern city of Capua. The terror of learning that men and women escaped their servile bonds, which had occurred twice in Sicily in recent memory, pushed Roman writers to hyperbolic heights of panic. Roman officials regularly equated the suppression of revolt with the eradication of infectious disease. The leader and mastermind of the Capua rebellion, which lasted two years and at its height encompassed some hundreds of rebels, of slave and freeborn status alike, was none other than the Thracian soldier and onetime exemplary Roman military recruit, Spartacus.

In the weeks and months after Appius's death, local slave hunters, a ruthless lot who scavenged Mediterranean lands to rake up foreign-born prisoners to sell at auction, had captured and imprisoned the twenty-something Spartacus. Because he lacked the protections of a Roman citizen, which would have guaranteed him an appeal to have his case adjudicated before a magistrate, the Thracian was shackled and loaded on a ship to Rome. Every day, the republic's military and its slave hunters hustled thousands of similar captives into the Forum for buyers to inspect and purchase.

At the height of Rome's conflict against North Africa in the third century B.C., Romans subjugated an estimated 20,000 Carthaginians and packed them onto ships. At the war's conclusion and after Carthage's military annihilation, an additional 55,000 men, women, and children were taken to Rome. Placards identified their birthplace, their price, and any caveats about their fitness for work. In tatters, they stood shoeless amid the muck of the ancient city, their feet daubed with silversmiths' powder— the same "cretaceous earth" that sporting officials used to "chalk the victory line in the circus races." The blot, marking their enslaved status, was affixed as a sign of shame. Chains prevented them from escaping.

Working conditions for Rome's enslaved population could be grim. One Roman novelist, writing later than Clodia's era, evoked their daily realities as he described the workroom of a bakery:

Bluish welts covered the whole surface of their skin. Tattered cloaks barely covered their backs. Some used the cloth to cover their loins, but mostly, they were just a heap of patchwork rags. With their branded foreheads, closely shaven heads, and shackles, they stared out from the haze of the bakery's workroom with a sallow look, their labor having left them caked with flour, like pugilists, dusted with white powder, ready to fight.

Men and women in domestic positions may have fared better. Spartacus's fate lay in between. The proprietor of a gladiatorial school in the southern Italian campagna acquired the Thracian at one such auction and brought him to Capua. There, Spartacus and his cohort of enslaved men would be trained to kill or die for the entertainment of spectators in the local stadium.

Tens of thousands of Oscan-, Etruscan-, and Greek-speaking families called Capua's historic streets home. Strategically positioned at the crossroads of two arteries that facilitated travel across the peninsula, the city had risen from humble beginnings to prominence as a local economic powerhouse. In the aftermath of the wars against Carthage, the republic took possession of the town. A feeder road led westward from Capua to Rome's busiest commercial harbor, Puteoli, on the Bay of Naples, less than a day's journey away. With the creation of the Via Appia, Clodia's great-grandfather's contribution, the town became an important hub in the Romans' burgeoning highway system. On the Via Appia's broad lanes, cart and carriage traffic came northward from Capua to Rome.

Anyone who embarked on an expedition across the peninsula valued Capua's location as a convenient, pleasant rest stop. Civil engineers calculated and posted the distance between it and many popular destinations, including Rhegium, on the southern coast: "Capua to Rhegium: 321 miles," one Roman highway sign announced. What started at Capua could easily spread.

Spartacus's rebellion started small. He and his fellow slaves purloined "kitchen knives and cooking skewers," Plutarch says, and in the uprising's first days, unleashed chaos upon the school. Then, Spartacus and his men escaped from their gladiatorial compound. Free of its walls but still legally the property of its management, they demanded emancipation.

Spartacus's cry for justice garnered immediate attention across the republic, whose enslaved population in Clodia's day has been estimated at between two and four million people. Some did backbreaking farm work; others served as tutors in elite households. Just as modern constructions of race were absent from the ancient world, so, too, were race-based notions of slavery. But dreams of emancipation consumed many enslaved people's nights and days. Roman masters learned to detect these absent looks. Ancient literature is filled with the findings of dream interpreters, who interviewed slaves and documented their musings. One enslaved man imagined being transformed into a heroic bronze statue. One enslaved woman imagined becoming a queen. Both fantasies, the experts concluded, expressed a deep desire for freedom.

Yet within weeks of Spartacus's escape, freeborn Roman men and women from the ranks of the economically disadvantaged and politically discontent professed support for his cause. A powerful movement was born. Rome, fearing the spread of unrest, sent troops.

Rome's politicians showed no forbearance to those who dared challenge its laws. Magistrates perennially boasted of having prosecuted escaped slaves. "After being elected to a judgeship," one man recalled on his tombstone, "I hunted down Italian runaways and returned the men to their rightful owners." Heavy-handed displays of force were expected. Since the Romans extracted their slave labor from conquered provinces and foreigners were considered ill-suited for civilized society, massacre of rebels was deemed an appropriate response. State-sponsored violence soothed the ancient Romans' xenophobic fears.

Yet what began as a routine act of policing in Capua turned into a protracted, embarrassing manhunt that would stretch for hundreds of miles north and south of Rome. From the very beginning, the military commanders underestimated Spartacus's ingenuity. After fleeing Capua, Spartacus had led his band of sympathizers up the perilous slopes of Mount Vesuvius, an inexplicable move that seemed to be an unforced blunder. They could see that many of Spartacus's rebels lay dead on the volcano's incline or were too weary to continue their march. The path down Vesuvius's opposite side would drive Spartacus straight into the maw of awaiting troops, or so the commanders thought.

That night, Spartacus devised a ruse to facilitate their escape from Roman hands. He instructed his men to rescue the corpses of their fallen brethren, the ones lying unburied at Vesuvius's base, and to prop up their bodies with wooden stakes. Like scarecrows, the corpses would create the illusion of living sentinels whose presence would deter the Roman army from pursuit while Spartacus ushered his followers to safety. The feint worked. Over the next eighteen months, Spartacus and his band repeatedly eluded capture. Battlefield engagements and hand-to-hand skirmishes produced few clear victories for either side. By the middle of 72 B.C., six Roman generals had earned the dubious distinction of having been humiliated by a foreign menace.

The Romans never showed the sort of historical imagination required to understand, explore, or sympathize with Spartacus's revolt, which means that Clodia's reaction to it remains murky. A full narrative of these years written by Clodia's near contemporary Sallust might have helped reconstruct the toll that Spartacus's revolt wrought on the Roman public. But the fragments of Sallust's text that survived antiquity are too threadbare to offer any insight. The straightforward, if unsatisfactory, analysis that the ancients advanced was that Spartacus was fighting for his freedom and that he aspired to return to his native land. It never occurred to the limited minds of Rome's intellectuals that a once-enslaved warrior might have wished to stay and fight to change the republic, rather than topple it.

In the end, whether Spartacus had been friend or foe to Clodia's father, his reckless disregard for the republic's law left many Romans shaken. The strength of his convictions, his charisma, and his fearless pursuit of justice inspired others in unforeseen ways. His fate followed

Clodia for a lifetime. Five years into her marriage to Metellus, Clodia was about twenty-four years old in 71 B.C. when Spartacus's revolt ended in brutal fashion. Stern, disciplined, and ruthless, the general Marcus Licinius Crassus trapped and captured six thousand rebels. As a deterrent, all were condemned to swift public execution. One was crucified every thirty-five yards along the shoulder of the Appian Way. Spartacus's body, says Appian, was never found. Social pressures at the time of the uprising, like Metellus's career ambitions, might have prevented Clodia from expressing the depth of her opinions about the matter. But the horrific scene along her family's road clarified Clodia's moral vision of the future.

CHAPTER FIVE

Clodia's Sisters

Our problems are more difficult than our husbands',
but we know how to make things work.

—EURIPIDES

With Clodia pregnant, the last years of the 70s B.C. were fraught with anxieties. Complications in childbirth were in the ancient world an omnipresent concern. Expectant mothers regularly visited healing sanctuaries, where, as archaeologists have deduced from the scores of anatomical votives women left behind, they prayed for a healthy pregnancy.

Fired into a bright orange terra-cotta, a dazzling assortment of objects were modeled into the forms of wombs, breasts, faces, even women's genitalia. Hundreds of thousands of these offerings embodied a young mother's hope that she would survive the ordeal of childbirth. Wreaths hung from the jambs outside a couple's door announced the joyful news of the safe delivery of child and mother. Hearths remained ceremoniously lit for days.

In the fanciful imaginations of Roman poets, the start of a young couple's family brought days of domestic tranquility. Newlyweds, it was said, enjoyed hours of resting a "dazzling foot on the worn sill, / pressing it with creaking sandal." After Clodia and her husband welcomed their first and only daughter, Metella, the couple's routines diverged, Clodia's to child-rearing, Metellus's to sating his career ambitions. A man of Metellus's pedigree expected to spend the next decade of his life setting foot on three continents.

By the 60s B.C., men of Metellus's age went east with the army, lured by dreams of conquest and plunder. For the past half century, the Roman

Women hoping for a successful childbirth and patients nervous about a medical condition went to sanctuaries and left clay-made body parts as votives for the gods. This assortment, excavated in Italy, includes heads, hands, feet, and in the center of the top row, a model of a uterus.

military's primary target in the region had been a slippery adversary, King Mithridates of Pontus. The king's family had inherited valuable land on the northern coasts of Asia Minor and, through conquest, gradually increased its holdings to include the shores encircling the Black Sea. From his fertile coastlines, Mithridates reaped enormous profits. Annual grain surpluses regularly stocked cupboards in Greece, Syria, and Egypt and replenished hundreds of thousands of bellies at home. Mithridates's opulent capital, the city of Sinope on the southern shore of the Black Sea, boasted an international reputation as a center of art, literature, science, and medicine. Emissaries who visited reported never having to use a translator. The king himself was "known to have spoken twenty-two languages."

With the republic's expansion into Asia Minor in the second and first centuries B.C., Rome and Pontus faced open conflict. Since the time of

Sulla, Mithridates had adopted an aggressive posture toward Roman encroachment, whether at his borders or in his sphere of influence. Three hundred warships policed the Black Sea on the hunt for spies and traitors. Pirates, who plundered and kidnapped brazenly in Mediterranean waters, never dared do so in the Black Sea unless the king gave explicit approval. At Pergamon, on the Asia Minor coast, which he claimed as his own, Mithridates once ordered his deputies to torture a Roman ambassador by pouring molten gold down his throat, to warn away the republic's armies. Then, in 88 B.C., to underscore his threat, he ordered 80,000 Roman citizens living in the region rounded up and slaughtered. Since that dreadful day, armed conflict between Rome and Pontus was a constant for every Roman soldier.

Almost two and a half decades later, the despotic king, in his late sixties as Clodia's husband prepared to deploy, remained on the throne, paranoid as ever. He was reported to consume a daily microdose of toxins to immunize himself against assassination by poison. (The blood of Black Sea ducks, his scientists discovered, carried a potent serum, effective at neutralizing pathogens.)

The conquest of Pontus promised astronomical levels of wealth, prestige, and reward. Roman women from well-placed families—Clodia's peers—used their connections to arrange this coveted assignment for their husbands, brothers, and cousins. Among the dizzying list of tasks that occupied young Roman wives, then, should be added the discreet, high-stakes inquiries necessary to secure these preferred military posts. Metellus likely received his commission due to the efforts of his half-sister Mucia. At the time of Metellus's deployment, she was the wife of the great general Pompey. To receive an appointment as supreme commander of the eastern front, Clodia's brother-in-law Lucius Licinius Lucullus sought help from his wife's resourceful friend Praecia. One supportive word from Praecia prompted "associates and companions to further her friends' political ambitions." Only after she intervened could Lucullus don his general's cloak.

Underwater archaeologists discovered this marble statue of a goddess, possibly Aphrodite, during the excavation of a shipwreck off the Tunisian coast. Its exquisite craftsmanship attests to the beauty of the artwork that decorated the homes of Clodia and her sisters.

Toppling the tyrant and returning with hoards of his treasure was every Roman soldier's fantasy. Already in these years a dazzling array of fine art bearing the craftsmanship of eastern Mediterranean artists had begun to enter Rome's markets. Much of it—sculptures, paintings, and objets d'art—was plundered. Judging from the unusually high number of shipwrecks in the Mediterranean Sea that nautical archaeologists have dated to the first half of the first century B.C., the precious pieces arrived by the boatload.

Bronze bedroom fixtures, stately candelabra, gorgeous marble statuary, elegant glassware, and fine ceramic lamps have been recovered from underwater excavations off the Italian, Tunisian, and Greek coasts. Generals would distribute a large part of the loot—that which didn't end up underwater—to loyal soldiers in exchange for their votes in a future election. A large part of the shipments was destined for retail.

꒰

Like the legendary Golden Fleece, purloined from Colchis—a fictional realm that the Romans located within the borders of Mithridates's kingdom—success on the battlefield was thought to bestow riches. Many men of Metellus's age hoped to turn their years of military service into profitable political careers. Once elected to the quaestorship, for example, one of twenty entry-level treasury positions that were filled annually, men received a lifetime appointment to the Senate and were made eligible for more prestigious, higher-profile offices such as judge and consul. Each rung of the ladder held the promise of further advancement. Years of lucrative overseas work, such as participation in the enforcement of tax contracts, typically followed.

By the middle of the 60s B.C., every male relation of Clodia's had embarked on this course of honors. Clodia's youngest brother, Clodius, served as Lucullus's none-too-obedient lieutenant, to judge from the rumors of insubordination that later circulated in Rome. Clodia's eldest brother, Appius Junior, traveled as diplomatic envoy to Armenia. Clodia's brother-in-law Quintus Marcius Rex deployed to the same military theater as Lucullus. The only unaccounted-for sibling is her middle brother, Gaius. Clodia's husband, Metellus, departed in 66 B.C. as adjutant to Pompey, the most talented military mind of his generation.

Roman law prohibited wives from accompanying their husbands on foreign business. One might assume the ban was implemented due to the rough, sometimes politically delicate nature of these postings. In a later period of Rome's history, however, slightly after Clodia's time, one of the city's Chosen Fathers may have revealed the unspoken depth of earlier men's fears. If wives were permitted to travel to the provinces, one senator exclaimed during a debate about repealing the law, women's luxuries and their sensitivities "would obstruct the business of peace and war." Their presence in the camp would "transform every military march into a decadent bacchanal." A wife on campaign might have every Roman soldier "at beck and call."

✂

Praising a man's valor was a popular topic for Roman writers. Early Latin poets like Ennius imagined soldiers dodging spears as they fell "from all sides like rain." The historian Sallust glorified the contributions of "eminent men" to the republic's past. How young mothers filled their hours as they endured their husband's absences for unpredictable lengths of time never rose to the level of men's literary concern. The popular stories of Clodia's day cast housewives in clownish comedies, as two-dimensional characters lacking emotional depth.

In Plautus's play *Stichus*, after two marriage-weary men make a pact "to try their luck as sea merchants," panic seizes their wives. Terrified by the prospect of their husbands' imminent departures, the women speculate about how they will support themselves should the men not return—a scene played to hearty laughter. The reality was that many marriages collapsed. One unsuspecting husband learned of his wife's wish to dissolve their union "on the very day he was scheduled to return from his province." Visions of a murderous homecoming, hatched by a duplicitous wife, terrified men. In Aeschylus's well-known *Agamemnon*, for example, the hero, returning from Troy, is stabbed in his own bathtub by a scheming spouse, Clytemnestra, with the help of her young lover. In Rome, men feared deadly mushrooms and poisons.

When Metellus left for Asia Minor and Syria, on a deployment that would eventually take him with Pompey to the walls of Jerusalem, Clodia assumed control of their family's affairs. In their husbands' absence, it was the wives who visited the bankers, balanced the accounts, and discharged the family's debts. When a husband wrote home to request supplementary financial assistance from the household savings, which Roman husbands frequently did when they mismanaged their expenses, wives arranged a courier to deliver the coins overseas. At least one classical playwright, the great Athenian dramatist Sophocles, gave voice— from a highly unusual angle—to the power of the connections that women might forge when the men were away in his dark tragedy about two siblings, *Tereus*.

Romans of Clodia's day knew the play, originally performed in Greek theaters in the fifth century B.C., from a revival brought to life in a Latin translation by Accius. Only fragments of Sophocles's original script, which took its name from its inscrutable antagonist, King Tereus, now survive. But from a handful of Accius's lines, a few helpful paraphrases from ancient critics, and a little sleuthing, scholars have pieced together a sketch of the plot—horrifying and heartbreaking even by the standards of the ancient theater.

As the drama opens, King Tereus rules the inhospitable kingdom of Thrace with his new bride, Queen Procne. The couple's marriage has displaced Procne from the familiar surroundings of her youth in Attica, where her sister, Philomela, still lives. In one of the play's opening scenes, a monologue on womanhood and on society's expectations for its young brides, Procne longs to reunite with her younger sister:

Nothing is what I've become. But
as a woman, that's no surprise
to me since, once we leave the comfort
of our father's house, we're told we
matter not at all. Born from the
follies of our youth are the best
times in life, after which they fix
our market price and force upon us
strange husbands and joyless homes,
hostile, unfamiliar surroundings;
instructed, in one blissful night,
to find our future contentment.

Hoping to enjoy her sister's company once again, Procne petitions her husband to arrange for Philomela to visit, a treacherous journey for a woman to make alone. The king consents, on the condition that he act as Philomela's escort.

While Procne awaits her husband's return and the moment of joyous reunion with her sister, audiences learn—in the typically oblique narrative style preferred by classical dramatists—of a ghastly development. The depraved king has sexually assaulted his sister-in-law. To silence Philomela's protestations, as well as to protect himself from accusations of rape, he has also sliced out her tongue. By the time the king and his entourage reach the palace, Tereus has disguised Philomela as a slave. Procne, puzzled by the trip's supposed fruitlessness, inquires in vain about her sister's whereabouts.

With Philomela trapped in the palace, unable to communicate with her sister, the play gathers emotional intensity. Philomela begins to search for an opportune moment to reveal the barbarity of what has transpired. Ancient theatergoers were transfixed as they waited to observe how the silent Philomela would reveal her identity and expose her attacker.

Seated at her sister's loom, unobserved by the palace retinue, Philomela picks up a shuttle and spools it with wool. Patiently, she passes thread after thread through the warp and slowly and determinedly spells out the name of her assailant—at which point Procne learns her sister's terrible fate. In the play's last act, Procne butchers her newborn son and, in an act of vengeance that unites the two sisters in a shared tragedy, feeds the child to the unsuspecting king.

Sophocles's story and Accius's Roman revival dramatized two women's traumatic experiences of adulthood, sisterhood, and marriage. In bringing these themes to the public's awareness, the playwrights made a bold literary statement. In a cultural environment consumed by the supposed universality of men's issues, the stories of siblings, female as well as male, merited attention.

Humanity belongs to a single
tribe. A single moment in our parents'

lives witnesses our births, preeminence
a distant dream, even then for siblings.

Sophocles's artistic statement—that the fates of women raised in the
same household might follow radically different trajectories; that brothers and sisters might share a connection by virtue of belonging to a
"single tribe," humanity—landed with no less emphasis on the modest
stages of Clodia's Rome than in the stately theaters of classical Greece.

Even in the 60s B.C., Rome lacked a dedicated venue for these artistic and cultural performances largely because the Fathers obstructed
its establishment. Any benefactor who possessed the wealth required to
realize such a monument's construction would, they supposed, be extravagantly lauded for commissioning it and, like a demagogue, would then
wield undue influence over the people. As a result, Roman audiences of
Clodia's day, rich and poor alike, were prevented from enjoying, as hundreds of ancient cities already did, their very own first-rate theater.

⁂

Clodia's husband returned to Rome, ran for office, and by 63 B.C. was
elected praetor, a prestigious judgeship. Metellus's future as an incon-
trovertible force in Roman politics looked assured, as did Rome's position of supremacy throughout the eastern Mediterranean, when, that
same year, confirmation of the death of King Mithridates reached the
capital. The news stunned the republic. Cornered by Roman forces,
cut off from his allies, the aging autocrat, nearing seventy and by then
immune to every naturally occurring toxin, asked a stoic bodyguard to
assist his suicide by plunging a sword into his chest.

The king's lands, which Mithridates's family had owned for centuries and which encompassed the entire belly of Asia Minor, fell into the
republic's lap. Cities across the east acknowledged Rome's indisputable
might. In the months that followed, twenty cities alone fell in the regions
of Cilicia and Syria. Turning south, Pompey brought havoc to Jerusalem
and its Jewish Temple, imprisoned its Jewish king, and sent mounds of

gold talents back to Rome. Before the year was over, the Fathers were devising plans to carve the king's holdings into governable provinces. Every inch—the ribs of the central Cappadocian mountains, the flat expanses of northern Pontus, the flank of Cilicia along the Mediterranean Sea, and Bithynia, on the northwest peninsula facing Europe—had become Roman taxable territory.

Pompey, who had, years earlier, replaced Lucullus as the region's supreme commander, proclaimed victory and returned to Rome expecting a hero's welcome. Before leaving Mithridates's palace, the general had stolen one of the king's prized possessions, a cloak supposedly worn by Alexander the Great. Pompey planned to don it for his victory parade. The Senate, which oversaw planning for all processions through the city and was dismayed by the meteoric rise of Pompey's reputation, delayed its approval.

Luster rained upon Rome. Among Pompey's reported loot were two thousand gemstone-encrusted goblets with gold appliqué, crates of ceremonial ivory drinking horns, gem-studded couches, chairs, and horse bridles. Birds including Mithridates's prized peacocks found a second life on Tuscan and Campanian farms, where they strutted through gardens like their newly boastful owners. Humble workers who never dreamed of tasting an Asian cherry, one of the agricultural riches of the east, suddenly found them for sale at the local fruit vendor. It took the Roman notaries thirty days to catalogue the entirety of Pompey's spoils, which included prisoners of war: satraps, generals, and Mithridates's five sons and two daughters.

While the Senate dawdled in approving a formal celebration, Pompey and his adjutants prepared for the most expensive parade Romans had ever seen. As was customary when an honored general processed through the city, colorful floats would escort the party and exhibit the spoils of war. There were informative hand-painted placards to be designed, each bearing a didactic label to describe the marvelous object or unusual prey on display. At a Roman triumphal parade in the 60s B.C., it was not uncommon to see a caged rhinoceros, tigers, and serpents of astonishing size. The circus-like atmosphere quenched the public's thirst for cursory knowledge about the republic's newly conquered lands.

The unrivaled nature of his success prompted even Pompey to reflect. Rome sorely needed an architectural wonder, a new public work of audacious engineering that would surpass the cities of the east and put the city on the Mediterranean map of cultural sophistication.

Meanwhile, Pompey's conquests turned Rome's fancier abodes into stunning museums. Inner courtyards on Palatine Hill featured recently acquired sculptures by classical Greek masters such as Apelles and Lysippus. Aviaries, fishponds, and gardens with exotic snails decorated the grounds. Upon retirement from his own military command, Clodia's brother-in-law Lucullus had returned with an unusual slab of red-veined black marble. Builders were soon inquiring about the source of the luxurious stone for their own projects. Stonemasons obliged, naming the material Lucullan marble.

New literature arrived in Rome's homes, too, crate upon crate of scrolls, many of them stolen from Mithridates's libraries. (Books—discrete artifacts assembled from cut and cleaned animal hides and sewn between leather covers, their pages awash with delicate illuminations—still lay decades in the future.) Women like Clodia and her sisters benefited from the lot. In an age when a wife's formal education ended at late adolescence, the arrival of foreign poetry and unheard histories reinvigorated many women's early love of the pleasures of reading.

There was a literary revolution awaiting Clodia in those texts. Born in the cosmopolitan world of the Greek-speaking east, the works that flooded Rome in the 60s B.C. were experimental, playful, and mischievous. Their themes embodied a radical ethos that spoke directly to Clodia's day. The group's leading authors—Callimachus, Theocritus, and Apollonius from Rhodes—transformed episodes from history and beloved myths into clever, quasi-epic plots. Literary critics named the collective the Neoterics, or New Writers. Unadventurous Roman readers accused them of producing the written equivalent of *contaminatio*, "muck."

The New Writers, who were read aloud in performance perhaps more than they were enjoyed in the privacy of a home, dazzled Roman audiences with their erudition. They quoted freely from Homeric epic, love poetry, philosophical treatises, and highly technical scientific writing. Often, they blended wildly different genres in the same work. With an ear for the rhythms of language, many packed their verses with an unusual combination of metrical beats.

The salons of Clodia's days were filled with women and men who appreciated these unorthodox, freethinking, and rebellious offerings. When Theocritus introduced two housewives who were oblivious to their Alexandrian comforts, the commentary pierced Clodia's present-day surroundings. "Every day's a holiday for people with nothing to do," one woman says within earshot of her slave. The dialogue forced audiences to recognize the vast chasms of experience that might exist between women of different social and economic backgrounds.

In another work, Theocritus offered a ridiculous reflection on romance, dramatizing what would seem to be an impossibility: the spiteful one-eyed monster of Homer's *Odyssey*, Polyphemus, finding a girlfriend. ("He loved Galatea," Theocritus writes. "Everything else was unimportant.") Exposure to this literature in translation fashioned a bold and versatile new Roman woman: "temperate, impassioned, sometimes even salacious," according to one contemporary. By the end of the decade, women were emboldened to write their own "verses, crack jokes, and hold forth on a range of topics."

Latin writers of Clodia's era embraced and experimented with the new mode of expression. The poet Cinna, from Brescia, north of the Po River, and the poet Calvus, in Rome, produced their versions of genre-bending works in the first century B.C. The movement's *enfant terrible*, Catullus of Verona—a city, like Brescia, on the Italian peninsula but technically located in Cisalpine Gaul—shocked audiences with his raunchy vocabulary and sexually explicit verses. His contemporary Lucretius was just then consumed with composing his most audacious work, an epic poem called *On the Nature of the Universe*. When completed, it would introduce Romans to the latest theories about indestructible particles, which the Greeks called atoms, from whose elemental beginnings emerged the material world.

As can happen in close creative circles, many of these New Writers disdained one another's works and did not miss an opportunity to deride their competitors. Cinna mocked the nine years that one of his peers was taking to finish a poem. The poor quality of another's writing he characterized "as befitting recital by a monkey." Some of the harshest estimation was directed at Cinna himself. His poetry, it was said, would never find an audience beyond Brescia unless someone carried his verses south on parchment as "wrapping for mackerel."

In Clodia's Rome, scrolls on every imaginable subject circulated freely. One afternoon might be spent appreciating a highly technical agricultural treatise while another might be absorbed by a philosophical dialogue. Even when enjoying more obscure or recherché texts, such as Aratus's wildly popular *Phenomena*, a discourse on astronomy, readers delighted in detecting and debating their philosophical resonances.

Women, undeterred by the movement's endemic machismo, offered their own contributions to this literature. Artfully blurring the genres of biography, history, and memoir, Pamphila, one of Clodia's near contemporaries, told a history of Rome's republic through the story of her thirteen-year marriage. She published it as a thirty-three-volume collection called *The Many-Colored Tapestry*. Widely quoted in antiquity, Pamphila's magnum opus circulated under the more anodyne title *Historical Commentaries* and earned high praise from the ancient world's later librarians. (Not until a half century after Clodia's day did the city offer citizens their first public library.) These later scholars saluted Pamphila's innovative combination of "first-hand insight with information she gleaned by research," and applauded the originality of her style, which "operated under a radical artistic principle that respected both the lines of her investigation and its gaps." The daunting task of unearthing documents outside her family's archive and of describing events outside her personal experience might have deterred a less deft writer from embarking on the project. But Pamphila's "interwoven approach" to the historical record, respecting the evidence and its silences, "created a more delightful experience than a dry presentation of facts."

The season's most anticipated readings debuted in private homes, where, in the absence of their husbands, women like Clodia and her sisters likely occupied the front-row seats.

❧

While those in Clodia's circle enjoyed a windfall in the wake of Mithridates's defeat, these were trying years for many Romans. Seasonal crop failures drove small farmers to seek temporary credit. Throughout the 60s B.C., the farmers' mounting debts outpaced their harvests. Tavern owners and merchants sought loans in order to cover Rome's rising rents, and also fell behind in their payments. By 63 B.C., with Clodia, her husband, and their daughter together in Rome, growing resentment at these financial inequities threatened to upend the republic. By autumn, a network of women found themselves in the unusual position of standing on the frontlines of the crisis.

With the year's campaign season well underway, a charismatic reformer, Lucius Sergius Catiline, stood for consul and pitched the need for economic aid. In ancient policy terms, the sale of government-owned land at competitive prices would bolster the treasury enough to allow for legislation to expunge these crushing debts. Catiline appealed to the angriest of the electorate, who shared his contempt for wasted wealth and such astronomical levels of patrician self-absorption.

Channeling the Roman people's economic disaffection into a powerful movement, Catiline asserted that the widening gap in wealth, if left unaddressed, portended a revolution which the republic's elected officials were foolishly ignoring. Yet, as one of the year's candidates for consul, Catiline himself fomented the populist ire. If Rome's cozy political class was unwilling to pass legislation to remedy the runaway economic disparity, Catiline told his supporters, then the people should send him to office with a mandate to overhaul the broken system. Among the

many painted slogans that appeared on Roman walls during the tense
months of the 63 B.C. campaign, one Latin phrase predominated: *Novae
Tabulae*, "A Clean Slate." Roman financial records were customarily tal-
lied on wax "slates" or tablets.

Catiline's platform appealed to struggling voters who hoped that
their debts would be erased. Yet the very year Pompey returned from
the east, tonelessly sporting Alexander's royal dress, Catiline lost the
annual election. The status quo prevailed. Had it not been for the eyes
and ears of a quiet, respectable, but otherwise unknown woman, whose
name is reported in the ancient sources as Fulvia, the second half of 63
B.C. would have taken a much bloodier trajectory. Roman writers never
specified the woman's father's family.

Earlier in the year, this Fulvia had contacted Terentia, the wife of
Cicero, one of the year's two consuls, to share news of a disturbing
nature. Fulvia's paramour at the time, the roguish Quintus Curius,
whose improprieties had led to disgrace and expulsion from the Senate, had made some unsettling casual remarks intimating that, in coming months, he stood to realize a large financial gain that would give
them the resources to start a new life together. Quintus anticipated this
change of fortune as an ally of Catiline and regaled Fulvia with promises
of future "gifts of the mountains and the seas," a proverbial expression
meaning anything her heart desired. During these fevered promises, he
let slip mention of an imminent attack on Rome in retribution for Catiline's electoral defeat. Terentia took the report to her husband.

That autumn, visions of heroically defending Rome from attack
occupied Cicero's every waking hour. Standing close by was Clodia's
husband, Metellus. As one of the year's urban praetors, he would pre-
side at the prosecution of any alleged conspirators. If necessary and if
Cicero authorized him, Metellus would also lead soldiers outside the
city to quash any domestic threat. Soon the names of seven conspirators surfaced—more dimwitted crooks than criminal masterminds—
among them senators and public officials. As autumn turned to winter,
the republic's spies reported that Catiline was amassing thousands of

armed supporters in the hills outside Florence, in Fiesole. Cicero, the first in his family to have ascended to consul, recognized an opportunity to secure his legacy.

Claiming the mantle of the republic's fiercest protector, Cicero delivered, starting in late October, a series of public addresses about the evolving threat, filled with graphic predictions of the coming slaughter. Although the first speeches were devoid of any corroborating evidence, Cicero's rhetorical prowess transfixed his audiences, rendering Romans of every class fearful of a coming, if vague, campaign of terror. On October 21, 63 B.C., a gullible Senate passed a law that vested the consuls with emergency powers, to safeguard the republic using all necessary force.

Every Roman house, which was to say, every woman, including Clodia, as vigilant protector of her family home, was on edge for signs of an impending terror attack. Sallust, in his history of these weeks, speaks of the "gloom" that befell Rome's citizenry as nightwatchmen patrolled the city. Clodia's husband, authorized to raise an army and to hunt down Catiline's conspirators to the east and north, left Palatine Hill that month. By November, Cicero had fashioned himself into the republic's only trusted voice of authority.

The first verifiable evidence of Catiline's intentions came from an unexpected quarter that month: an embassy of Gauls on a mission to lobby the Roman Senate for lower taxes. A handful of Catiline's associates had contacted them while crossing Tuscany en route to the capital, and urged them to join the rebellion. The Gauls left the meeting noncommittal and relayed the information to the Senate, agreeing to return to Tuscany to act as double agents.

Before dawn on December 3, 63 B.C., and with the Gauls' cooperation, Cicero commissioned Roman deputies to intercept their caravan and confiscate a sheaf of incriminating letters that Catiline's men had entrusted to them. The letters, in the conspirators' own handwriting, confirmed the details of Catiline's plot: to set fire to Rome and its Senate, to murder the republic's leading politicians, and to seize power through a coup. Cicero brought the Gauls into the Senate to testify.

By midday, five of Catiline's associates were arrested and hauled before the Senate. Under the emergency powers granted to Cicero, all were charged with conspiracy against the state. Julius Caesar cautioned restraint, but Cicero's ego and his impetuousness led him to insist on immediate execution. He strong-armed the senators into approving the death of the conspirators without a trial—an unprecedented breach of the rule of law. On Cicero's orders the Catiline five—Lentulus, Cethegus, Statilius, Gabinius, and Ceparius—were strangled in a jail cell on December 5, 63 B.C. With the conspiracy exposed but its mastermind still at large, Cicero waited anxiously as Clodia's husband pursued the remaining outlaws in Tuscany.

As Cicero prepared to leave the office of consul at the end of the month, many Romans were already eager for change. When Cicero requested an opportunity to address the Senate that December to deliver one final self-congratulatory speech, a parliamentary maneuver was used to block him. He fumed to friends and colleagues: How dare he be silenced? How dare lesser men obstruct his hard-earned moment of triumph? Absorbing the brunt of Cicero's rage was Clodia's brother-in-law Nepos, who had voted against Cicero's victory lap. The episode, Plutarch noted, not only exposed Cicero as brittle and petty but confirmed how unhinged and self-absorbed with his own legacy Cicero had become: "People grew tired of hearing him continually praising and magnifying his achievements."

The cat-and-mouse chase of Metellus and Catiline ended in early 62 B.C. when the two men's armies faced each other for the final time near the hills outside Pistoia. When the fighting concluded, light spears and wooden stakes littered the battlefield, a coarse grid plotted with hundreds of fallen on both sides. With them died Catiline and his push for reform.

⟊

Her husband home, then gone; home, then gone—perhaps Clodia found solidarity in these years with women of her circle, many of whom were admirers of the memory of the Roman widow Julia. Dead at sixty as the decade dawned, she had been the wife of the statesman Marius, Sulla's fiercest rival. Like her husband, she had inspired those who recognized the republic's flaws but fought to realize, for all, the nobility of its principles.

After her husband's death by disease on the eve of Sulla's dictatorship, Julia had remained unmarried but never retreated from the public eye, even while Sulla's antidemocratic laws barred the sons of Marius's supporters from election to higher office. Few Romans of Clodia's day, not even Catiline, would have dared to mention Marius's name. But Julia attended social events and cultivated her husband's network—a provocative stance for an outlaw's widow. In the years preceding her death, she was a living witness who symbolized her husband's most popular political commitments as an advocate for a higher quality of life for all, a guarantor of economic security, and a fighter for wider enfranchisement. In her youth, likely of her own volition, she had financially underwritten Marius's career. Even as she lived in fear of arrest, harassment, or assassination at the hands of Sulla's sympathizers, her devotion inspired a movement to repeal Sulla's prohibition on her husband's memory, a victory she never realized. When Julia died in 69 B.C. of old age, her thirty-one-year-old nephew, a relatively unknown Julius Caesar, ascended the rostrum to lionize her as a stateswoman. In recounting the richness of his aunt Julia's life, Caesar subtly reminded citizens never to waver in their fight to change the status quo.

That fight had taken an unexpected turn with Catiline's decision to wage war against the republic. Violence was an extreme response to a lost election. But in the months and years ahead, there would be more opportunities to press for economic reform and constitutional change as another generation of Roman men came of age to stand for office.

CHAPTER SIX

Clodia's Fortunes

The moon has set / and the Pleiades.
Hours elapse, midnight comes, / and I sleep alone.

—SAPPHO

In July 61 B.C., after a monthslong campaign, Metellus went to Rome's voting halls to cast his ballot in the annual elections for consul. Denied the franchise, Clodia waited with her husband and their daughter for the announcement of the results.

Every July, the republic's officials prepared for this important civic event. (Clodia knew the month as Quintilis. Julius Caesar's efforts to rectify the calendar by adding additional days to the year lay more than a decade away. The month was renamed for him posthumously.) At dawn, priests would ascend the city's most sacred hill, the Capitoline, to observe the day's auspices and confirm whether the gods looked favorably on the pending election. By morning, a red flag would be unfurled atop the Janiculan Hill. Intended to be lowered only in the event of a sudden siege, the flag declared the opening of election day. Over a long, twelve-hour summer day, voting would bring hundreds of thousands of citizens to the plains of the campus, the verdant parklands on the city's western edge. Romans queued under the wooden roof of a rustic enclosure affectionately known as the Ovile, the Sheepfolds.

The blare of the military trumpet summoned citizens to their civic duties. Volunteers stood ready to assist the voters, shepherding the throngs along the lines, watching them deposit their ballots in the urns, and staying behind to tabulate them. It was a tremendous honor, the Romans said, "to take the oath and participate in the counting of votes." Eagle-eyed ballot observers, deputized to detect suspicious similarities of handwriting, hunted for duplicates and other potentially fraudulent votes while candidates and constituents alike passed the nervous hours in the promenades of the Villa Publica, the pleasant gardens nearby.

Voting, done in secret as decreed by Roman law, lasted until sundown, when soldiers lowered the flag on the Janiculan Hill to announce the successful completion of yet another peaceful election day. Then, the names of the victors, including next year's two consul-designates, were announced.

There was no organized party system in Rome, no bosses to demand partisan loyalty or party chairs to dole out favors. But two broadly opposed platforms informed politics in Clodia's day, and their existence helped the Roman electorate identify its preferred candidates. On one side were the Populares, the representatives of the "people's interests." They fought to boost the average worker's precarious economic standing and advocated for the expansion and protection of voting rights. Whenever crops wilted, debts climbed, or new voters entered the census rolls, a member of the Populares was sure to respond by proposing a government program to assist them. Opposing this reformist coalition were the Optimates, the republic's self-styled "best ones." Usually drawn from families of landed wealth with large inheritances, they protected the political and economic interests of the ruling class.

By Clodia's day, rich, well-educated, property-owning slave-owners filled both the populist and the conservative ranks. But despite these overlapping demographics, the ideologies of Rome's two political factions offered starkly different visions for the republic.

More than seventy government offices stood vacant every year. Although the term of office was only one year, elections had consequences for implementing policy. Competition was fierce, and a campaign demanded money and an extensive level of commitment. The first step in declaring one's candidacy was to file a *petitio*, a "request" to seek elected office, which included a list of supporters. Reputation did not guarantee success. Politicians needed Hope—a sixth sense about the possibility for a better future preposterously at odds with ancient life's cruelties and capriciousness. Hope was considered a divinity, and two temples in Rome were devoted to the goddess. Bronze and marble statues personifying Hope stood in private gardens. Coins inscribed with Hope's name circulated daily in the markets. Only such divine reassurance could have persuaded a candidate to launch a grueling campaign.

No "companion of solitude," wrote Plato, willingly sought election to public office. Only men with a "submissiveness to injury," the philosopher speculated, had the physical and mental fortitude to withstand the toll of a campaign. Advisors recommended that candidates hold events in as many towns across the Italian peninsula as they could reasonably expect to visit, as many times as possible. Each appearance in a town was a chance for a candidate to introduce himself to voters again. In a world without formal political debates, every interaction with a voter mattered, and a likable personality and an approachable demeanor left a valuable impression. Some candidates began their marathon campaign two years before their election. By Clodia's day, veterans of these campaigns had traded so many lessons and tales that an anonymous Roman writer collected and published them in a helpful pamphlet, *How to Run for Office*, which promised frank advice, expert analysis, and a laundry list of suggestions for converting handshakes into votes. The odds of an outsider's success were low. Rome's notoriously fickle electorate rewarded name recognition above talent and established households above newly acquired wealth. Yet self-importance and cultural elitism made urban and rural voters alike bristle. Romans valued candidates who listened and treated people's individual concerns as their own.

"Always be seen traveling in large groups," the pamphlet recommended. Humility had never won a Roman election. "Every day when you descend into the Forum, you must repeat to yourself: 'I'm new here. I am campaigning for consul. This is Rome,'" the anonymous author advised. "Consider what you're seeking, who you are, and how special this city is."

A campaign brought heightened scrutiny to candidates and their families. The annals of Roman history are filled with candidates who suffered early missteps and never recovered the voters' trust. One, short on financial resources—never a reassuring look—had been caught selling slaves to raise campaign funds. Another was surreptitiously strolling the slave market for a same-sex lover when constituents recognized him on the streets. The "gossip that most poisons one's public reputation," though, as pundits warned in Clodia's day, originated "within one's household." Unfortunately, a scandal involving Clodia's thirty-year-old brother, Clodius, nearly upset her husband's campaign before it started. The details emerged in January 61 B.C.

Clodius, as radical and nonconformist as his sister, was an unrepentant populist. A mischief-maker, as Plutarch later described him, he was a "lover of all things new and novel." After he supposedly mutinied in the east during his brother-in-law Lucullus's advance against Mithridates, a cloud of disgrace followed him home. Then, in the winter of 62–61 B.C., his name came to the public's attention in unusual circumstances again when, it was alleged, he had donned a silk gown and a veil to infiltrate a popular nighttime gathering.

The Bona Dea Social Club, an exclusive, women-only annual affair, brought Roman high society to the house of the city's chief priest, whose wife played hostess as decorum required the priest's absence for the evening. Women of every social and economic class gathered in similar neighborhood associations. Surrounded by friends, they dined, socialized, and mobilized to claim their voice in the city's affairs. In a republic that restricted women's enfranchisement, these private clubs sustained women's activism. Many, like the Association of Women's Good Fortune, founded five hundred years before Clodia's birth, owed their existence to civic leaders whose example still inspired.

When, in the fifth century B.C., fears arose that a seditious soldier, Coriolanus, was planning to attack the city, a respected matron, Valeria, convinced Coriolanus's wife, Vortumnia, and mother, Verturia, to intervene. (These are the names Livy records. In Plutarch's retelling, which Shakespeare followed, Coriolanus's wife's name is given as Vergilia, not Vortumnia.) When Coriolanus's assault was successfully averted, the

Senate decreed that a temple of Women's Good Fortune, *Fortuna Muli-ebris*, should be built on the residential Aventine Hill to commemorate the patriotism of the three women. Its association still gathered there in Clodia's day. As with the Bona Dea Social Club, men were banned from the festivities.

Excluded from their wives' recreational gatherings, resentful husbands let their imaginations run wild, picturing witches' séances and toxicological experiments behind closed doors. Some believed the Bona Dea Social Club was little more than an excuse for a salacious sex party. The goddess Bona Dea, they said, "hated the eyes of males."

Although Clodius suffered no consequences at the time for having allegedly intruded on the event, in January 61 B.C. a partisan band of legislators leveled a charge of sacrilege against him. A conviction for impropriety, they hoped, would deter the already disreputable lad from pursuing a career in public service. So it happened that, six months before election day, Clodia's husband found himself on the defensive side of a growing scandal involving his brother-in-law.

When a witness came forward and attested that he had observed Clodia's brother "elsewhere" on the evening in question—the telling Latin adverb being *alibi*—Clodius was acquitted, the case dismissed, and the final stretch of Metellus's campaign cleared of distractions.

Observing from a distance, volunteering behind the scenes, cajoling friends and neighbors: The wife of a political candidate could facilitate her husband's campaign with any number of public or private conversations. Some couples, however, sought more equality in their political fortunes. Had Clodia and Metellus chosen to do so, they might have pursued a career in public office together. A quirk in the republic's laws permitted husbands and wives to serve simultaneously as priests of Jupiter. Alongside the Vestal Virgins, the opportunity constituted one of the few avenues in Rome by which women could participate in public life.

Solemnly veiled, with an authoritative mien, and instantly distinguished by her six rows of braided hair, religious women, like the Vestal seen here, figured among the most publicly engaged women of ancient Rome.

Lacking any notion of the separation of church and state, the Roman Republic's constitution encouraged its citizens to interweave their personal pieties with their civic beliefs. One traditionalist of Clodia's day described the arrangement this way:

> Among the many features of the Roman constitutional system which our ancestors had the foresight to establish, none was more noteworthy than our founding Fathers' wise decision to use the power of the state to enforce our religious values. In this way, the best, brightest minds of our republic have been put in positions of authority to protect and preserve our traditional Roman mores.

Rome's Fathers exploited this feature to impose their paternalistic ideologies and moralities on society. They did so through the government appointment of priests.

Every year, the members of Rome's distinguished College of Pontiffs announced their selections to fill open seats in the city's priesthoods.

Every year, more than fifty Roman men served in a priestly role, which came with important, highly visible civic responsibilities.

An augur watched the skies for auspicious or ill-omened patterns of birds. A pontifex presided at the city's grand outdoor sacrifices on important religious holidays and examined the animal's entrails for good or bad omens. During times of crisis, a team of fifteen Roman priests was tasked with consulting the Sibylline Books. Roman tradition attributed these enigmatic verses, a collection of writings akin to the Delphic pronouncements of Greece, to a local prophetess. Jewish and later Christian forgeries of them abounded, preserving the Sibyl's cryptic style—assigning numerical values to individual letters of the alphabet, for example, to obfuscate the identity of a loathsome or divisive political leader. Romans believed the verses contained coded information about the future.

Unimpeachable integrity was a key qualification for these roles, for, in addition to religious duties, Rome's priests served as quasi-parliamentarians. In his capacity as augur or pontifex, for example, a priest's public pronouncements might affect the constitutionality of this or that bill as it moved through the Senate or the assemblies before going before the citizens for a vote. Judiciousness and collegiality were essential to the job.

Even Romans who aspired to powerful secular offices, like consul, coveted these religious appointments since they furnished important introductions to men from other well-established, well-connected families. Most priesthoods, despite their religious nature, demanded from officeholders no sacrifice of their comfortable lifestyles. A Roman priest could be married, live at home with his wife and children, and his family did not need to worry about following a scrupulous set of religious prohibitions so long as the man performed his public duties.

By Clodia's day, however, couples rarely expressed an interest in serving as the married priests of Jupiter. The Flamen and Flaminica Dialis, as the husband-and-wife positions were known, prohibited the Flamen from leaving the city's perimeter overnight. The Flaminica was banned from Rome's streets during funerals. At meals, the couple was expected to follow a strict regime of ritual purity, refraining from the consumption of raw meats, goat meat, and all varieties of legumes. Yeast was forbidden in their kitchen.

It is easy to appreciate the origin of these strange rules and regulations. Many preserved the morals and mores of a much simpler day. Yet by the first century B.C., so few couples were willing to accept such antiquated impositions and arbitrary restrictions on their domestic lives that these offices had lain dormant for two decades—unfilled, unappointed.

The neglect was symptomatic of dire problems. The republic had outgrown its own constitution, and an undue reverence for archaic principles and outdated laws had paralyzed any search for remedies. The uncritical worship of tradition had its champions, men who used their influence to stymie the will and the imagination of the people and to dissuade others from undertaking reforms. "Foul a clear well, and you will suffer thirst," the Athenian playwright Aeschylus had written. By the time Clodia's husband embarked on his campaign, an unsustainable level of partisan stress, corruption, and ill will had poisoned every institution in Rome's republic.

Within the past decade, a bribery scandal had upended the careers of two consuls-designate. Public pressure forced the men's resignations before either could take office. Since Rome's constitution made no provisions to elevate a pair of alternates, like vice consuls, to replace disgraced or deceased officials, the Fathers in these unforeseen moments turned to an age-old custom whose origins lay in the distant monarchy. They appointed an *interrex*, a short-term manager, to govern until new elections could be scheduled. In principle, the temporary measure allowed the republic to function. Its practical effect delayed the people's business.

Had a Roman at the time wished to consult the republic's foundational charter for guidance—a document conceived by lawmakers, ratified by the people, and drafted in fine calligraphy, which moderns might recognize as a constitution—such an artifact was nowhere to be found.

High-minded theories of statecraft never appealed to Rome's Fathers, who neglected to express their government's ways in print. Comity between gentlemen and a respect for tradition were thought sufficient for a healthy republic. Or so they naively presumed.

In the 60s B.C., the republic was unraveling at its seams. Even the most basic government functions were subject to the personal whims of elected officials. What should have been routine tasks, like the taking of a census, now flared partisan tempers. The republic relied on its census to collect tax payments. It also used the registration data to assign the year's newest voters to the thirty-five electoral districts so that new citizens could exercise their vote. For centuries the practice had run smoothly, but by the time Metellus stood for election, an inexcusable fifteen years had elapsed since the republic last collected the necessary demographic information to complete a census. Fearing a rise in the number of progressive votes in the electoral colleges—those of freed slaves and Italians who had won the franchise—a series of conservative politicians used the power of their office to block the appointment of a census director. By postponing the census, they suppressed the votes of the new citizens.

When a coalition of forward-thinking Romans, led by the tribunes, succeeded in passing a new law that guaranteed voting rights to these disenfranchised groups, opposition senators mobilized against the cause. The Optimates passed new legislation repealing the popular voting rights legislation. The policy debates that Clodia's great-grandfather Gaius had predicted might cause the republic's demise remained, one hundred years later, unsettled.

The prospect of a republic with new geographic borders, more ethnic groups, new scientific and philosophical discoveries, and newly enfranchised citizens had incapacitated the formerly reliable institutions of the Roman Republic. Consensus was understandably hard to find in an age when Sulla's law still banned the descendants of his political enemies from holding elected office. Unwilling to embrace these first-century realities, the Fathers instead worshipped the idea of tradition and defended their visions of an imaginary, harmonious Roman past. Reformers grew restless.

Such was the situation in the spring of 61 B.C. as Clodia's husband entered the last leg of his race for consul. That he spent exorbitant sums to win election in such a patently inequitable, fracturing society speaks to the intensity of his day's conflicts and the ferocity of citizens' desire to implement change or, in Metellus's case, to maintain the status quo.

≫

During the final months preceding an election, unable to avail themselves of mass media, candidates were forced to think creatively about when and where to disseminate the details of their biography and their political platform. In court, in a speech before a crowd, or at a dinner with members of a workers' guild, a carefully cultivated eloquence projected the right notes of professionalism and self-assurance.

In a world that expected superior oratory from its public speakers, there was no concealing a lesser candidate's flaws. A man with a noticeable speech impediment—Latin words with an *r* stymied even the best native speakers—practiced until he could deliver a flawless performance. Discerning audiences easily differentiated a superlative candidate, *perfectissimus*, from the average, or *mediocris*, one. Good posture conveyed seriousness of purpose. A solid stance communicated reliability. Candidates who swayed and teetered while speaking distracted voters. "He seems to be speaking from the deck of a boat," was a Roman advisor's expression of alarm.

Without anyone to provide honest feedback, many candidates failed to realize how unsuitable they were for public life. Applauding himself for the apparent moment of gravitas he had woven into his speech, one man walked away under the impression "that he had aroused the audience's pity." When he asked a colleague whether he thought the speech successful, the colleague said, "'Oh yes, it certainly aroused plenty of pity.'"

The smartest Roman campaign managers were the ones who harped,

"Always be counting." Even in an age before data-driven science, electioneering in Rome allowed little room for intuition or guesswork. Turnout could be carefully calibrated, and success on election day demanded a rigorous attention to math. Every candidate in Rome recognized how the electoral system manipulated the raw numbers of the popular vote, laundered them through the electoral colleges, and confirmed a mathematical outcome that safeguarded the establishment's interests.

Still, in an electorate fast approaching half a million people, votes were also there for the taking, provided that a wise candidate surrounded himself with ruthless number-crunchers. Their job was to identify where to find these crucial voters.

> Make a demographic canvass of the whole city [of Rome], its social clubs, its hills, its neighborhoods, its suburbs. Find the influential citizens, then recruit them to your cause. The multitude will follow their lead . . . Let there be no town, no colony, no rural district, or any place in the Italian peninsula where you have not cultivated a sufficient level of this support. Inquire and seek out voters wherever you can. Meet them, get to know them, secure their vote. See that they campaign in their own localities for you and that they act like candidates on your behalf.

A campaign staff's most important homework was learning the worm-eaten shapes of the republic's thirty-five electoral districts, along with the number and profile of the voters registered within them.

The most undisciplined error, one that both novice and experienced campaign managers might make, was for their candidate to lose the support of his own electoral district. Given that Roman political commentators often mention it as a real possibility, it must have occurred with humiliating regularity. The anonymous campaign manual offered a succinct solution: "Commit the electoral map to memory."

On a July morning five months after Clodius's scandal, voters went to the campus to cast their ballots. The "merest whisper of a rumor" might, at the eleventh hour, change a voter's preference. When the people stepped up to deposit their ballots, as one elitist Roman put it, "Their stupidity is often on full display. Romans regularly elect men unfit of office for no other reason than on the supposed strength of a man's name." Oftentimes and without explanation, turnout proved disheartening. By one scholar's estimate, the average hovered around the appallingly low rate of 2 percent of the eligible population.

The outcome of an election frequently left prognosticators baffled. At night, a candidate might dream of delivering a victory speech to the glow of an enthusiastic Forum. By morning, he could be composing his concession speech. "Nothing is more dispiriting than an election," went one Roman adage. Platitudes provided little consolation to the defeated.

That July, Roman voters chose Metellus and another former lieutenant of Pompey's, Lucius Afranius, as consuls-designate. On inauguration day, January 1, 60 B.C., Metellus took the oath of office in a bright white toga and was joined in celebration by his daughter and his wife. Stepping into the most visible role of her thirty-five years as her husband claimed one of the most august titles in the Roman Republic, Clodia entered the history books as a consul's wife, an honor she must have felt deeply, to judge from the one bit of unsolicited commentary that survives. After her husband's election, the former consul, Cicero, refused to congratulate her. In a letter to a friend, he neither acknowledged nor said Clodia's name, writing, "I can't stand the confident airs of that woman."

Metellus's one-year term passed uneventfully. The scale of Pompey's triumphs absorbed public attention. Julius Caesar, enjoying a moment of widespread acclaim after the moving eulogy he had delivered for his aunt Julia, had declared his intent to run for consul the following year. Metellus and his colleague in the consulship, Afranius, had approximately six months in which to make their marks on the capital.

A bare-bones entry in an ancient Roman almanac glosses their year in office, 60 B.C., as the period "when Metellus and Afranius served as consuls." By March of their term, Romans in everyday conversation were referring to Afranius as "the other guy." Barring any foreign or domestic crisis that might require the republic to mobilize its armies, a Roman executive's agenda was fairly uncomplicated. Routine tasks and minor city problems filled the start of Metellus's year. When an aging wooden bridge that serviced the working-class Trastevere neighborhood collapsed and "people were thrown into the Tiber," his government responded with expenditure on infrastructure. When violent storms uprooted trees and dislodged roof tiles, the government assisted its citizens with money and manpower for repairs.

That spring, a thorny policy matter required Metellus's attention: how to provide benefits for veterans of the wars against Mithridates. In the early Roman Republic, the age of the selfless citizen-soldier, armies were levied from men who could afford the equipment required for combat. Upon completion of duty, they returned home to their own estates. By the first century B.C., with Rome's elite ensconced in the comforts of their farms and military units increasingly comprised of men with more modest incomes, a soldier's homecoming was precarious. One of Marius's most popular policies, implemented at the turn of the previous century, had been to award land grants to veterans in gratitude for their service. This program applied only to those who had seen combat in Marius's wars.

Pompey's veterans expected the same reward, but their general's extraordinary charisma complicated the situation. Any land bestowed upon his soldiers by the government would create for Pompey, as it had for Marius, thousands of loyalists, all of whom could be mobilized to vote for their benefactor in future elections. Veterans' relief stalled as the elites in the Senate indulged their hostility to Pompey.

No one opposed the land grant legislation more vehemently than Clodia's husband. Although their shared military service should have made the two natural allies, the friendship between Metellus and Pompey had deteriorated after the general declared his intent to divorce his wife, Metellus's half-sister Mucia, "in spite of having had children with her."

Pompey's next wife, whom he married the following year, was Julius Caesar's daughter Julia.

By summer, temperatures were rising on Palatine Hill. Irreconcilable differences exploded into open altercations in the Forum, and they mirrored a growing marital conflict. Clodia and Metellus were observed sparring over state and family matters in public and at private dinners. Lines were drawn over social issues, such as how to extend voting rights to the residents of the North Po region or whether to draft an aid package for debt-saddled Romans. Clodia, a committed populist, pressed her husband to do more. Metellus hemmed and hawed.

Metellus found himself with few defenders and, to make matters worse, at least one outspoken enemy. In June, Lucius Flavius, one of the tribunes, literally came to blows with Metellus outside the Senate building and dragged him to a nearby holding cell used for common criminals, where he barricaded Metellus inside using wooden benches from the Forum. Enraged and humiliated, Metellus smashed a hole in the cell's wall and demanded an emergency meeting of the Senate to adjudicate the dispute.

By then, Clodia and Metellus's stormiest marital rows concerned Clodia's brother Clodius. Six months after the Bona Dea Social Club affair, Clodius remained undeterred by the shadowy network of Optimates who had tried to destroy his reputation. Determined as ever to enter public life, he had become committed to government reform. How could the Roman Republic ever solve the crisis faced by its poorest citizens if not with legislation that authorized the distribution of subsidized food? Protections were needed for the city's workers, too, who wanted to organize as a group to safeguard their economic interests.

At thirty-two years old, still too young by a decade for highest office but showing his characteristic impatience, Clodius raised the possibility of standing for the board of the tribunes. The office, as the scrapes on Metellus's knuckles could confirm, was often won by mavericks. While Clodia found her brother's proposal intriguing, Metellus immediately vetoed the idea, and the feud between the year's consul and his wife

made its way into the correspondence between Cicero and a friend of
Clodia's, Atticus.

> June 3 in the year of the consulship
> of Metellus and Afranius [60 B.C.]
> News from Rome

Dear Atticus,

Metellus is turning out to be quite the patriotic politician
and, as I predicted, showing himself to be a trustworthy ally.
What's the ironic term of endearment Greeks use for Egypt's
ruthless kings, *philopatres*, "lovers of their country"? Well,
Metellus hasn't murdered anyone yet, but that label might suit
him just fine.

Clodius and I, on the other hand, are locked in an ongoing
exchange of jests and jibes.... He tells me his sister has been
keeping his own ambitions on a tight leash. I said, "I bet she
has a whole cabinet of devices that could keep a man in line."
Not my finest quip, I'll admit. "Unbecoming of a former consul.
Beneath your dignity," I can hear you chide.

But I can't stand the confident airs of that woman. How does
that famous song go? *She fights with her man. She's trouble,
trouble . . .*

Whatever inappropriate tune Cicero was humming that summer—even
scholars are unsure what lyric he was straining to recall—less than six
months into her husband's term, the image of Clodia as a force operating at
her consul husband's side had burrowed deep into the psyche of the family's fiercest detractor. From her husband's time in office, Clodia almost
surely gained firsthand knowledge of the daily workings of the executive,
of the crafting of legislation, and of the uses and abuses of power.

By the middle of June, the election for the following year's posts was
weeks away. Any projects that Metellus had hoped to complete were

scuttled as Romans began to evaluate the new slate of candidates. As workers erected the voting bridges—elevated planks across which the citizens walked to ensure that they cast their secret ballot in the appropriate urn—the public's attention drifted back to the world of campaign theatrics. Clodia remained supportive of her younger brother's ambitions, but Metellus did not relent in his opposition. To endorse a radical reformer at this stage of Metellus's career would mean lost contracts, lost overseas posts, and lost promotions once he left office. No consul, not even a retiring one, could afford to alienate his colleagues. The couple's disputes continued. Less than four months after he left office, sometime in early April 59 B.C., Metellus died.

Proud son, accomplished soldier, loving father, Quintus Caecilius Metellus Celer was forty-three at the time of his death. Judge, augur, and consul, he was survived by his brother, Quintus Metellus Nepos; his half-sister Mucia Tertia, the third wife of Pompey, presently divorced; his beloved daughter, Caecilia Metella, soon to be married; and his wife of seventeen years, Clodia. The cause of death was not reported. There are reasons to believe that Clodia inherited her husband's estate.

That the onetime consul died intestate—that is, without any estate planning, possessing in his study neither a last will and testament nor any stipulated financial trusts—was not just unusual for a man in Metellus's position; it was scandalous. Of the more than fifty million people who lived in the Mediterranean in Clodia's day, comprising citizens, freeborn foreigners, and slaves, only an estimated 10 percent drafted a will. The majority saw no need. Disposing of one's wealth was largely the prerogative of Metellus's set. The thought of dying without a plan to distribute their wealth horrified Metellus's peers. Those to whom much had been given were expected to gift to others what was no longer theirs to enjoy. Wealthy Romans took this duty very seriously; it brought great relief to friends and family when a man announced that he had notarized and filed his last will and testament. A common follow-up question to the news of a dear friend's sudden death was when, exactly, the family's executor might expect to share the details of the deceased's estate.

Formal invitations were sent to the elaborately choreographed and highly anticipated ceremonies at which a will was read. Attendees arrived in their best dress, and sudden changes of fortune were always possible. At the reading of the last will and testament of one freed slave who had become a successful businessman, the valuation of his estate surprised the crowd: 7,000 strong-necked oxen, in excess of 250,000 cattle, cash reserves totaling 60 million sesterces, and 4,116 enslaved domestic laborers across the man's farms and villas.

Lawyers took care to apportion an estate according to the dead man's wishes, and the distribution of inheritances and legacies—financial gifts to a deceased's relatives and friends—constituted a lucrative industry. The due diligence of investigatory work rooted out pretend beneficiaries. Determinations had to be made as to whether a spurious codicil had been added or a line surreptitiously emended. A swipe of the thumb across an ink-soaked parchment could erase fortunes. When the wax seals were broken and the tablets read, the theatrics alone set everyone on edge, not the least of whom were the legacy hunters. "Weasels," the later Roman poet Lucan called the lot. A "chirping brood" awaiting morsels from the swallow's mouth, they swooped in like "vultures at a corpse."

The Fathers had for centuries allowed freeborn Roman women to be named as beneficiaries and to inherit some, none, or all of a relative's savings. That permissive arrangement ended, however, with the passage of an important piece of legislation in Clodia's grandmother's day: Voconius's Law. Named for the Father who proposed it, Quintius Voconius, it was debated and eventually ratified in 169 B.C. under circumstances that seem suspiciously undocumented, despite the fact that it affected fully one half of the Roman population. The law prohibited men in Rome's wealthiest income brackets from designating women as their heirs. Investments, properties, enslaved human beings, and liquid assets: All the holdings of a man's estate were required to pass into the possession of men. Sons, nephews, and grandsons would not have to go through a woman to access the wealth that would finance their own futures.

The law, in effect, eliminated a well-established route by which wealthy women had participated in civic society. In the ancient world, charitable institutions and civic projects, in addition to cash-strapped husbands, all benefited from women's philanthropy. "I wish to be immortal by arranging a just and sympathetic trust," one woman, Phaenia Aromation, would declare on her tomb. Hailing from a family of prosperous merchants, she announced that she would endow a local gymnasium. From the interest on Phaenia's four-figure gift, the facility was able to purchase, among other necessities, its annual supply of olive oil, which trainers and athletes used to exfoliate and moisturize. The details of the trust stipulated that any excess jugs of oil be distributed to enslaved residents of the town at no cost. "No one should dare, either in a private or public capacity, to neglect my donation," she warned, the lesson being that when a woman had means, she could make men listen. The passage of Voconius's Law, by limiting the income that women could receive by inheritance, had ended most public gifts. Though the specifics of Clodia and Metellus's marriage contract are unknown, the law would have expressly forbidden Metellus from naming either Clodia or their daughter as his heir. With no man to support her, a widow was compelled to remarry—and quickly at that—if she lacked financial resources of her own.

Although the Fathers were silent about the motivations behind Voconius's Law—whether the social and economic inequities it introduced were accidental or intentional—men of Clodia's day still praised its impact. The "advantages . . . bestowed upon men" at women's expense, Cicero admitted, were substantial. For more than a hundred years, Voconius's Law was included in the annual publication of the magistrate's law code, to be enforced by that year's elected judges. A wealthy wife had little recourse for avoiding its penalties—that is, unless her husband conspired with her to circumvent the law.

Scholars are sufficiently informed about Roman society to offer a plausible set of reconstructions of what might have happened after Metellus's death. One strategy for wealth preservation was for the family to hide its assets from the census director. In another scenario, a husband might deliberately forget to prepare a will, at which point a loophole in the statute ensured that the widow's marriage dowry passed into her possession provided that her father was not alive to reclaim it. For couples who held joint property, this strategy offered an added benefit, in that common law would recognize the widow as one of the beneficiaries of her husband's estate; no guardian need be involved in the probate. It would take the Fathers another generation before they closed these loopholes by mandating that every Roman woman bear three children before she claimed her financial freedom.

With Metellus's death, it's highly probable that Clodia inherited not one but two fortunes: her dowry and some portion of her husband's estate. Having escaped by mere decades the Fathers' increasingly pathological desire to limit women's autonomy, Clodia in 59 B.C. was, perhaps for the first time in her life, free to act according to her own desires.

PART II

Experience

CHAPTER SEVEN

Clodia's Second Start

On a windswept seaside cliff I lie,
contemplating the many ships that pass . . .

—ISAIS, MERCHANT AND MOTHER OF TWO

In what had once been open fields surrounding Rome's walls, the messiness and disorganization of everyday life had by Clodia's day taken root and blossomed. Cramped apartments, colorful temples, sprawling office structures that housed the republic's growing bureaucracy, fountains, townhouses, and every imaginable market—flower sellers, vegetable sellers, livestock traders—lined streets. The imposing gates that had once marked the line where rusticity ended and urbanity began softened into inconspicuous archways that became the charming centerpieces of local neighborhoods. With few local threats, periphery and city center blurred.

Roads, named for their destination, at least sent you in the right direction if you were trying to leave the capital. The Via Ostiensis exited Rome to the southwest through the city's industrial-looking warehouse district, where depots with pier-and-beam floors protected the city's precious grain supply from the soil's mildew and mold. Framed by stacks of ceramic shipping containers holding wine imported from Sicily and olive oil consignments from Spain, the road charted a course along the low, winding banks of the river Tiber until, sixteen miles later, pleasant stone-pine streets and the brick construction of Rome's harbor, Ostia, rose into view. An unpretentious town of fewer than ten thousand residents and a port with modest facilities, just large enough to handle important domestic shipments (international vessels docked in the better-equipped Bay of Naples), Ostia contained a sizable population of ordinary Romans: longshoremen, barkeeps, middlemen who booked passage on departing vessels, butchers, bakers, and ceramic lamp makers, whose trade included the necessary linen wicks.

At the eighth milestone of the Ostian Way, long before it reached that noisy destination, a small road turned inland again, surfing through the countryside's green-gold fields. At the twelfth mile of poplars, maples, holm oaks, and juniper, the hamlet of Solonium appeared. After her husband's funeral in April, Clodia retreated to the bucolic setting of her family's estate about a half day's journey in the direction of the coast. There was a welcome solitude in the Roman campagna, fewer interruptions by tangential acquaintances or the unpredictable distractions of life on Rome's Palatine Hill, and more time for planned, sustained interactions with friends.

Metellus's death, for all its financial benefits, put Clodia in an unusual social situation. For Roman men who lost a spouse, a second life could start quickly—as quickly as he identified another woman to wed. But the death of her husband robbed a Roman woman of any immediate control over her future. A widow, largely regarded by the Fathers as a placeholder for her deceased husband, was legally required to remarry after ten months, obligated in the meantime to grow her hair as a public display of grief, and expected to remain faithful, chaste, and devoted to the memory of her spouse, whose name she was required to honor until she took her next husband. In the interim, custom labeled her a *vidua*, a word whose initial consonant native Latin speakers pronounced as if it started with the *w* their alphabet lacked. For a bereft husband, there was no comparable term, the classical world's paternalistic assumption being that for adult men, brides were aplenty.

Clodia was lucky not to face financial hardship. Their fathers deceased, their husbands gone, many less fortunate Roman women struggled to pay the landlord, provide for their children, or settle the monthly meal tab at the tavern. Women faced slim prospects for employment, as regulations restrained a free Roman woman's access to work. Picking up a trade—fruit seller, vegetable seller, hairdresser, nurse—was an urgent necessity for some. Women adept at accounting or supervising might fulfill the position of *vilica*, farm manager. Country estates required year-round upkeep during their wealthy owners' seasonal absences. Setting the workloads for the staff, stocking the larder, storing leftovers, planning menus for the servants as well as for the master, mistress, and their guests, were tasks that fell to women as well as men. Frequently, these positions went to trustworthy slaves. When a worker took sick, decisions about whether to sanction a doctor's visit or demand continued labor lay with these supervisors. They watched the sky for downpours and, when it rained, shifted the staff to indoor duties. The most pragmatic implemented strict regimes of hourly sweeping and cleaning, to keep idle farmhands busy.

⤜⤛

If the farmhouse staff anticipated a somber stay when Clodia's horses pulled into the estate at Solonium sometime in early April 59 B.C., their mistress's demeanor surprised them. Clodia instructed her servants to prepare the villa for guests; an Appius family council had been called. The whole clan of brothers, sisters, and spouses descended upon the farm on April 16 or April 17. At the top of the agenda was a debate about Clodius's aspirations.

Clodius's populism irritated the traditionalists in the family, chief among them Clodia's older brother, Appius Junior. Clodius had been a modestly successful provincial treasurer in Sicily and during his days in the military had found that he had the eloquence to amplify the voices of the disgruntled. His talents could attract votes. Since becoming the household's elder statesman, however, the thirty-nine-year-old, practical-minded Appius questioned his younger brother's enthusiasm for working- and lower-class causes. Clodius's talk of implementing an expanded government program to feed the republic's neediest citizens, in particular, risked alienating the republic's wealthier households. Their electoral backing would be essential if, as everyone in the family assumed, Appius Junior planned in coming years to stand for consul.

For the son of an establishment family, the easiest path to political power meant adhering to Sulla's conservative platform.

Ambitious and confident, the thirty-three-year-old Clodius threatened to upset his elder brother's political hopes with his aspiration to become a tribune. By law, only members of the plebeian caste were eligible to run for that office—but Clodius had a plan. Restricting the office to lower-income candidates had, during the early republic when a wide income gap separated patrician and plebeian families, increased economic diversity among elected officials. But over time, as military conquest and the accumulation of intergenerational wealth increased the prosperity of plebeians and patricians alike, the wealth gap narrowed. Gradually, many plebeians boasted patrician-sized financial portfolios. Depending on the family, the distinction between the two groups might be meaningless.

The election for tribunes, held in the autumn, was a highly consequential moment in the republic's balance of power. By the first century B.C., it was not uncommon to find affluent plebeians who subscribed to the same conservative ideology as their patrician peers. Senators cajoled, connived, and coopted the wealthier candidates for tribune to endorse the elite's legislative priorities. A constitutional office that had once championed and safeguarded the concerns of Rome's lowest classes now regularly subverted them.

Amid Solonium's farmhouse luxuries, Clodius announced that he had persuaded a plebeian household, the Fonteius family, to propose a formal adoption that would annul his status as a patrician. The move between the two legal categories—a technical maneuver called in Latin a *transitio*—required the government's imprimatur but would open a path for this privileged son of the house of Appius to circumvent the law and stand for election as tribune. Two high-placed government and religious officials had recently authorized the move.

The forty-nine-year-old Pompey, whose peers resented his rapidly rising popularity, and the forty-two-year-old Julius Caesar, one of that year's consuls and an avowed reformer, shared Clodius's desire to weaken the political establishment. In the early months of 59 B.C., both men—Pompey in his capacity as an augur, Caesar in his role as the republic's chief priest, which he held concurrently with the post of consul—held positions of significant influence. Both offices had the power to stall government business. Either could have rejected Clodius's transition.

As Caesar and Pompey well knew, obstructionism was a frequent threat in the bitterly divided republic. No problem was more urgent than an overhaul of the filibuster technique that enabled religious officials to suspend business by claiming to have seen inauspicious signs. A version of this "motion to oppose," a wordy, six-syllable procedural term in Latin befitting the legislative congestion it unleashed, the *obnuntiatio*, was particularly abused. Authority to deploy it originally lay in the hands of the augurs, who were tasked with consulting the sky for unfavorable omens in advance of legislative business. From the direction of lightning flashes, peals of thunder, or flocks of birds on a disconcerting path above the Apennine Mountains, they deduced whether a bill met with divine approval. When these portents were interpreted favorably, a legislative vote could proceed.

Because augurs were appointed from the Fathers' ranks, in practice they were rarely called upon to register their objections; a broad consensus among senators reached during the preliminary drafting of a bill usually propelled a law to passage. During divisive deliberations, however, partisan augurs shamelessly stalled the government's work. By Clodia's day, other officials, including consuls, regularly invoked the augurs' authority to stall legislation they personally opposed.

By March 59 B.C., obstruction had already dealt Pompey and Caesar a series of legislative defeats. Pompey continued to advocate with a stubborn Senate for the welfare of his veterans, to no avail. Caesar, who tried to spearhead the passage of land distribution through the Senate, faced opposition. When a motion was proposed to repeal Sulla's ban on the descendants of his political enemies from holding office, that proposal, too, was stalled. The partisanship was manifest to all that year when Caesar's colleague as consul, Bibulus, used his augural power to object to the legislation. An augur customarily stood on Capitoline Hill, which offered sweeping vistas, to take the auspices, the majesty of the site reinforcing his authority. In a mockery of protocol, Bibulus announced his opposition from the window of his townhouse.

The deadlock rendered the Senate, Rome's most august body, dysfunctional. Three months into Caesar's term, people flooded the Forum to protest the corruption of "do-nothing Bibulus," chanting, "Caesar will do what Bibulus will not!" At the end of one afternoon—as the Romans styled it, "at the ninth hour" of the working day—Caesar put the government's stamp of approval on the technicalities of Clodius's adoption. Pompey had already given his blessing.

So it was that, in mid-April, the Appius clan gathered to learn Clodius's next intentions. There was a rumor circulating among Caesar's allies that Clodius might be persuaded to lead an embassy to Armenia, as a sign of goodwill between Rome and the kingdom. After Mithridates's demise and Rome's acquisition of his Black Sea territory, an agreement had been made with neighboring Armenia to respect its sovereignty in exchange for its political and military support in the region. As collateral, Pompey had kidnapped the Armenian prince Tigranes, and placed him in the home of a political ally in Rome. Clodius supported the young man's return home, and the assignment to lead the embassy to the Armenian king would raise his profile as a statesman. But why should a newly declared plebeian, on the doorstep of a promising domestic political career, leave the peninsula now? For the first time in a generation, a more progressive Roman Republic—the dream of both Clodia and Clodius—looked achievable.

During the family meeting, Clodia's endorsement of her brother's campaign came swiftly, her support unequivocal. Clodius's wife, Fulvia, a formidable woman in her late twenties whom he had recently wed, also expressed enthusiasm. Although born to aristocratic parents, she shared her husband's commitment to addressing the republic's injustices and brought appreciable talents. She was later remembered as a strategist, a communicator, and an organizer with insight beyond her

years. Plutarch condemned her brio in his later biography of her third
husband, Marc Antony. "Neither weaving nor women's usual domestic
chores held [Fulvia's] interest, nor was she content to give orders . . . at
home. What she wanted was to lead a leader, to command a general."

Clodius, Clodia, and Fulvia's wishes prevailed. Within days, word of
the result of their deliberations trickled out, along with snide second-
hand reports from the adversarial Cicero of the Appius family's "displays of remorseless extravagance." Clodia "sounded the charge," as one
source puts it in military idiom, for her brother's campaign launch.

From a letter preserved in Cicero's posthumously published collections, modern historians hear the first ripples of that consequential
meeting, as news of Clodius's plans reached a drinking establishment
thirty miles from Rome.

> April 19, in the year of the consulship
> of Caesar and Bibulus [59 B.C.],
> 4 p.m.
> News from Tres Tabernae,
> outside Rome

> Dear Atticus,
> I was just leaving the coast at Antium and had reached the
> Appian Way outside Tres Tabernae, right during the start of the
> Harvest Festival for Ceres, when my young friend, Curio, runs
> into me on his way from Rome and along comes a young man
> with letters from you. *Synkurema*, as the Greeks say. Synchron-
> icity! When Curio asked me if I had heard the latest news, I cau-
> tiously said no.
> "Clodius is standing for tribune," he said.
> "You can't be serious," I said.
> "I am. He's intimating that he wants to topple the whole edi-
> fice of the republic's government."
> "What does Caesar have to say?"

"He denies having anything to do with Clodius's adoption. Caesar, Memmius, and Nepos confessed shock and surprise although regret might be a more accurate description."

I thanked the messenger, saw him off, and rushed to crack the seal on your letters.

Some people, I know, prefer to hear news as it happens, but nothing pleases me more than consulting your commentary about the rumination and the cogitation happening in Rome on a daily basis: Clodius's planning, and his sister, Rome's own Cow-Eyed Hera, sounding the trumpet on his behalf. That mercurial number two of theirs, "Athenio,"* or whatever Sicilian rebel slave's name I imagine he carries, also appears to have enlisted as their banner-carrier, to judge from Gnaeus's letter and Theophanes and Memmius's conversation. I'm ravenous for more details about that family gathering at Solonium you've mentioned but understand why you might prefer to keep mum. Can't wait to join you to learn more.

I'm drafting this note at 4 o'clock in the afternoon immediately after having read yours, but I will likely send it by messenger tomorrow, first thing in the morning.

Terentia was pleased to receive your note, by the way. She sends you her love.

In the *Iliad*, Homer applied the epithet "cow-eyed" to Zeus's spouse, Hera, who moves about Mount Olympus as the hypervigilant queen, apprised of every divine and human scheme. However much the Greeks admired Hera's charm and intellect, praising a Roman woman for her near-360-degree vision was no unambiguous compliment—even if, as the ancients well knew, a cow's eyes could be quite striking and comely.

Clodia's brother's candidacy fired up supporters and convulsed the

---

* Though scholars are unsure of the identity of Clodius's associate in this passage, it's conjectured that he might have been a man named Sextus Cloelius.

establishment. Clodius indicated that his first legislative priority would be a food relief bill. Many of the capital's poorer citizens required assistance to meet the rising cost of grain, a daily essential. Suspecting that such a generous subsidy would fail to win support in the Senate, Clodius's team promised to offer, if elected, a second bill: a constitutional reform of obstructionism.

Clodius's third proposal would boost the fortunes of the city's working classes by restoring their rights to assembly, a liberty that the Fathers had, in just the past decade, revoked. For generations, bakers, carpenters, dockhands, shipbuilders, masons, merchants, and artisans had possessed the freedom to gather in *collegia*, or guild halls. Community centers, financial safety nets, and social clubs, the city's *collegia* provided meals to their members, connected them with financial patrons, and mobilized workers in advance of important votes in the assemblies. Many members were freed slaves. Fearful of workers' gatherings during the debt crises of the 60s B.C., the Fathers had shuttered the city's *collegia* by senatorial decree. Repealing that law, Clodius expected, would restore worker solidarity.

The fourth, final plank of Clodius's platform was reform of one of the more antiquated procedures of the Roman census. The precise language of the reform, a targeted, scalpel-like intervention into the complicated process by which the republic verified income, was calibrated to win broad support among both elite and non-elite constituencies. Whether voters heard Clodius's call for nuance was another matter.

On the Roman campaign trail, mention of the census, however benign or restrained, perennially stirred passions. The last attempt to hold a census—in official terms, to make a complete demographic and economic registration of the republic's freeborn male population for the purpose of enrolling new voters—had been slated for the year 65 B.C. But it had ended prematurely when census officers could not agree on whether the republic should extend citizenship to the residents of the North Po valley. They also disagreed about how newly freed slaves should be assigned to voting districts. Almost three decades after the civil war, partisan recalcitrance was still disenfranchising large parts of the electorate. At the root of the impasse was the Fathers' fear that new voters would unseat the establishment.*

Within weeks of Clodius's declaration of candidacy, resistance hardened. Caesar's co-consul, Bibulus, resorted to an egregious gambit to blunt Clodius's electoral momentum. Invoking the augur's authority, he postponed the year's elections. The modest delay—perhaps a few weeks—would allow Clodius's field of rivals a short-term reprieve during which they could sharpen their attacks. But it was not a long-term solution to the rising tide of elite resentment. By April's end, Cicero, in a letter to his and Clodia's mutual friend Atticus, articulated his peers' increasingly dire concerns and his own instinct for self-preservation.

> April 26, in the year of the consulship
> of Caesar and Bibulus [59 B.C.]
> News from Formiae,
> at the Latium coast

Dear Atticus,

How great my expectations to hear your report. What has Bibulus told you? Can you pass along what Cow-Eyed Hera said? What transpired at your recent dinner party with her? My ears are thirsty for news.

Recent events have left me unnerved. How would you say it in Greek? I'd prefer that we were "tyrannted" (Is that a legitimate Greek verb?)—by which I mean, I'd prefer our side resurrect Sulla's old style of governing. Strongman politics seems a far better solution to our predicament than trying to resolve hopeless partisan differences.

---

* Clodius eventually proposed forceful legislation to resolve both these issues. Whether he articulated his plans as early as the summer of 59 B.C. remains a point of debate.

Two days later, in a follow-up letter, Cicero underscored that last point. "Bibulus's action in holding up the elections may be very noble," he confessed to Atticus. "But what does it achieve except a personal protest which offers no solution to the country's troubles?"

An earlier generation of scholars was often reluctant to invest these mentions of Clodia in Cicero's letters with any significance. Given the strictly gendered parameters of Clodia's day, when men's voices predominated and only men's votes mattered, ancient documents have seemed most legible as straightforward sources for the lives of Roman men. But over the past century, feminist calls to read between the lines of paternalistic narratives have enabled us to see them as hidden transcripts preserving the forgotten experiences of important women.

Reading the corpus of Cicero's letters with more magnanimity allows us to see Clodia as a determined power broker and unavoidable go-between for her brother's campaign. The implication behind Cicero's stream of inquiries is that Clodia and Atticus enjoyed an unusual parity despite their differences of age, gender, class, and frequently, distance, since Clodia resided in Rome and Atticus was usually in Greece. For a widow to command his attention—and Cicero's—on the printed page testifies to her prodigious influence. Clodia occupies nearly a quarter of the correspondence addressed by Cicero to Atticus during the remaining eight months of the year. The only other matter that fills the men's letters in 59 B.C. to a comparable extent is Rome's preoccupation with the deteriorating situation in Egypt, where the Macedonian-born monarch, Ptolemy the Twelfth, heir of Alexander the Great—incompetent militarily, politically, and financially—was facing growing unrest and revolution.

✧

Fifty-two years old in 59 B.C., fifteen years Clodia's senior, Atticus would have been younger than Clodia's father but older than her brother Appius. Politics had never held much appeal for him. His upbringing among Rome's equestrian class, a well-to-do group of citizens theoretically eligible for higher office but less affluent than senatorial households, inculcated in him an epicurean sensibility for living well but avoiding unnecessary conflict. A love of fine art and culture accompanied him throughout life. After his parents' death, he resolved that the finer aspects of the Mediterranean table should take priority over the perennial race for public honors.

In the 80s B.C., as Sulla's regime became ever more authoritarian, Atticus found himself constitutionally incapable of tolerating the Roman Republic's descent into madness and moved to Athens. By his twenties, he had become a well-regarded bon vivant, a shrewd businessman, and a sworn Hellenophile. In those early years of the European conflict with Mithridates, he purchased dilapidated apartments in Athens and transformed them into lucrative rental properties. His days were spent poring over ledgers of real estate and shipping transactions. For friends seeking paintings, marble friezes, or bronzes from Asia Minor to decorate their townhouses and villas, Atticus arranged the acquisitions, inspected the crates, and deducted an appropriate commission. He was known for his integrity.

In a world that valued practicality, Atticus embraced the life of the mind. After the capture of Mithridates, when eastern Mediterranean lands opened to Roman merchants, financiers, and tax collectors, he leveraged his knowledge of the emerging markets to become an avid collector of scrolls. Teams of secretaries, tutors, and research assistants drafted lists of multivolume works for Atticus to acquire. With the efficiency of a modern assembly line, he instructed his slaves to copy each one as it entered his collection. Then they made duplicates to fulfill requests for reproductions.

Atticus's reward was a leisured life, removed from the republic's manic policy debates. When business brought him to Rome, he dined with Clodia and dined well. Cicero professed jealousy of the pair's convivial meetings. But Clodia and Atticus likely shared an awareness of their existence on the republic's margins. Atticus's greatest satisfaction was the purchase of a ranch on the Adriatic coast, in Epirus, where the land held varietals of sweet-scented apples and myrtle berries, and there were spacious fields to raise cattle and graze horses. The entrance to his ranch lay well removed from Epirus's main road.

Clodia, too, knew what it meant to inhabit an in-between space, adjacent to power. Atticus lived there by preference, Clodia by necessity.

⌖

By summer, the election for tribune was accelerating the public's desire for political change. Clodius's message resonated. Younger voters and passionate, sometimes volatile, partisans styled themselves Clodiani, creating a nickname for their movement from their rising political hero. One commentator, in a snarky aside about Clodia's agility as a dancer, observed that she and her brother "anticipated each other's every move." As the campaign entered its final stretch, Clodia was her brother's consigliere. When the election was finally held, Clodius won his seat. The inauguration was scheduled, as was customary, for early December.

Most Roman politicians prided themselves on preserving and protecting the status quo. (A popular refrain heard upon leaving office was, "With scarcely any noise, scarcely leaving any rut, the wheel of the state has made its revolution.") The prospect that Clodius might improve the quality of life for ordinary people generated renewed interest in the campaign, and speculation abounded about his ambitious agenda as tribune. According to observers, Clodius began to intimate that no Roman—not even a former elected official—should be immune to prosecution for past crimes. That included consuls who might have executed citizens unlawfully.

Cicero, who less than four years previously had executed Catiline's alleged band of insurrectionists without a trial, recognized in Clodius's veiled language a cause for alarm.

Late July, in the year of the consulship
of Caesar and Bibulus [59 B.C.]
News from Rome

Dear Atticus,

Why didn't you stay in Rome? I know, I know, you would have
stayed if you had foreseen what was going to happen. To think,
you and I then would have been easily able to keep watch over
Clodius or at least would have been able to divine his intentions.
As things go, he's turned volatile, secretive, and his plans uncer-
tain. He's been on the attack in recent days and seems likely to
pursue whatever chance or opportunity will dictate. . . .

There's a stream of friends coming and going from my house.
Acquaintances run up to greet me on the street. I have to say, in
some way, it's just like old times, back when I was sitting in the
consul's chair. . . . But apart from your friendship and trust, I'm
hard-pressed for your wise counsel. How quickly do you think
you can get here? There's a lot I can learn in the meantime from
our mutual friend Varro although your presence might make
my inquiries proceed more smoothly, and there's a lot to be dis-
cerned from Clodius himself. . . .

But when it comes to discerning the thoughts of other influential men, such as Caesar's confederates, Crassus and Pompey,
your presence would benefit me immensely, especially since
you might provide access to Cow-Eyed Hera's thinking. Am I in
legal jeopardy?

Still clouded in the stale euphoria of his accomplishments as consul
four years earlier, Cicero had presumed that no one would dare prosecute him for his illegalities. But by the time of Clodius's election as
tribune, which empowered the People's Coalition, or Populares, it no
longer seemed certain that Cicero could evade the consequences of his

action. Ordinary Romans, discontented with the Fathers' inability or unwillingness to hold one of their own to account, wanted justice. The rising political temperature in the streets contributed to the fraying of Cicero's nerves. Toward the end of the month, Cicero predicted to Atticus, "There's going to be an eruption soon."

By August, many of the Optimates, staunch traditionalists who saw governing as their birthright and reform as anathema, adopted "a widespread contempt for anyone [else] in a position of power." Cicero's writing became outright panicky.

> August, in the year of the consulship of Caesar and
> Bibulus [59 B.C.]
> News from Rome

> Dear Atticus,
> Don't be alarmed that this letter has arrived penned by an unrecognizable hand. You can only imagine how preoccupied I am. There's no moment to spare. My voice is gone. I'm dictating this while I'm walking. . . .
> Cow-Eyed Hera and her brother are planning something sinister, I just can't say what. Clodius admits it, then denies it when asked by Pompey, then repeats it and confirms it when asked by someone else. . . . If you're there, I need you to wake up and return as fast as you can. Sprint, gallop, fly. . . . If you can't be back in time to vote, at least try to be here for the announcement of the election results. Your presence in Rome remains of the greatest import to me.

Cicero resented the public for turning against him and disparaged it for not acknowledging the efforts he had expended on its behalf. "I've done my part," he confessed to Atticus. The thought of ever again serving as "captain of the ship of state to a group of such ungrateful passengers," as he put it, was inconceivable. Two additional letters from Cicero requesting Atticus's presence follow. But for the remainder of the year, there is no indication that Atticus ever left his ranch in Epirus.

On December 10, the patrician-turned-plebeian Publius Clodius Pulcher officially commenced his one-year term on the republic's board of ten tribunes. Romans would always remember these months as a pivotal time in the evolution of their republic, when three of the day's richest, most powerful men—the so-called triumvirate of Julius Caesar, Pompey, and Marcus Crassus—struck an alliance to protect one another's interests and, collectively, to exercise their authority over Rome's weakened institutions. This "band of three men," Romans said, was like the arrival of a "three-headed monster," rivaling the beasts of classical myth. Overlooked, or at least underappreciated, were the year's three underdogs: Clodius, Fulvia, and Clodia.

The celebrity politician quickly proved himself a capable legislator, passing all four planks of his reformist platform within weeks of the new year, 58 B.C. The next order of business was to identify what financial resources were available to fund these ambitious proposals. The estimated first-year cost for Clodius's state-subsidized food program, which would allow every resident of Rome ten years and older to claim five full measures of grain per month, has been calculated by modern scholars in excess of one hundred million sesterces. No source of revenue in the republic's budget could cover such expenses—except a military invasion.

Clodius, angling for establishment support, proposed the annexation of Cyprus. In January 58 B.C., the island was one of the last two autonomous territories in the Mediterranean world, along with the much larger and wealthier kingdom of Egypt. The island, tucked in the northeastern corner of the Mediterranean and the sea's third largest after Sicily and Sardinia, lay about a half day's journey by merchant vessel from the southern coast of Asia Minor. The coast of Egypt was reachable in two days. Mountainous on both its northern and southern sides, Cyprus boasted a broad central fertile plain whose nutrient-rich soils were farmed with the three core Mediterranean staples: olive oil, wine, and whole grains. It was rich in other resources as well: timber and aromatics and precious stores of copper, which, alloyed with tin, made bronze, the metal that was fashioned into a range of essential tools, from weapons to domestic accessories. From the island's interior came a highly prized, oregano-scented marjoram oil, a "divinely seductive perfume," befitting the birthplace of Aphrodite, the Greek goddess of love. Ancients regarded the island's salt as of the highest quality, no modest claim when gourmands could list 120 different colors and varieties. Wine from Cyprus had an earthy nose, as divine as the island from which it was harvested.

Cyprus featured a rich mix of native customs and imported cultures, spanning thousands of years of ancient history. For nearly three hundred years, since the death of Alexander the Great, Egypt's Greek-speaking dynasts, the Ptolemies, a family of lavish-living monarchs who styled themselves the successors to the pharaohs and whose land holdings and financial assets ranked them the wealthiest family in the ancient world, had governed the island as a personal protectorate. A Roman invasion of Cyprus would immediately test Egyptian–Roman relations.

In February, the Fathers appointed one of their own, Cato the Younger, as supreme military commander for the island's annexation. Rome would seize the island's assets, which it would liquidate to fill its coffers and finance, or at least stabilize, Clodius's plan for annual grain subsidies. Roman authorities delivered their demands to the island's administrator and representative of the Egyptian crown, Ptolemy of Cyprus, the younger brother of the colorful king of Egypt, Ptolemy the Twelfth, nicknamed the Musician. The demands were simple. In exchange for Cyprus's cooperation and, of course, its governor's immediate resignation, Rome was prepared to offer a prestigious lifetime appointment, priest of Aphrodite, in the new territory that the republic would administer. Humiliated by the proposal, threatened by military invasion, and unable to marshal an effective military response, Ptolemy committed suicide. His brother, who watched the events unfold with great apprehension, declined to intervene.

Throughout Egypt, anger mounted at the king's dereliction. Little did the Egyptian people know that in his two decades in power their king had assumed an astronomical level of foreign debt, borrowing upward of 6,000 talents from overseas Roman creditors—the equivalent of the kingdom's annual income from its collection of taxes on crops and imported goods—to bribe Roman senators and earn their assurance that Egypt would remain a free, independent territory. That is, if the payments kept coming. Corrupt and cowardly, Ptolemy had few options; sending the Egyptian army to defend Cyprus was unthinkable, confronting his Roman creditors impossible. Protesting their government's incompetence, 300,000 people poured into Alexandria's promenades and plazas from their taverns, shops, houses, and warehouses in the summer of 58 B.C. They flooded the palace quarters near the harbor, to demand their wayward ruler be held to account.

On the nearby island of Pharos, the hub of all maritime arrivals and departures, Alexandria's lighthouse soared 330 feet above the harbor. At its top burned a powerful lantern whose artificial star, mariners reported, dipped below the horizon of the sea at an impressive fifty miles' distance from shore. It was the Ptolemies' mathematicians who were the first to infer a round earth, using little more than a set of measuring sticks, a basic familiarity with the sun's shadow, and a knowledge of the theorems of geometry to calculate the planet's circumference. They accomplished it with an accuracy within 150 miles. This planetary curvature, the Alexandrian scientist Eratosthenes wrote, explained why "sailors, as they approach their destination, behold the shore continually raising itself to their view, and why objects which at first seemed low, begin to elevate themselves"—an optical phenomenon that explained how Egypt's most familiar landmark would have disappeared from the view of a distraught monarch fleeing under the cloak of night.

The Egyptians chose his eldest daughter, eighteen-year-old Berenice, to rule in her father's place. Meanwhile, Ptolemy the Musician sailed for Rome to meet his creditors—among them, Pompey—and plot to reclaim his kingdom, accompanied by his eleven-year-old daughter, her father's darling, Cleopatra. Her future was as blank as the horizon.

CHAPTER EIGHT

Clodia's Romance

Journeys, my kinsman, are oft ill-timed.

—SULPICIA

Sometime that spring or summer of the year 58 B.C., a workman came to Palatine Hill with buckets and brushes to add a rental sign, in paint, to the frescoed surface outside one of the neighborhood's luxury townhouses. It advertised an unused space available for rent on the top floor of a quiet residential mansion. Archaeologists have found and photographed similar vermilion-inked painted signs preserved on the yellow exterior walls of ancient homes throughout Roman territory. Here's one example, from Pompeii:

FOR IMMEDIATE AVAILABILITY.

At "The Venus Baths," a five-year lease starting August 13th.

An elegant suite of rooms adjacent to the baths, including the option

for shops, with luxury quarters, including a second-floor apartment.

In the property owned by Julia of Spurius.

Prestige clients only.

Inquire within.

The range of amenities often determined how quickly these offers were taken up, with some properties, like Julia's "luxury quarters," offering the tenant access to delightful gardens, tranquil orchards, and mosaic-tiled pools. Some boasted proximity to a tavern, for lodgers who enjoyed taking their meals in a sociable setting and with a pitcher of wine.

The landlords and landladies who managed these properties belonged to a world of leisured entrepreneurs who kept themselves unusually well-informed about local business and politics. Many were women, smart, established, and well-connected, who owned more space than they could occupy, and sometimes had more free time than they cared to admit. Most sought lodgers whose social qualifications—an accomplished lecturer, a man of letters, or better still, a promising youth embarking on a career in the law—enhanced their own repute; some hoped for a presence that would enrich the neighborhood during its waking hours.

A Palatine Hill address in Rome, even without Pompeii's pools and nightlife, offered any young man a desirable foothold from which to craft the next chapter of his career. For twenty-six-year-old Marcus Caelius Rufus, recently returned from a year-long stint as a junior government officer in North Africa, it fit the bill perfectly. Born in the 80s B.C. on the far side of the Apennine Mountains, in the hill towns of the central Adriatic coast, he was raised by a modestly well-to-do father. He was sent to Rome in his adolescence to study rhetoric under the leading practitioner of the day, the wealthiest man in the republic, Marcus Licinius Crassus. In Rome, Rufus joined a flock of young men of similar economic background and lofty, if unspecified, ambitions who, in adulation of long-dead giants, pretentiously lugged around copies of *The History of Alexander the Great* by Cleitarchus of Colophon. In those days, men twice Rufus's age still trekked hundreds of miles to stay in roadside inns across the Parthian deserts where Alexander was known to have once enjoyed repast and repose. Standing in the presence of the general's statue, few men measured up.

Under Crassus's tutelage and, more significantly, with Crassus's letter of recommendation, the young Rufus, barely twenty, made his debut on the Roman political scene. Earning a coveted overseas appointment from the government, he took up a post as adjutant on the staff of a provincial magistrate in Carthage. Personal and professional connections likely led to the opportunity. Rufus's own pluck allowed him to survive.

Even a century after the conclusion of Rome's last Carthaginian War, a North African assignment posed considerable personal and professional risk, as Romans were seen as occupiers and colonizers. When the army left, boatloads of civilian contractors and rapacious merchant-men had poured onto shore to extract every imaginable profit from the land's agricultural riches. Rufus's father's investment portfolio conveniently held properties inland from the Gulf of Tunis, whose soils were highly esteemed for the quality of their olives and grapes, and where Rufus's family's knowledge of the terrain was helpful to local Roman authorities. Three years later, having earned high marks from his superior officers, Rufus boarded a vessel back to Italy, the sea journey home prompting bright-eyed, if nervous, dreams about his future.

Rufus was raised to see the value in every public legal dispute and, like other men his age, was allured by visions of holding forth in the Forum as a well-respected orator and statesman. That year, the young Rufus filed a corruption lawsuit against a retired politician. Impressed with his argument, the jury ruled in Rufus's favor. Although Clodius and Cato's plans to annex the island of Cyprus were then still being formulated, every man of Rufus's upbringing and aspirations imagined the day when he, too, like Sulla from Athens or Pompey from Pontus, would parade through Rome's streets with his own batch of looted Greek marbles and precious bronze artworks. Cartloads of spoils constituted every Roman man's definition of success. For those who could boast of having received a prestigious education under Marcus Licinius Crassus, lucre was a birthright, a political career their due.

Within months of returning to Rome, the young Rufus, to his family's delight and his father's approval, was elected to his first public office, city manager of Interamnia, his hometown. The idea of acquiring a residence in Rome, appropriate to Rufus's broader aspirations, dawned shortly thereafter: economical, temporary, and above all, if possible, free from his father's oversight. When the Romans remarked that successful men lived in the Forum, the comment was no idle figure of speech. Claiming a Palatine Hill address advertised a young man's drive to achieve success. A rental unit close to the center of town, an unassuming place where he could retire at the end of a busy day in the Forum, would be ideal. And so, sometime in the summer of 58 B.C., scholars have deduced, he came to be the tenant of an apartment held by Clodia's family. The monthly rent, 10,000 sesterces, was paid to Clodius.

Rufus was tall, radiant, and strikingly handsome. Friends described him as down to earth, easygoing, and jovial in company. It would prove difficult for a thirty-seven-year-old widow not to notice him.

In Clodia's Rome, heterosexual sex, if not paid for, meant procreation. It's difficult to find any contemporary Roman writer who allowed for the possibility that passion could make an appearance in the life of a Roman woman past the usual age of marriage. Even the most liberal-minded men, such as many of the ancient Roman poets, tended to parrot traditional expectations. "Play as you please, and very soon / produce children," Catullus wrote. Arranged marriages and sexual partnerships forced upon their scandalously young daughters—those were the Fathers' acceptable ways. Widows, divorcees, and women of a certain age who sought satisfaction from romantic pursuits flirted with the reputation of whore or high-class madam.

Puerile and polysyllabic, often in the same poem, Catullus and his sharp wit have for centuries held an immovable place at the center of Clodia's story because, according to later Roman tradition, he had an affair with an enigmatic noblewoman thought to have been Clodia. The woman, called Lesbia, and her sexual allure lurk behind several of Catullus's love-addled verses: "Lesbia whom alone Catullus / Loved more than self and all his kin"; "no sooner ... / Do I look at you than there's no power left me." The second-century-A.D. writer Apuleius titillated his readers by claiming that this Lesbia was a pseudonym for the first-century-B.C. Clodia. Descending into seedy imagery, Catullus declared that Lesbia was notorious for seducing men "at every street corner and back alley." Her multiple lovers, he claimed, included himself and Rufus. But neither he nor Apuleius ever provided any corroborating information, and with so many Clodias in the historical record, skepticism abounds. When Catullus published his poetry collection after returning from a post in Bithynia in the 50s B.C., his Lesbia was still a married woman, with hobbies more befitting a young bride than a mature wife. At this point Clodia's husband, Metellus, was already dead.

The literary mystery deepened in 2012 when researchers at Oxford announced an overlooked candidate for Catullus's Lesbia: Appius Junior's daughter and Clodia's niece, also named Clodia. A younger contemporary of Catullus, she was married at the time to one of Pompey's sons, Gnaeus, whom multiple writers, including Catullus, described as *fatuus*, foolish or insufferable. Whether the new identification can ever be substantiated, in the end Catullus's poetry offers only thin, unconvincing evidence that Clodia had multiple liaisons. Her more reliably documented romance with Rufus must stand on its own.

Role models were scarce for a widow of thirty-seven who entertained the thought of a consenting relationship with a man whom she was free to pursue on her own terms. While upper-class divorcees and widows were expected to take second or third or sometimes fourth husbands, the motives were pragmatic and the woman's wishes an afterthought. A woman who remarried might do so to cement a business alliance between her brother and a rival's family, for example, or to guarantee a more stable financial future for her fatherless child. In these elaborate schemes, a Roman woman never rose past the role of pawn. So absurd was the notion that a woman could fall in love that the trope drove the plots of the classical world's best-loved comedies, where the loose women who worked in the city's sex shops came as close to the idea of a sexually liberated woman as the Roman Fathers' ideology would allow. Unheard of was the mature woman who, unconcerned for a husband or her heirs, dared to assert control over her own body.

Youth was another matter. Roman literature tells of smitten teenage girls and their young paramours who often met at the beach town of Lanuvium, a vacation spot for rich Romans. There, under the moonlight, the couples would seek the seclusion of a local cave, the supposed dwelling place of the goddess Juno's sacred snake, and convenient for evading the prying eyes of parents. A visit to the site on strictly pious terms involved a curious dare. A girl who entered the darkness and came out untouched was thought to ensure her chastity for another year. Clinical reports were filed from the scene of the so-called miracle, where girls, Roman writers observed, blushed at the slippery touch of "a serpentine tongue." Young lovers knowingly indulged in amusements that, if pressed, their parents probably would have remembered playing, too.

Something of those fleeting, impressionable years of summer love survive in between six and eight poems—some forty-odd lines of Latin in elegiac couplets—attributed to a nineteen-year-old, Sulpicia. Composed in the late first century B.C., they were discovered by scholars among the papers of a famous Roman elegist, Tibullus, who is known to have shared Sulpicia's wealthy literary patron. Sulpicia's deft musings, although published too late for Clodia to have read them, offered Roman audiences a rare literary insight into a young woman's view of romance. They told a familiar coming-of-age story: picnics with girlfriends in the Roman countryside, trysts with the sons of her father's associates, and platonic friendships in spring that blossomed into memorable summer affairs.

In her verses, Sulpicia coifs her hair, wraps herself in the finest Tyrian purple, and fastens the clasp on an expensive set of Indian Ocean pearls in anticipation of meeting her admirer, Cerinthus, a rugged woodsman and hunter. After his sudden illness prevents a second clandestine rendezvous, a dejected Sulpicia pines to see him again in time for his approaching birthday. "Let Love in a thousand ways devise / the stolen moment of our embrace," she writes, a prayer that expresses her longing to languish in her sweetheart's arms—"Love, if you are just a god, then enslave / us both, or release me from my chains, if not." As the excitement of her relationship takes hold, she discovers a confidence she never knew. "Our masks removed, plain to all, a perfect fit, / he's the mistake I never feared of making." The experience overjoys her and leaves her grateful, which, in turn, informs her poetry. "May the joys that others lack, my own now fill." Uptight Roman men diagnosed such confessional expressions of affection as an illness, a disease.

Women overwhelmingly bore the brunt of men's criticism, with satirists lampooning wives who cheated on their husbands and "shamelessly deserted [their] wailing children" to pursue extramarital flings. Rare indeed was the Greek poet Apollonius of Rhodes, who broke literary convention and imagined the romance between Medea and the hero Jason from Medea's perspective ("No one, / she knew . . . could ever match him. His charm, / like his voice, lingered when he was not there.")

Ancient intellectuals, regardless of school, decried love's stranglehold on otherwise well-adjusted lives. Rational study, they postulated, regulated the unpredictable oscillation of the passions. Even-keeled temperaments were a prerequisite for happiness, and volatile emotions were decidedly lowbrow, especially those of the heart. To those who followed Stoic philosophy, life's unpredictability made the enjoyment of worldly pleasures and the satisfaction of physical appetites vain pursuits: unreasonable, excessive, unnecessary. Such passing satisfactions distracted from the development of one's moral compass. Even the Epicureans, notorious for their pursuit of pleasure, avoidance of pain, fearlessness about approaching death, and indifference to religious judgments, condemned sexual overindulgence as an illness requiring a cure.

Nonetheless, then as now, philosophical teachings might offer solace, but living life often meant setting abstract principles aside, as we know from the fact that ancient writers enjoyed gossiping at length about their neighbors' affairs and trysts. That is how it came to be known that a well-born widow and an ambitious young tenant were an item in the summer of 58 B.C.

꙰

Politically, the spring of 58 B.C. had been busy for Clodia's brother. After the republic supported his plan to annex Cyprus—it passed with resounding senatorial support in February—Clodius introduced a bill to address abuse of power, articulating clear standards and judicial guidelines by which elected officials could be prosecuted for overstepping their authority. The bill gave teeth to the republic's much-vaunted ideal of equality before the law, a principle respected in theory but ignored in practice. That bill passed in March, with language that applied it retroactively to previous officeholders. Risk-averse senators, who in other circumstances might have frothed at the full extent of Clodius's reforms, held their tongues and waited patiently for the profits from the Cyprus invasion to pour in. Almost immediately, a third bill was introduced, identifying Cicero as a target for criminal prosecution. The man who had once predicted the plot of a band of insurrectionists needed no divine help to surmise his own coming fate. That spring, Cicero packed his belongings, left his wife, son, and daughter behind, and fled to Greece.

By the first week of April, the streets and byways of Clodia's usually sedate Palatine Hill neighborhood thronged with rambunctious parade-goers, revelers who had ascended the hill to celebrate the city's annual Great Goddess holiday. Held every spring over the course of ten days starting on April 4, the freewheeling event pushed the boundaries of acceptable public behavior, no mean achievement in a city with a reputation for the exuberance of its numerous holidays. The ancient Romans celebrated their gods throughout the year with dependable regularity. Exhilarating chariot races, festive parades, and raucous gladiatorial matches closed shops and markets and paused work. Spectacles abounded: of priests and attendants who sprinkled incense offerings at outdoor altars, ritually slaughtered cows and pigs to honor the gods, and oversaw the distribution of a bountiful array of butchered meats.

Two hundred years earlier, the Romans had instituted the Great Goddess festival during the darkest hours of their republic's conflict with Carthage. Concerned citizens lobbied the government to embark on an expedition to the Phrygian mountains of Asia Minor, to bring the relics of the venerable deity to Rome. Her presence in the city, believers insisted, would turn the tide of the war. Senators responded enthusiastically. As Hannibal was ravaging the peninsula in the third century B.C., the vessel carrying the goddess's statue arrived at the harbor. When the skiff was caught in the river's muddy undertow, a distant relation of Clodia's who was attending the ceremony, Claudia Quinta, dislodged it to great cheering. The goddess's statue was eventually enthroned in a temple that overlooked the Circus Maximus and the neighboring heights of Palatine Hill. With the celebration of Hannibal's defeat in 202 B.C. and the relaxation of wartime tensions, her holiday came to signify a second founding of the republic. Her festival was a time to commemorate Italy's independence from Carthage, which had paved the way for Rome's supremacy over the lands of the western Mediterranean.

Now, every April, Romans flocked to the Great Goddess's temple in advance of theatrical performances, held on the temple's steps, and games, organized in the circus. Riotous crowds of tourists thronged the streets, banging cowhide tambourines and jangling cymbals in the goddess's honor. The "thunderous" expressions of "maddened minds" overran Clodia's neighborhood. They blasted bone and ivory horns, chanted hypnotic melodies, and played sprightly tunes on flutes and recorders. Male celebrants donned the goddess's characteristically tall bonnet and danced from the temple to the circus. In their flowing saffron- and purple-dyed gowns—a transgression that infuriated the Fathers, with their conservative notions of masculinity—they sashayed through the streets. The goddess's most ardent followers, nicknamed the Galli, grew trellised locks of hair, jangled rings on their fingers, and exaggerated their walk to showcase their bejeweled cloaks and necklaces studded with expensive gems. Many of the Galli depilated their calves and arms to leave their skin "smoother than Aphrodite's own salt-smoothed seashells." Rumor was that the men castrated themselves to serve the Great Goddess. To disparage a man, you called him a Gallus. In the classical world's strict gender binary, the fluidity of the goddess's followers left most people puzzled and eventually prompted Roman writers to invent the category of *tertium genus*, a third gender between male and female. Hostile men categorized the Galli as women.

One affluent pair chose not to be a part of the pageantry that spring of

Springtime on the cape of Misenum, Italy; its northernmost coasts, forming a sheltered recess along the Bay of Naples, allured many Romans for its delightful mix of quaint fishing villages and resort life.

58 B.C. By mid-April, Clodia and Rufus shuttered the Palatine Hill house and departed along great-grandfather Appius's road for a tryst in Naples and the countryside around Mount Vesuvius. For them, Greece was not an option. Though the policy's origins are obscure, Roman law restricted women of Clodia's day from leaving the Italian peninsula; the ban remained in effect, scholars believe, until at least A.D. 21, when the Senate amended it. Until then, Aegean islands, Iberian beaches, and the pebbled shores of Gaul were, for Clodia, unreachable destinations. She did not need a man's permission, however, to frequent the stylish spas in Naples and to take the thermal baths in the Crater, as the Romans affectionately referred to the sulfurous stretch of seismic land that lined Italy's coast beneath Mount Vesuvius. The charming resort towns of Pompeii and Herculaneum catered very well to elite visitors like her.

Calming groves of myrtle trees scented the hills between the coastal

cities of Cumae and Baiae. Legend has it that one entered the under-
world at the shore of nearby Lake Avernus. More than a century before
Vesuvius's eruption, the region's geological volatility was believed to
have swallowed entire towns. Thrill-seekers took to the hills to roam
the barren, primordial landscapes outside the bay's metropolis, Puteoli (modern Pozzuoli), where beyond the city center the ground vented
its pungent volcanic steam. Fishing villages like Baiae lured sun-kissed
Romans with the prospect of a calm stroll at the water's edge, where
oysters were farmed and local mussels harvested. Roman intellectuals
enjoyed days of quiet study and nights of intimate conversation, a welcome departure from the incessant chatter of the Forum.

Clodia owned a villa on the bay, inherited either from her father or
from her husband's estate. Gossip notoriously preoccupied the Crater's
social set, and the gossip that was written down—primarily, Cicero's
later courthouse references to escapades at Baiae—confirms that Clodia
and Rufus enjoyed their seaside house that summer. Life at the Crater
was lived outdoors, preferably on the water: swimming, boating, and
shuttling between the islands of Procida and Ischia and the bay's southernmost island, majestic Capri, which, though it would later pass into
the private hands of Rome's emperors, in these decades still tempted
Romans with publicly accessible beaches.

There was a truly disorienting amount of history here, embedded
along the Crater's coastal roads, visitable from its peninsula's cliffs, and
sunk beneath its waves. A mind-boggling eight hundred years before
Clodia's era, this was the world of the first Greeks during the mythical
age of Homer. In the eighth century B.C., Greek seafarers, driven by famine and dreams of owning land, sailed to the Mediterranean's western
territories and found enchantment beneath southern Italy's olive trees.
Within decades, colonists had established the first settlements on the
island of Ischia. By the start of the seventh century B.C., an acropolis
was built on the dramatic cliffs of Cumae, on the mainland opposite the
volcanic island. The rustic stone temple in the Doric style, dedicated to
Apollo with colorfully painted terra-cotta, was already a tourist desti-

nation for Clodia's contemporaries. A Roman in the first century B.C. could stumble upon remains of that ancient time: the once elegant hand-painted jugs that Greek artisans adorned with mesmerizing geometric patterns or the once prized dinnerware decorated with sketches of fantastic gryphons and birds. Fragments of the Greek past were strewn across the Crater's surfaces, like the remains of some seaside soiree, and awe-inspiring Greek monuments were still standing at nearby Paestum, just a short journey inland.

Like an invasive species, the Romans altered whole swaths of this formerly pristine coastline, changing the ecosystem. In the first century B.C., the Latin verb "to build," *aedificare*, acquired its secondary, pejorative meaning, "to develop." Astronomical levels of Roman wealth transformed the bay, turning once sleepy towns and undisturbed fishing villages into popular, crowded resorts. In less than fifty years, the coast became a string of mansions, one architecturally daring cliffside villa with private dock after the next. To the Roman geographer Strabo, the Crater gave the appearance of a "continuous city," which may not have been a compliment.

Financiers and senators all had homes on the water's edge. Every night brought a different social gathering in a different location along the roughly twenty-mile strip of rugged land from the northern edge's Cape of Misenum to the south's Cape of Sorrento. Pompey lived here. The tyrant Sulla's grandson had a house here. Caesar occupied a property above the bay. Rome's much loathed cohort of amateur fish-farmers—the preferred pastime of the republic's moneyed elite—had their own estates. So, too, did circles of artistic and philosophical patrons, Caesar's father, Piso, among them, who sponsored nightly meals, arranged introductions between guests, and stimulated highbrow conversation. Moralists loathed the excesses of the scene and the attitudes of its denizens: disengaged, self-absorbed, comfortable among their own set. The nightlife lured curious young men who, desperate for a glimpse of the extravagance, crashed the parties. Many homes would lie dormant for months, with only a skeleton crew of servants, until, as suddenly as the previous summer's delights had ended, the grounds of an estate would come roaring back to life once more.

"There are so many people here," Cicero once complained, "the whole place is like a tiny version of Rome." The boating parties and dinner parties, the precious free moments stolen with a volume of poetry or the scandalous hours of doing nothing, had a way of sticking with the Crater's visitors, just like the sand from its beaches. The bay brought, at least to some, a "contentment of the soul and of the mind," as the philosophers phrased it, a feeling that ordinary Latin speakers simply called *relaxatio*. In antiquity it was not uncommon to overhear a returning vacationer mention a newfound desire to change their garden or renovate their rooms, as if to bring the memory of the Crater home with them. A phrase referencing the bay's most exclusive resort, "As they do it in Baiae," became the proverbial Roman expression for achieving one's lifestyle dreams.

Here, too, were the less glamorous aspects of life that Rome's elite vacationers preferred not to acknowledge. East of the shoreline lay the region's sprawling, unsightly brickyards, where, in row after row of factories, workmen fashioned the building materials needed for temples, townhouses, apartments, and shops. The republic's formidable western fleet would, in years to come, be headquartered at the Roman naval base off Cape Misenum; sailors on shore leave caroused in Puteoli's taverns and brothels. The city was western Italy's largest international harbor and arguably its most ethnically diverse metropolis. Every day the Mediterranean's largest vessels docked there, and waves of Thracian, Syrian, Delian, and Egyptian crews came ashore for provisions. Roman xenophobes and agoraphobes alike avoided its crowded marketplaces.

⁂

Clodia, still riding the crest of her brother's legislative victories, no doubt believed during those months away from Rome that she and Rufus shared a progressive political outlook: a belief in the efficacy of government service, a moral commitment to improving the fortunes of others. The practical-minded man of twenty-six, well versed in the minutiae of government administration, was highly regarded as a magistrate by villagers back home. An apparent dedication to populist reforms, if not constitutional change, made him a rising star. A generous woman of thirty-seven—the accomplished, if uncredited, architect of her younger brother's phenomenal success, with resources to lavish on causes and candidates of her own choosing—might well have found in Rufus a project, a future leader, as well as a like-minded companion. History can wring its hands that not a single hour of Clodia's summer is documented, but it's easy to imagine how these two passed their time.

In the mornings, Clodia and Rufus could recline in the garden with a scroll of philosophy, history, or the latest theatrical offering. Before lunch, there might be time to draft letters, dabble in verse, or put the finishing touches on one's memoirs. Sulla, in his last months, completed his autobiography at the Crater. Cicero, in one of his letters to Atticus, uses a Latin phrase that might best be translated as a "working vacation" to describe the voluminous output of his own Neapolitan peregrinations. Afternoons could be spent at literary readings, which debuted a mix of original Roman verse and translations from Greek. Sarcastic skits, a genre of playacting that the Romans called mime, were popular. The Crater's own colorful locales inspired at least three now-fragmentary farces by Clodia's contemporary Decimus Laberius: *The Fisherman, Lake Avernus,* and *Hot Waters.*

Serious, challenging dramas found an audience, too. One of the most celebrated literary events in these years was the completion of the first Latin translation of *The Journey of the Argonauts,* originally written in Greek in the third century B.C. by Apollonius of Rhodes. An otherwise obscure Latin translator, Varro Atacinus, brought Apollonius's story to audiences who were unable to experience it in its original language, and teams of scribes would create multiple handwritten copies of the text for distribution to readers. Virgil, the author of Rome's national epic, just a sprout of a boy when *The Journey of the Argonauts* circulated, was raised on Apollonius's voice.

No Greek writer since Homer had so effortlessly matched the bard's dusty-sounding dactylic hexameters. Apollonius's narrative combined a scholar's deep love of learning with literary taste that ran to the shamelessly popular. From the much-maligned ancient genre of romance, for example, which intellectuals perennially demeaned as a second-rate form of literary expression, the poet conjured a quest for eastern riches that leads to a steamy love affair between the poem's young, brawny protagonist, Jason, and the resourceful, smitten, unmarried Black Sea princess Medea. Medea's love, as well as her skills as a magician, ensures Jason's success.

Everyone in classical society knew the outline of Medea's story thanks to Greek tragedians like Euripides, who centuries earlier had dramatized Medea's murderous rampage for the Athenian stage. What won Apollonius praise was the stylish way in which he reimagined that narrative. Instead of rehashing the horrific but by then tired story of the final chapter of Medea's life—when, as Jason's wife, as the mother of his children, and as a foreigner in Greece, she plots the murder of her sons as revenge for her husband's infidelity with a local princess—Apollonius surprised his audiences by dramatizing Medea's first encounter with Jason, providing, as it were, a prequel to the myth. Even in a world without audiotape or film, the ancients could appreciate this high-concept notion of rewinding a narrative; after all, reading for the ancients meant rolling a papyrus in reverse. For writers like Apollonius and his Hellenistic contemporaries, who had inherited centuries of classical storytelling from giants like Homer and the Athenian tragedians and wondered whether their own literary output would ever equal it, this ingenious technique offered a way to enhance the present with the prestige of the past and invest the past with modern energy.

Like most ancient literary offerings, Varro's translation of *The Journey of the Argonauts* would have been read in salons as well as in theaters, where wealthy patrons sponsored public performances. Many of the Crater's cities, Misenum, Pompeii, and Naples among them, boasted venues that could seat between five and six thousand spectators, both men and women.

⁊☙

At dinner, the tables, like the wine, overflowed. There were cheeses, fresh sardines, oysters, and the local Campanian vintage. Judging from the exquisite cups and plates on display in the region's local archaeological museums, Clodia and Rufus dined in sumptuous style. They drank from goblets fashioned from imported rock-cut crystal and from cups of hammered Spanish silver. The party season usually lasted through September, when the weather around the bay cooled, senators returned to work, and owners began shutting up their houses for the winter.

From the Crater, if lovers wanted, there was always the slow boat back to Rome. From Puteoli to Ostia, in a modest transport vessel, ancient writers said, the journey took three days and had the benefit of avoiding the congestion on the road. Gaining a few more days on the water and a few more hours of gazing at the sea's endless horizon, couples could stretch their holiday just a bit longer.

CHAPTER NINE

Clodia's Cross-Examiner

Under every stone, my friend, look out for a scorpion.

—PRAXILLA

Since May, Cicero had been alone in exile in the northern Aegean harbor town of Thessaloniki, a prosperous Greek city but remote from Rome. That slow-rolling crisis upended Terentia, his wife, a forty-one-year-old mother of two, and the couple's close-knit family: their son, seven-year-old Marcus Junior; and their elder daughter, twenty-one-year-old Tullia, already a widow but engaged to be remarried when the reality of her father's pending indictment became apparent. Cicero would speak about this period in his letters as the family's "shared calamity." For Terentia, it acquired an existential dimension. Disgrace attached to the public image of any exiled Roman politician's wife. But with Clodius adamant about using his veto power to block any government aid to Cicero's family, whispered sympathies followed Terentia and her children as they tried to continue their lives.

That autumn, in one of Clodius's first acts as an elected official, the Roman government confiscated three of Cicero's most expensive pieces of real estate, located in the nearby towns of Formiae and Frascati, and in Rome. The republic put the properties up for auction, then retained the proceeds. The family's residence in Palatine Hill, the multimillion-sesterce mansion where Cicero had enjoyed taking his exercise, was leveled to the ground. By summer, a construction crew was clearing the site to erect a new community center, a building dedicated to the goddess of independence and self-determination, Libertas, or Freedom.

Terentia and her children were forced to take up residence in properties whose titles she had retained from before her marriage.

The most beatific biographies have been written about Terentia's husband. It took twenty-one centuries before scholars finally acknowledged Terentia's centrality to Cicero's future success. A woman of immense wealth and extraordinary emotional resources, she brought both to their decades-long relationship. While he languished in exile, Terentia captained her family's ship, paying the bills and lobbying for her forty-eight-year-old husband's return. Even with much diminished prestige, she had access to sources of power. When, that year, Terentia was summoned to appear before a tribunal in the Forum and publicly berated for her husband's clandestine departure, Terentia's half-sister Fabia, a Vestal Virgin, intervened with the diplomacy expected of her position.

Had not fate and politics intervened, superficial similarities between Clodia's and Terentia's upbringing might have been enough to warrant a friendship. Affluent, successful, cultured without being aloof, educated without being impractical, Terentia shared a great deal with Clodia and her sisters. Born into a slave-owning family in the 90s B.C. to a father who could trace his ancestry to the wars against Hannibal, Terentia had been betrothed around 79 B.C., just as the tyrant Sulla retired from politics. With her sizable dowry, she made Cicero's future possible. Her parents had given her a portfolio of apartment complexes, properties near the city center and beyond its outskirts, ranches in the hill country near Antium, villas on the coast. Upon her marriage, nearly 400,000 sesterces, the precise sum required to elevate a citizen's income level to the elite status of senator, was deposited in the couple's accounts. Even with his own appreciable talents as a speaker—one who turned heads in the 70s B.C. as a critic of Sicilian corruption—young Cicero would have gone nowhere had not Terentia purchased her husband's entry into society. Hers was the more recognizable family name.

Years working as a scrappy, clever defense attorney showed Cicero's promise. He courted men with influence and compiled a mental index of useful connections. When he declared his campaign to run for consul, Terentia's help proved invaluable. It was from her, and her social circle, that Cicero learned the alarming news that Catiline was plotting to overthrow the republic. Clodia's husband, Metellus, parlayed his role in that affair into a successful run for higher office. For Cicero, everything that followed was a chance to burnish his reputation.

In the end, though, for all the natural points of compatibility between Terentia and Clodia—storied lineage, impressive siblings, powerful husband—the women's relationship might best be characterized by detachment, sparked by the occasional prickliness and enlivened with a dash of bemusement. It was widely known that Cicero had an almost irrational obsession with Clodia's authoritativeness. Rumors circulated that the onetime consul was smitten by Clodia's intellect and charm and that he kept his amorous infatuation secret from Terentia, as we know from Plutarch's much later biography. The urge to include such a salacious absurdity must have been irresistible.

To Terentia—self-assured, faithful, trusting her husband's fidelity—gossip was inconsequential. Throughout the nearly three decades of marriage before the mysterious circumstances that led to the couple's divorce, she would let few household matters or unfounded suspicions unnerve her—unless the talk concerned her husband's prospects for power. She was "ambitious," Plutarch said, "more inclined to take a share in her husband's political concerns than to give him a share of her own domestic ones."

Cicero wrote from exile to comfort her. "My beloved, my heart's longing, my dearest Terentia, how it saddens me to no end to hear that you, who has always been the safe harbor in everyone else's time of trouble, now find yourself so tormented and so alone." When he heard that his wife was considering selling some of her properties to finance their son Marcus Junior's education, Cicero expressed horror. He floundered to maintain the Roman male posturing as head of their house. He had loyal friends, rich friends, he reminded her. Surely, they would step forward to lend a hand. He could see his star was dimming before her eyes.

Terentia did not wait for her husband's associates to come knocking. Seven months after Cicero's flight into exile, the destructive consequences of his actions became fully apparent to him. His mood turned despondent. A guilty conscience gnawed at him. "I'm to blame for everything," he confessed to Terentia in November. Four days later: "I'm ashamed," he wrote. "The blame for this disaster is all mine." Yet his wife's acumen and resourcefulness, her sensibility and, above all, her unyielding belief in the temporariness of her husband's setback pulled the family through the second half of 58 B.C. She kept young Marcus engaged, if not exactly focused, on his studies. (During a much later academic year in Athens, progress reports would be relayed to the family in Rome of the lad's excessive drinking.) She accompanied their daughter to social functions: the theater, the races, the games, birthday parties of friends. She continued to set the table and to arrange flowers gathered from the garden. She wrote weekly, sometimes daily, just as Cicero requested, and provided him "the most comprehensive and detailed accounts" of happenings in Rome. In her letters, she played a role something between wife and mother, taking every opportunity to remind her husband to express his gratitude to his most loyal friends, a recommendation that he, of course, dutifully heeded. ("I have thanked the persons you wished me to thank.")

Come tumult, she would be the family's ballast. She was "indefatigable," an English adjective that derives directly from the Latin verb that Cicero uses to praise his wife's tireless spirit. She would spend the better part, if not the majority, of the next year petitioning the Fathers on her husband's behalf, patiently awaiting December 9, 58 B.C., the end of the term of those politicians who had supported the law, motivated by Clodius, that had forced her husband into exile. With the inauguration of a new slate of magistrates—newly sworn consuls, newly sworn tribunes—Terentia left little to chance. In a fevered burst of energy at the start of 57 B.C., she advocated for her husband's return. If the most influential atriums and dining rooms of the republic had not heard her cause by then, she debated the merits of his case and counted the votes in support of a motion to recall. "From every piece of correspondence and every casual conversation comes word of your incredible fortitude and your courage," Cicero wrote in one of his gloomiest moments, embarrassed but teeming with pride. His letters were preserved by his freed slave and secretary, Tiro, for posterity. Terentia's letters do not survive.

Before his exile, Cicero had expressed to Terentia his dream of retiring to the ranch outside Antium, whose wooded surroundings reminded him of one of the ancient world's most peaceful sites, the religious sanctuary at Dodona, hallowed by the ancient Greeks. It had a venerable oak tree that, believers asserted, delivered spoken predictions about the future. "All our ranch needs is that talking tree," Cicero was fond of joking. "We'll have ourselves a real sanctuary then."

On August 4, 57 B.C., conservative senators made the decision to rescue the exiled politician. Fearful that growing support for Clodius's progressive policies might diminish the Senate's authority and wary of Pompey's growing popularity, the Fathers forced a bill through the assemblies that nullified Clodius's ethics law and made explicit their desire to recall Cicero from Greece. His dream of returning to his refuge at Terentia's Italian farmhouse took one step closer to reality.

Within hours of the news breaking, Terentia hurried the children into a carriage for the journey to Italy's southern Adriatic-facing harbor, Brundisium, arriving, thanks to her expert planning, before Cicero's ship docked. The day he traversed the gangway onto Italian soil, August 9, coincided with a local citywide festival and with their daughter Tullia's twenty-second birthday. For the first time in sixteen challenging months, the family embraced and celebrated their reunion.

❧

By early September 57 B.C., Clodia's onetime neighbor was splitting his residence between Terentia's multiple properties and a slightly older house in the Esquiline Hill neighborhood that belonged to his family.

The move alerted Clodia and her brother that the disgraced politician intended to reclaim his position at the center of public life. Revenge looked imminent. Any Roman who had done Cicero a personal or professional injury would have received that message. But Cicero's far more immediate concern was the state of his finances, which were in shambles. Real estate holdings in Rome bestowed self-worth, and Cicero's portfolio upon return from exile was an embarrassment, especially next to Clodia's—and especially given that her brother had demolished Cicero's Palatine Hill townhouse.

Clodia's every step taunted him, whether she and Rufus were in Rome, enjoying the Solonium estate, or shuttling between venues on the Bay of Naples. In late September 57 B.C., a public hearing was announced before Rome's College of Pontiffs to adjudicate the legitimacy of Clodius's "Freedom Center," whose foundations had been poured on the Palatine Hill site. In a city where piety influenced every facet of civic life, the College of Pontiffs functioned as the republic's supreme oversight board, their judicial remit not dissimilar to a high court of appeals. The arguments would mark Cicero's first appearance in the Forum and his first public address in more than a year.

Speculation about the outcome of the case spread through Rome's taverns and townhouses, as the public debated whether the man who had made his name by beating the odds could replicate his past success. If the members of the court denied Cicero's appeal, their ruling would subject the formerly exiled politician to another humiliating legal defeat. Cicero would have to draw upon his wife's finances, yet again, to cobble together the resources for a second start in public life. If, on the other hand, the court invalidated Clodius's laws and declared the Freedom Center an illegal construction, the verdict would hand Cicero a much-needed vindication. A summary judgment in Cicero's favor could potentially amount to a onetime payment of millions of sesterces.

Competition was Cicero's second nature, interwoven with episodes of delusion and fed by increasing self-aggrandizement, over his sixty-three years. But he was socially as well as intellectually gifted. Early on, acquaintances had marveled at his preternatural ability to retain strangers' names without the use of a *nomenclator*, a hired prompter, and at his capacity to recall inconsequential details about people's personal and family lives: where they lived, where they vacationed, with whom they regularly dined. After modest success as a trial lawyer, in the 70s B.C. he won an unexpected victory over Hortensius, Rome's leading trial lawyer, who was thought to be invincible. After election to consul, vanity instilled in him the regrettable habit of demanding space at the center of every story. If colleagues spoke of weekends at a friend's delightful country ranch, he parried with weeks-long stays at expensive villas. If you mentioned high-placed friends, his were inevitably placed higher.

Even by his culture's low standards of decency—a lawyer's work in the Forum practically required crude comments and "cruel jokes" to be persuasive—Cicero's "propensity to attack anyone for the sake of raising a laugh" found few admirers. The man's childish longing for affirmation, wrote Plutarch, "aroused a good deal of ill-feeling against him." Cicero shamelessly relished the inappropriate quip. His efforts at humor were legendary both for how often they fell flat and for how mean-spirited they made him appear, as when he quoted a lost comedy to denigrate a fellow senator for the physical appearance of his daughters ("Apollo clearly never meant for him to beget").

During the 70s and 60s B.C., when Clodia's male relations were soldiering overseas, Cicero perfected his craft in the service of the law. This was not a career path most Roman parents imagined for their sons. Lawyers were assumed to be bookish, overeducated, and lacking in the kind of practical awareness needed to support themselves or a family. Studying statutes, rehearsing arguments, and drafting rebuttals consumed exorbitant amounts of time and energy. Financial security was never guaranteed. Without large firms of attorneys or even modest collective enterprises to provide litigators with steady remuneration, a lawyer's income depended on a client's wherewithal and sheer chance. Custom dictated that attorneys represent clients without charging a fee. Payment, if it arrived at all, might arrive years, sometimes decades, after a case in the form of a bequest to be distributed upon the reading of a will. For Romans interested in the law, profit accrued only to those who could afford the leisure of practicing it. Still, with the right network and a talent for selecting clients with serious financial resources, court appearances could provide a living. "Law puts bread on the table," commoners crowed. Few in antiquity could have hoped to acquire Cicero's argumentative prowess and rhetorical finesse.

As an acutely self-conscious outsider and budding showman, Cicero had understood the importance of following and breaking, when appropriate, the tried-and-tested rules of public speaking. Without a prestigious family name facilitating his entry into public life, Cicero knew at an early age that craft, not connections, would determine his success.

Clodia was fifteen when Cicero made his first memorable appearance, at twenty-six. His client, the young Roscius Amerinus, was accused of murdering his own father to accelerate his inheritance. Few court-watchers expected the relative unknown to prevail. The prosecutor disparaged his opposing counsel's abilities, but when Cicero rose, he turned the slights to his own advantage. "As soon as our prosecutor found out that the defendant was being defended by someone with limited ability and experience, like me," Cicero began, "you and I watched him become so impatient with the court, he couldn't sit still, stretched his legs, even summoned an assistant—presumably to request a bite brought from the tavern, assuming the trial's quick conclusion." The folksy charm and intellectual humility worked in Cicero's favor, as did his own ingenious investigative work, which exposed members of the prosecution for having planned the murder and framed Amerinus in a scheme to steal the millions that rightfully belonged to his client.

The Roman public learned to anticipate when the wunderkind performer would agree to argue in court. Ordinary people who faced extraordinary, unusual, or novel legal charges sought out his services. On behalf of the downtrodden, he fought against corruption and greed, successfully bringing a suit in the 70s B.C. against Verres, a disreputable governor of Sicily. Idealism suffused his early appearances in court. At the end of the day, he was known to tell jurors, every account needed to be balanced, every wrong righted. "Who could be so unprincipled as to realize what has transpired and still remain quiet and turn a blind eye?" he said in one moment of moral exasperation. "It's your responsibility to cure the sickness that is afflicting our republic," he would tell juries. "Every hour that passes after we learn of some new horrible event, even for the calmest, levelheaded person, is another hour wasted that strips us of our humanity."

Jurors recognized in the strength of his convictions a noble desire for fairness. In the case of an unidentified woman wrongly accused of misrepresenting her new citizenship status, "I argued rather vehemently," Cicero later explained, "that Roman citizenship rights could not be taken away." He used his success to sing the virtues of citizens who lacked his own access to a speaker's platform. Caecilia, a generous woman who had supplied one of Cicero's desperate clients with clothes, food, and a roof over his head when he faced outrageous murder charges, was a "model for others," Cicero told his jury. "When everyone else had given up on my client, she came to the help of her friend in trouble." She was "a *femina* beyond compare, a superlative example of womanhood," whose illustrious relatives—her father, uncles, and brother—would benefit from her example.

In the 60s B.C., as Clodia navigated life as a young mother, Cicero commanded the public's attention. The size of his crowds swelled. Clodia's Rome knew no better orator. Eschewing legal jargon—the desiccated-as-dry-parchment style of communicating that passed for his field's intellectual contribution—Cicero fashioned, with studious attention to language and structure, a uniquely endearing public voice. "Now everything you're hearing from the other side has been dressed up with legal absurdities," he would tell the court, pausing in the middle of a speech to lament how common sense had been "twisted and perverted by the [other] lawyers' ingenuity." With their fancy educations, a bemused Cicero would say, nudging jurors back to the larger picture, "they still haven't managed to tell us whether it's more proper for us to say 'two days from now' or 'the day after tomorrow,' have they?" A consummate entertainer with an ear for complex layers of rhythm and sound, he crafted his speeches around emotional hooks, defended common sense, and hinted that long-windedness would never substitute for talent. In the summer of 64 B.C., he pivoted from winning the hearts and minds of jurors to gaining the sympathies of voters when he ran for consul—and won.

Being at the center of power changed the boy from the hills of Arpinum. So, too, did Catiline's threat of domestic terror during his consulship. By December 63 B.C., when Cicero faced the dilemma of how to punish the members of the insurgency, while some members of the establishment proposed leniency, Cicero was preoccupied with his own image, desirous for accolades as the republic's finest hero. In seeking and ultimately securing the death penalty for the conspirators without a trial, he may have proved his toughness to the Senate. But he misjudged the sentiments of the Roman people, the ones who had supported his early career.

Where Cicero's maturity would later manifest in a truly impressive way was in his insistence that every case needed a story. If recognizable character types could be joined to simple or at least familiar plots, the portrayal of a drama with a sympathetic protagonist or a suspicious villain would win more minds than any insufferable lawyer's misguided attempt to appear the smartest person in the room. "I think poets and writers invent stories," he once mused, "so that we see our own behavior mirrored in other people and are shown a realistic depiction of our own daily lives." Yet where once he appreciated the power of artful storytelling to generate compassion for the complexities of other people's experiences, his decades in law and politics now equipped him to understand it in a different light: as a means to manipulate sympathies and to serve his own interests—and perhaps, his appetite for vengeance.

꠲

Clodia, in September 57 B.C., ignored this man at her own risk. He thrived when audiences underestimated him. He still had the instinct to rise to a challenge.

On September 29, 57 B.C., Cicero demanded that the College of Pontiffs indemnify him for the entirety of the 3.5 million sesterces that, at the height of his public acclaim, he had paid for a prestigious Palatine Hill mansion, on which he had spent an additional 20,000 sesterces in improvements and artwork. More consequentially for the city's planned community center, Cicero petitioned for the return of his title to the property. Incensed at Clodius's demolition of his property and angry that looters had ransacked his two country homes, Cicero was perhaps most of all frustrated by the sixteen months of cultural and political irrelevance he had suffered in Thessaloniki.

That day, the resentful orator packed a year and a half of grievances into a long-winded, testy, rancorous account. The looters had stopped at nothing, Cicero howled. The columns of his home had been smashed, expensively carved cedar doors ripped from the hinges of bedrooms and closets. Foundation stones had been hauled away from the perimeter wall. People in the streets were defaming his memory, calling him a threat to the capital, "an enemy of the gods who protected Rome's hallowed Capitoline Hill," forgetting that six years earlier he himself had saved it from insurrection. Assuming that every courthouse listener was eager for his insightful commentary on current events, Cicero prattled, preached, and pontificated. He had heard that the Fathers had recently voted to depose the king of Cyprus, and he launched into a diatribe about foreign policy. On what legal grounds had the republic annexed the island? Was it solely to claim its natural resources? Had anyone paused to consider how such a questionable military intervention might destabilize the east? In the republic's haste to remove the king of Egypt's brother from Cyprus, Cicero implied, the Romans risked losing access to a vital source of imported grain.

Cicero's views on the perils of interventionism were already known. He had communicated them years earlier in a speech called "On the Alexandrian King," a now-fragmentary text that excoriated the Fathers' thinly disguised greed. "If money has truly so consumed, so obsessed, so blinded our way of thinking..." The thought, like the text of the jeremiad, trails off. But that September before the College of Pontiffs, Cicero resumed the thread. He denounced the opinion then circulating that Rome should use its military might to annex Egypt's riches, too. So much chaos had been unleashed in his absence! Somewhere on the seaways and highways between Thessaloniki and Rome, bitterness had consumed his sense of decency.

> These people have accused me, supposedly in good humor, about those occasions in the past where I referred to myself in lofty terms as the god Jupiter or where I might have used imprecise language to imply the goddess of wisdom, Minerva, was a relative of mine. But at least Jupiter's daughter was a chaste virgin, Clodius, unlike your sister. And if in your jubilation you are thinking of claiming the mantle of the king of the gods yourself because of your recent string of successes, I would caution you against it. I hear your family's house is a veritable Mount Olympus these days, where the reigning queen also plays the role of both "sister" and "wife."

In Greek and Roman mythology, the king and queen of the twelve Olympian gods, Zeus and Hera (or Jupiter and Juno), were siblings as well as spouses.

Both Greeks and Romans considered incest taboo, but even educated men, like Cicero and Plutarch, hurled it as a rhetorical smear. By the first century B.C., it was a slur that Romans also cast on the Egyptians, who for hundreds of years had used sibling marriage among their pharaohs to suffuse their earthly power with an unambiguous mystique. Sycophantic court poets compared Egypt's rulers to Zeus and Hera, to do

the same. To Romans, the accusation of incest between siblings like Clodia and Clodius was a high-flown way of suggesting that they exerted
a tyrannical power antithetical to the Roman Republic. (Cicero, again
without evidence, would repeat the specious charge against Clodia and
Clodius in his defense of Rufus, from which it has falsely and distract-
ingly entered both scholarly and popular accounts of Clodia's life.)

Clodius, having enacted the laws that had caused Cicero's exile, must
have expected that he would find himself a target of such vitriol. For
Clodia, the rebuke must have been bracing. Cicero was revealing the
depth of his own disillusionment. Truth, to its onetime defender, no
longer mattered.

That fall, the College of Pontiffs ruled against the constitutionality of Clodius's community center. They also granted compensation
for Cicero's two properties outside the capital to the tune of 750,000
sesterces—a disappointing sum given that the orator had paid upward
of 1.2 million sesterces for the land, although scholars speculate that it
may have been a fair insurance value. For the 3.5-million-sesterce mansion on Palatine Hill, he was indemnified to the amount of 2 million sesterces. And he regained the title.

At the beginning of November 57 B.C., flatbed wagons loaded with
the ash and aggregate required to make Roman cement, timber planks
used to erect the scaffolding for constructing Roman walls, and clumps
of Rome's characteristically square bricks, made the daily journey up
and down Palatine Hill's tree-lined roads as construction began in earnest to rebuild Cicero's home and reputation. On November 11, 57 B.C.,
outraged Romans flooded the streets of the Forum to protest, if not the
court's absurd absolution, Cicero's return to public life.

CHAPTER TEN

Clodia's Resolve

*If the two compounds do not bind, if the volatile substance is
incapable of combining with the non-volatile one, the results of
the experiment will not go as planned.*

—MARIA THE ALCHEMIST

Having returned to Rome from the Crater, Clodia and Rufus
would have settled into familiar habits: For him, legal work
and visits to the Forum to build relationships; for her, lunches
and dinners with friends and associates who wanted a bit of her time.
The Palatine Hill remained central to the couple's social calendar, but
Clodia also owned property on the Tiber's right bank, at the base of the
Janiculan Hill. There in the district of Trastevere, weary Romans sought
calm under a verdant canopy of trees without sacrificing their proximity to power. Evergreen holm oaks soared above them. Deciduous oaks
rained acorns in abundance, which for their bounty the ancients considered a sign of the bygone Golden Age, a prosperous time before the
hardships of the present. Julius Caesar, then serving a five-year post in
Gaul, would later figure among Clodia's closest Trastevere neighbors.

By night, there were dinners on couches and a regular round of after-
dinner amusements with friends. Word games and puzzles delighted
convivial Roman couples, as they teased, tested, and taunted each other's literary and historical knowledge. One partner would select a letter of the alphabet at random; the other would have to give the name
of a famous fighter from Troy or of an exotic city on a distant conti-
nent. Redoubtable consumers of literature, elite partygoers dared one
another to recite verses that started and ended with the same letter.
Brainteasers kept them on the edge of their cushioned seats. "Shall I
say the sweat from the Bromiad spring?" "Shall I say the dewy stream of

the nymphs?" "Shall I say the redolent breath of cassia coursing through the air?" Participants competed to be the first to shout the answers: "wine," "water," or in the last case, "myrrh." Penalties involved a stiff draft of *vinum*. According to the ancient cultural chronicler Athenaeus, author of *The Learned Banqueters*, these lighthearted evenings united friends, allowing them a reprieve from the pressures of professional life, a time "to enjoy reciprocal affection." Plutarch tells the story of a couple who, quoting Andromache's speech to her husband Hector in the *Iliad*, amused each other by extemporizing humorous answers to its popular opening phrase, "But to me, you are as . . ."

Relationships in Rome required care and cultivation, which the thirty-eight-year-old Clodia was in a unique position that autumn to give. Unapologetic opulence characterized her lifestyle as it did those of other upper-class Roman women, as Rome's archaeologists can attest: silver bracelets, deep red carnelian necklaces, gold pendant earrings with translucent agate. The once-precious pieces are occasionally found in the most surprising locations, for example, during the excavation of drainage pipes in Roman baths, where their owners lost them. A wealthy woman might don the elegant wrappings of a wool stola for the day and early evening, and before bed change into a diaphanous nightgown from the Aegean island of Cos, its indigenous silkworms being the equivalent of the fashion world's most sought-after seamstress. (Chinese-manufactured silk would not arrive in Mediterranean markets for another five hundred years.)

The phrase often used to describe the overspender's predicament in every age, "to find oneself in debt," translates into Latin as "to hold another person's money," which many of Rome's youngest political strivers raced to do. There was plenty of money to be lent in the 50s B.C. Men with a financial cushion could take risks and make spectacular profits off their investments. Bribery to secure a lucrative contract overseas or an influential position at home was rampant in the Roman Republic. When Rufus inquired about a loan, Clodia, thinking nothing of it, obliged. Generous gifts between romantic partners were common in Clodia's Rome. We don't know when these two met, but the law considered a man and a woman duly wed once they had cohabitated for a continuous calendar year.

Ambition kept Clodia's younger brother focused on politics. Disappointed by the decision of the College of Pontiffs, who had authorized the return of the contested Palatine Hill lot to Cicero, Clodius announced his intention to launch a second campaign, as aedile. Part mayor, part city manager, aediles were tasked with the essential daily oversight that maintained Rome's basic city services. They repaired roads, enforced a set standard of weights and measures in the markets, ensured the quality of the city's water supply, and inspected the baths for public safety. They also supervised the regular schedule of games at the circus. No office in the republic was more scrutinized by the public for lapses of judgment or ineptitude than aedile. Clodius's loyal constituents stood ready to support his campaign.

That fall, whether directed by Clodius or on their own initiative, partisan mobs vandalized the house of Cicero's brother. Cicero was harassed in the streets. In the usually staid environs of Palatine Hill, thieves ransacked the property of Titus Annius Milo, one of Cicero's most vocal supporters. There was talk of postponing the upcoming elections for city manager. Cicero's allies, led by Milo, threatened to file a series of lawsuits against Clodius for disturbing the peace. Joining Milo were Clodius's long-standing political enemies, some of whom had been desperate to drive him from public life since the early days of the Bona Dea Social Club scandal. Clodius would need to win immunity—a perk that came with election to higher office—if he hoped to avoid prosecution for his complicity in inciting the recent spate of public violence, which, given Milo's vindictive nature, looked imminent.

⁂

There is no hint in the fall of 57 B.C., as there was during Clodius's campaign for tribune two years earlier, that Clodia was propelling her brother's efforts. Cicero no longer mentions Clodia in his letters to their mutual confidant, Atticus. We have to wonder why. With Rufus in the city for work, the rooms of Clodia's far-flung estates in Naples and at Solonium likely sat dark for much of the season. Clodia's slaves were asked to tend their hearths.

In one of Clodia's homes stood a bust of Venus—the Romans' name for the Greek goddess of love, Aphrodite—whose delicately carved features Clodia used to display her jewelry. It is one of the few pieces of her décor to merit mention in first-century B.C. sources. Cicero, in a disapproving aside, calls Venus the patron goddess of Clodia's sexual conquests and intimates that her statue, bedecked with Clodia's gold and semiprecious stones, functioned like a talisman for a soldier girding for battle. The statue's magic, Cicero implied, empowered Clodia to work her woman's wiles.

That women donned this armor unnerved Rome's commentators, who saw such accoutrements as proof of a woman's power to beguile, bewitch, seduce, and deceive. A considerable portion of a Roman woman's weekly outlay went to pay the *pigmentarius*, the cosmetics dealer. Powdered kohl darkened lashes, lampblack lined the eye, ground saffron lent it a colorful shadow. Red ocher, red chalk, or red dye extracted from lichen gave a touch of healthy color to the cheeks. Rows of delicate glass vessels, compact containers, and tiny boxes covered the surface of women's vanities. Used excessively, the products created risible caricatures for caustic love poets, who never tired of bewailing their own beloved's overreliance on her dresser's "thousands of colors." Used thoughtfully and delicately, they fashioned their wearers into the beautiful, confident, sexually desirable partners many Roman women, married and unmarried, dreamed of being. The sunshine yellow elecampane flower with its woodsy scent, *Inula helenium*, was prized for its potency as an aphrodisiac. Women in Clodia's time bought it under its ancient brand name, the Tears of Helen.*

In the morning, applying a cleanser derived from imported crocodile

---

* By the twentieth century, Rome's botanical gardens would occupy the hillside and riverbank where Clodia's villa stood—a quirk of urban planning that might have delighted the women of ancient Rome.

dung might restore a rejuvenating glow to the skin's complexion and, if the ancients can be trusted, leave a pleasing fragrance, since the reptiles who generated the substance in their intestines thrived on a diet of sweet, "odoriferous flowers." For blemishes, spots, and wrinkles, countless clever techniques helped a woman cover, conceal, and smooth. With a little Corsican honey or a generous smear of tallow from a swan, spots might, as if by magic, be erased before the pressures of the social calendar called.

A cosmetics dealer sold not only beauty products but what we moderns would now consider pharmaceuticals as well. *Medicamentum* was the Latin word for a wide range of naturally occurring curative drugs and remedies. Romans used the same word for "poison."

Roman law tightly restricted the distribution of illicit substances, many of which arrived in Italy from exotic locations where their potency had long been feared. The Athenians of the fifth century B.C. knew of hemlock's deadly effects. Kings in Asia Minor grew poisonous henbane and hellebore in their royal gardens. In Rome's republic, a handheld jar of eye cream and one housing a deadly powder were frequently indistinguishable. In later periods of Roman history, a cosmetics dealer could be held liable "if they recklessly hand over to anyone hemlock, salamander, monkshood, pine grubs, . . . the venomous beetle, mandragora, or the Spanish fly, except for the purposes of ritual purification."

The farther east one traveled from Rome, the more complex the science of poisons became. Scythian women of the Black Sea coast ambushed their victims with darts dipped in the toxic bacteria that leached from limestone or in decoctions of nightshade, mandrake, and yew. Farther still, in the snow-capped Himalayas, poisonous secretions from birds' nests were thought to deliver a quick death. In the locked cupboards of the apothecaries of Persia was stored the tasteless, odorless *zamikh*, arsenic, whose properties made it a weapon of choice for the ancient world's scheming palace murderers. When the deceased King Mithridates's effects were transported to Rome following the republic's conquests in the late 60s B.C., decades' worth of the eastern king's own

A generation after Clodia, the ancient writer Dioscorides produced an authoritative treatise on the medicinal and narcotic properties of plants. This page from an early medieval illustration of his work depicts two types of mandrake, known to induce anesthesia.

most deadly curiosities sparked a cottage industry of amateur interest in the pharmacological dark arts, guided by a colorful two-volume illustrated encyclopedia on medicinal plants and herbs edited by one of the king's chief scientists, Crateuas of Pergamon.

Pompey's enslaved Greek secretary, Lenaeus, was responsible for preparing the first Latin translation of Crateuas's text. It was not uncommon in Rome to find a Syrian-born slave who had practiced medicine. Raised in the more cosmopolitan eastern Mediterranean, many also had a facility for translation. "No great accomplishment ever came from a slave," Pliny would later claim, but reality belied the prejudice. Many enslaved Greek speakers were highly sought-after tutors for the children of the Roman elite.

Over time, thanks to Lenaeus's efforts, knowledge of serums and poisons penetrated the curriculum of Rome's medical schools and the laboratories of its herbalists and alchemists. By the time of Rome's fall in the fifth century A.D., questions about whether garlic or anise or rhubarb might neutralize a toxin circulated in the form of Greek and Latin manuscripts, which traded hands in remote medieval monaster-

ies. Much of this scientific information would be preserved, for readers across the medieval Islamic world of the Middle East and Africa, by
Arabic translators.

꜠

While they might have begun to catch up on some eastern knowledge
of science and medicine, an aptitude for geography and an appreciation
of the world's cultural diversity largely escaped the Romans of Clodia's
day. The average Roman had neither seen nor heard of Egypt's pyramids.
The Roman elite could barely contain their contempt for the Egyptian
monarchy and dismissed its capital, Alexandria, as corruptingly cosmopolitan. In the middle of the first century B.C., Rome was still decades
away from the publication of Strabo's landmark series *The Geography*,
seventeen volumes that would offer Romans their first extensive introduction to the contours and peoples of the eastern Mediterranean world.
Under Strabo's guidance, Roman audiences would encounter, for the
first time and in the comfort of their homes, the cities of the Black Sea
region where he was born; Arabian lands, Ethiopia, Libya, and Egyptian oases that were like "islands in the open sea"; and, positioned at the
northernmost point of the Nile delta, Egypt's opulent capital with its
unparalleled cultural amenities: a library, a museum, palaces, a broad
central boulevard, and man-made canals that facilitated the distribution of goods to desert cities in the interior. Alexander the Great was
buried there, a point of pride. His successors, the Ptolemies, were the
ancient world's richest monarchs.

After Rome's annexation of Cyprus, which had led to Ptolemy the
Twelfth's exile along with his younger daughter, Cleopatra, Alexandria's new ruler, the eighteen-year-old Queen Berenice, was determined to inform the men of the Roman Republic that under no
circumstances should its government involve themselves in her kingdom's sovereign affairs. So, sometime that autumn or early winter of
57 B.C., the pageantry of international statecraft consumed Italy as one
hundred ambassadors dispatched by the queen arrived at Puteoli, the

large harbor near Naples. Sailing in winter was treacherous, but the mission was urgent.

As prosecutors would later allege, Rufus showed a keen interest in the Egyptian delegation and may have traveled to witness its arrival. Its leader, Dio, was a distinguished educator and philosopher, comfortable at the lectern, accustomed to public scrutiny, and a formidable sparring partner. He shared the latter two qualities with his brother, a prizewinning wrestler. As an intellectual, Dio adhered to the Academic school of thought, a loose group of scholars who scrupulously documented the origins of contemporary literary and philosophical ideas in the works of overlooked writers and thinkers. By virtue of his stint as a tutor and dinner guest in the houses around the Crater, he was fluent in Latin.

While Queen Berenice hoped to convey her uncompromising position, Roman supporters of her father, the exiled Ptolemy the Twelfth, remained bullish about his eventual return. Leading military men, foremost among them Pompey, had been quietly pressing the Senate to authorize a full-scale invasion of Egypt. There would be financial and political rewards for toppling the regime.

When Dio and his delegation arrived, unnamed rioters—partisans of Pompey and supporters of the exiled Alexandrian king—met them at the harbor with heckles, shouts, and stones and other projectiles. Riots erupted in the markets and streets of Puteoli and Naples. Arson destroyed one property on the bay. An untold number of ambassadors lost their lives in the ambush while Dio barely escaped, managing to secure transport to Rome where he was given shelter in the mansion of a certain Coponius. After a would-be assassin managed to sneak past Coponius's doormen, Dio was transferred to another house, where he died from poison. An unknown man named Publius Asicius was arrested and charged with the murder, but as soon as the proceedings were called to order the case was adjourned and the defendant exonerated. To the jurors, it seemed evident that this random defendant was someone's pathetic idea of a scapegoat.

In that same blur of events, during the six- to eight-week window on either side of January 1, 56 B.C., the priests responsible for interpreting the Sibylline Books—the cryptic writings Romans consulted in times of state emergencies—announced an objection to any imminent military action in Egypt. So dire, so unusually direct were the Sibyl's verses, the priests exclaimed, that they had taken the extraordinary step of petitioning the Senate to share them with the public. The Senate granted this unusual request. "If the king of Egypt comes requesting any aid, refuse him not friendship, nor yet succor him with any great force, else you shall have both toils and dangers," was the Sibyl's advice. After a pause for self-reflection, the Fathers reversed course and withdrew their support for the exiled king. Military hawks tempered their enthusiasm for an invasion.

These were panicked weeks. Because of recent famine and price manipulation by merchants, residents of Rome learned that their city's already depleted grain depots, from which the neediest received their free rations, were facing yet another shortfall. Then, adding insult to injury, fire consumed the Temple of the Nymphs, where the relief program was headquartered. According to archaeologists, the blaze gutted the building and rendered everything in it unsalvageable beyond a few drums of marble. (In coming years, a new temple would rise on the same site, reusing this older material.) Valuable census records, held inside the temple, were destroyed.

Cicero's letters fix the dates of a few key happenings in late January 56 B.C.; Plutarch provides an occasional dash of color; the historian Cassius Dio, writing two centuries later, covers the historical record with his own indelible fingerprints. In the weeks after Dio's murder, Clodia's older brother Appius took to the city's pavements to support Clodius's campaign for aedile, and he won election on January 20. In early February, Rufus stepped boldly into the Forum to assume the role of lead prosecutor in a corruption trial against an elder statesman, a case he lost.

February 7, 56 B.C., noon: As Clodius addressed a crowd of citizens in the Forum, he was heckled with lewd, unrecorded remarks about his sister Clodia. Two hours later, Clodius returned to the Forum with an energetic call-and-response routine that whipped his own supporters into a frenzy over recent domestic and international policy lapses. "Who is starving the Roman people?" "Pompey," they shouted. "Who wanted the commission to Alexandria?" Again, "Pompey!" By three o'clock in the afternoon, the anger reached a boiling point. Partisan opponents pushed Clodius from the rostrum and provoked additional rounds of editorializing and recrimination. The Forum that day, says Plutarch, was filled with "a rabble of the lewdest and most arrogant ruffians." The impression that the later writer Cassius Dio gives of this episode is of a formerly dignified republic descending into civic madness.

The Alexandrian king Ptolemy, desirous of more agreeable surroundings, boarded the next ship from Ostia. As soon as the halyards raised sail, he fled to the halcyon shores of Asia Minor.

⟩∞⟨

The Romans believed that lovers grew more intimate when their lives and fortunes "intertwined." Yet after the tumult in the Forum and the Alexandrian king's abrupt departure, the relationship between Clodia and Rufus frayed. At the Palatine Hill property, sometime in early spring 56 B.C., slaves reported an unusual disturbance: Thinking himself unobserved, Rufus had surreptitiously hauled away a large swathed lump that looked to be a corpse.

The discovery put Clodia's slaves in a difficult ethical position. They had apparently come to believe that Rufus was experimenting with contraband substances in his apartment and that he was planning to murder their mistress. Roman masters treated their slaves' reports with great suspicion, but nonetheless, Roman law required that slaves relay such information. Failure to do so could result in corporal punishment that would not be inflicted on freeborn citizens. Torture of enslaved men and women to extract testimony was routine; crucifixion was a very real possibility for those who refused to assist the authorities.

In one egregious instance, a contested inheritance dispute between a wealthy mistress and her son, the woman used her authority as head of the household to torture her slaves and extract false testimony against her own child. Her disregard for the slaves' well-being offended her contemporaries, who rejoiced when attorneys exposed her cruel scheme. The most sadistic Roman slave-owners stretched the limits of human depravity. The horrifying fact behind the gruesome practice of *crematio* was that it consumed still-breathing bodies—not, as the English cognate would imply, dead ones.

Slaves' lives did not belong to them, nor were their stories theirs to tell. But Roman law allowed enslaved men and women to hold savings accounts in their own names. Generous masters could make regular donations or pay the equivalent of wages. When the balance reached a mutually agreed-upon sum, slaves could purchase their freedom. Magnanimity could also change fortunes overnight. Pompey was said to have manumitted the linguist Lenaeus, for example, as compensation for his impressive translations. Hundreds of thousands of the Roman Republic's enslaved men and women gained their freedom due to these and other measures. Although their manumitted status excluded them from public office, they gained the right to vote in all elections. Their children achieved full citizenship status.

The abolition of slavery, as Spartacus learned, was never a real possibility. Neither before nor after Clodia's time did the Romans ever willfully consider terminating their slave-based economy. Such a radical thought was, to quote one modern historian, too "cerebral" an exercise for the ancients to consider. Liberating one's slaves in Rome would always remain a transactional enterprise. Only "after eight years," said one man's last will and testament, could his slaves be manumitted.

If loyalty could win emancipation, it should have been awarded to Clodia's slaves in March 56 B.C., when they intervened to alert her to their suspicions that her lover was plotting her murder.

Petite but precious, this hand-carved cosmetics container, with scenes of tiny cupids and a Roman woman's portrait on its ivory lid, still fits comfortably in the hand.

⁂

To be an accomplice to a crime, in the parlance of the Roman street, was "to carry the lantern" for one's confederate. Based on testimony later delivered in court, Rufus picked two, who failed him spectacularly. Only one, Publius Licinius, is known by name. They conspired to meet in the steamy rooms of a bathhouse, where Publius was expected to hand over a small jar of poison.

Clodia's slaves, alert to the time and place of the exchange, hid in the changing room, witnessed the delivery, and valiantly tried to apprehend the two men. Although the conspirators dropped the poison and managed to escape the premises, the public skirmish led to Rufus's arrest.

In late March, three litigators of varying age and experience—Lucius Sempronius Atratinus, Lucius Herennius Balbus, and an otherwise unknown Publius Clodius—announced their intent to prosecute the case against Rufus. Allegations circulated almost instantly about Atratinus's motives, given that Rufus, in February, had unsuccessfully prosecuted Atratinus's father for bribery. Even before the trial opened, then, the affair had the unwelcome appearance of settling a family score. Herennius Balbus, a voice of wisdom and a seasoned public speaker, brought much-needed gravitas to the inquiry. Atratinus was reportedly only seventeen.

The republic had never established an independent Department of Justice nor paid a government salary to a district attorney whose mandate might include bringing criminal charges on behalf of the state. Yet in 56 B.C., with the legality of a possible Egyptian invasion still unsettled and politicians growing bolder by the day about their intent to annex the kingdom, many Roman citizens were concerned that powerful forces would prevail over the rule of law. In their government, it was the responsibility of citizens to hold malfeasance and criminality to account. Some degree of principle likely compelled the three prosecutors to act.

The men charged the twenty-six-year-old Marcus Caelius Rufus with five counts of criminal behavior: conspiracy to incite the riots that had disrupted the Egyptian delegation and devastated Puteoli and Naples (two charges), participation in the destruction of private property (one charge, involving alleged arson at an estate outside Naples), intent to commit murder (of Clodia) with an illicit substance, and one count of murder (Dio's assassination). Whether for lack of evidence or lack of a corpse, there was no charge regarding the unidentified body Rufus had allegedly removed from his apartment. The trial was announced for the first week of April.

Clodia agreed to deliver the crucial testimony. She had lent the defendant money which funded Rufus's involvement in the sprawling conspiracy to assassinate Dio, the prosecutors alleged. Thanks to her slaves' careful oversight, Clodia also could confirm that Rufus had tried to murder her in a desperate attempt to cover his financial tracks.

That spring before the trial, less than a year away from celebrating her fortieth birthday and against the backdrop of an Italy scarred by the memory of violent slave uprisings, Clodia emancipated her household's enslaved men and women. Cicero claimed in court that she acted only "after receiving the input of her brothers"—Roman women were legally required to confer with a male conservator when freeing their slaves. Yet it's hard to imagine that Clodia needed anyone's permission to express her gratitude.

CHAPTER ELEVEN

Clodia's Testimony

I saw a figure use great force to steal
and deceive, a practice most brilliantly done. What did I witness?

—CLEOBULINA, RIDDLER

On April 3, 56 B.C., upward of 200,000 residents of Rome packed the valley between the Palatine and Aventine Hills to fill the wooden stands of the Circus Maximus for a day of horse races and gladiator games. Dressed in colorful tunics, drawn from every quarter of their city, and representing every rank of Roman life from senator to slave, they came to honor the Great Mother goddess and celebrate springtime's most raucous festival. Ordinary business in the Forum and the markets was postponed for the occasion, which had begun with the customary procession of the Galli, the grand marshals of the parade. They drummed, strummed, and filled the air with their hypnotic recorders. Throngs of spectators crowded the streets at the base of the Palatine Hill, in the vicinity of the racetrack.

A fifteen-minute walk away, court was called to order in an unusually vacant Forum in the murder trial of Marcus Caelius Rufus. Judge Gnaeus Domitius presided. That this courthouse alone remained open during the public holiday signaled the gravity of the proceedings.

The four courthouses that surrounded the Forum's central square wore their age well, given that they had been constructed more than a century ago. One part covered portico, one part hall, the spaces, which the Romans called basilicas, saw regular use throughout the year. Long and narrow, with rows of windows at the roof line, they provided a blueprint for later Christian churches. Judges oversaw the proceedings from a platform at the far end, calling cases to order then largely remaining silent. Weather permitting, a case might also be heard outdoors in the Forum.

By Clodia's time, the judiciary divided its criminal docket into seven broad categories: homicide, bribery, treason, extortion, citizenship disputes, forgeries, and political violence or sedition. A different magistrate oversaw each class of proceeding. The prosecuting party was responsible for bringing the matter before the relevant judge. When crimes and categories overlapped, it was up to the prosecuting party to select the most appropriate venue. For Rufus's trial, the prosecutorial team bundled the charges of murder, attempted murder, rioting, and arson, and argued them before the court of sedition.

Litigants stood beneath the judge's dais to deliver their arguments to the jury. While courts that adjudicated charges of treason and bribery empaneled seventy-five jurors, cases of sedition sat fifty-one. They were chosen by lot from the top income categories of the census and likely sat on benches for the duration of the trial. The accused and any relatives or interested parties occupied the rows behind them. Bystanders shuffled into the back or took a seat on the extra benches that were provided for high-profile cases.

Hearsay, slander, rhetorical posturing, name-calling, joke-cracking, and character assassination were expected in a Roman courthouse. There would be no motions to sustain, no objections to overturn, no instructions read to the jury. Since evidence was delivered through prior deposition, which lawyers read aloud at the appropriate moment during their arguments, there was no witness stand in a Roman court, though witnesses could and did observe the proceedings along with the spectators.

After the jurymen swore their oaths to hear the evidence impartially, the three prosecutors presented their arguments and their evidence. Clodia listened as they read her testimony into the record. The following morning, April 4, with the defendant's father among the spectators, it looked as if Rufus was headed for the maximum sentence, lifetime exile. Then the defense began its rebuttal.

Rufus had not hired just any no-name defense lawyer. He had managed to enlist the wealthiest man in Rome, former consul Marcus Licinius Crassus, the financier of Caesar and Pompey, and the best legal counsel, Marcus Tullius Cicero. Flanked by these two heavyweights, Rufus rose first to speak in his own defense.

The strategy struck many as odd. His risky decision to sport a toga trimmed with expensive purple, which communicated an arrogance unbefitting both his station and the gravity of the proceedings, was an error to start with, Romans whispered, like a man who dresses in "necklaces and pearls" or a woman "in a general's cloak."

Irritable and disorganized, Rufus botched his opening statement and delivered a lamentable speech that was still being discussed a century later in Roman rhetorical classrooms. He wasted no time in launching an attack on Clodia, savaging the prosecutors' star witness as a "knockoff Clytemnestra" and "an honorary member of the island of Cos by day but a citizen of Nola by night." The reference to Clytemnestra cast Clodia as a mythological murderer from the Athenian stage, thereby defaming her as her husband's killer—but the allusion was at least accessible to most of the jurors. His riddle about Cos and Nola, however, left many of the spectators perplexed. Very likely, what he had intended was a comparison between the soft, silky fabric of Cos's nightgowns and the famously pugilistic gladiators from the southern town of Nola. Such abstruse allegations should be avoided in all capital murder cases, Roman textbooks cautioned, along with riddles, "frequent metaphors, antique words, newly coined terms ... and rhythms as far removed as possible from the practice of everyday speech." Lucidity, teachers reminded budding law students, was a virtue.

By the time the defendant finished speaking, many in the courthouse were wincing at his amateur performance and concluding that he had lost. Crassus is presumed to have delivered a suitably statesmanlike speech that reclaimed the momentum. Then, Cicero spoke: calm, gracious, and sympathetic to the jurors, who had been asked to report for trial duty during a holiday. Since classical antiquity, the Latin text of his speech, which history has preserved under the title *Pro Caelio*, "On behalf of Marcus Caelius Rufus," and which runs to thirty-nine pages in the standard modern edition, has been transcribed, preserved, and endlessly studied. Fragments of it have been unearthed in the most far-flung places—pulled, for example, from the papyrus trash heaps at Oxyrhynchus, a city in Middle Egypt, where it was once likely read in a Roman imperial schoolroom. In medieval Europe monks copied and recopied it for their libraries. During the Renaissance, a friend of the manuscript hunter Poggio Bracciolini found evidence that an entire version of Cicero's "Speech in Defense of Rufus" had circulated in the abbey of Cluny in the region of Burgundy for several hundred years before it vanished in the eighth century. In the ninth century, a near-perfect version existed in Carolingian France, a copy of which found its way to Paris's National Library, where it still resides. Other libraries across Europe acquired and copied their own editions.

With each new copy, however, came problematic variants—the term scholars use to describe the mutated words, corrupted phrases, and missing sections that can infect later editions of a manuscript, altering its meanings. The array of inconsistencies can usually be attributed to benign factors, like the drowsiness or distraction of the copyist. The flicker of candlelight or the rumbling of his stomach might challenge even an educated copyist's ability to distinguish a sloppy scribe's version of the Latin verb *potuerunt* ("they were able") from the Latin noun *potionem* ("poison"). Significant errors entered the text of Cicero's speech and proliferated until the modern period, when scholars tasked themselves with examining, comparing, and collating every manuscript. Like patient prosecutors who have double-checked every link in their evidentiary chain, they have preserved, as closely as possible, the original transcript of Cicero's words—here abridged in my own translation.

Gentlemen of the jury, I'd like you to imagine for a moment that someone has come to Rome unfamiliar with our laws, our customs, and our way of life, and I'd like you to picture how this trial looks from their perspective. What kind of unqualified atrocity do you think they would let themselves imagine has taken place here, one that has dragged us into court on a holiday while the roar of the games can be heard from the Circus Maximus, the businesses are shuttered, and this one court remains in session? I think you'd agree they'd conclude that we were here because of an egregiously heinous act that, if ignored, might threaten the foundation of our law-abiding republic. Rome is, after all, a city of laws, as any visitor would understand, where armed men who assault their leaders or besiege the Senate House or attempt to overthrow the elected government can and have been brought to trial for their seditious behavior. . . .

But when that outside observer finally realizes that the matter before you today rises to none of those levels, that it involves neither a matter of sedition nor a grave crime nor even an act of violence but rather centers around a smart, talented, hardworking young man who has been brought into this complicated proceeding by a young, disgruntled prosecutor as payback for his father's legal troubles, then, gentlemen of the jury, the real story of why we're gathered here should reveal itself. Our young prosecutor's eagerness to defend his father's own reputation might even be misdirection. What's at issue, frankly, is that financial freedom has empowered a certain high-class woman, motivated by the kind of insatiable lust associated with women of ill-repute, to harass my client. Her escapades must be stopped. . . .

Now, I know you have heard [Cicero begins again, regaining the thread of his argument and addressing the defendant's own questionable reputation] that some people have criticized my client because he made the choice long ago to leave his father's house. Well, I think we can all agree, can we not, that at my client's age, a change of residence should be deserving of our praise. Moving out is a sign of a young man's maturity, especially one with aspirations in public life. It's never too early in Rome to prosecute and win a case in a court, and it's not every day that one of Rome's sons receives his parents' blessing to venture out on his own career. Furthermore, since my client's childhood home was a natural distance from Rome, far removed from the Forum, it's eminently reasonable, then, that Rufus rented his own apartment—on the Palatine Hill, yes, but a modest residence, to be sure—from which he would be regularly able to visit my own house, for example, and cultivate relationships with friends and acquaintances. . . .

Now, at this point in the story, I know what you're thinking. You're saying to yourselves exactly what my distinguished colleague, Marcus Crassus, was recently reported as having said, albeit in a much different context, when he learned a few years ago about the arrival in our country of that troublesome Alexandrian king. "If only the tree had never fallen . . . " Meaning, I suppose, in Crassus's mind, that if Egypt's domestic problems had never come to Italy's shores, how much more uncomplicated our republic's current affairs would be. Well, gentlemen of the jury, I believe that tragic line about the manufacturing of the *Argo* can be applied equally and quite aptly to the present case, too, don't you think? The sentiment is strangely the same if we reflect on what my client has been forced to endure these past few months, no? Maybe we should modify the song to say, "If only *Rufus* had never left home . . . !" After all, ever since he embarked on his move to Rome, one problem has trailed the next, sending up a wake of unsubstantiated rumors. There's a Medea in our city, too, living up there on Palatine Hill. . . .

All of us who are fathers and heads of households will concede that young men deserve the rewards of a little recreation. It's natural for someone my client's age to have these desires. But I think we can also agree, can we not, that as long as they restrain themselves from wrecking someone's home or interfering with the trajectory of someone's career, we can overlook

their youthful indiscretions as harmless, innocent behavior—
tolerating them without too much cause for concern.

So, let's come to the two charges that seem to me the most
crucial of the case: the first, the allegations of borrowed money,
the second, the very serious allegations about murder. Each
rather coincidentally, I should also note, happens to involve the
same woman. The money was received from this woman; the
poison was, according to the prosecution's theory, procured to
be administered to her. Let's stay focused on these two issues
for just a moment more because any additional accusations you
might hear, as I promise to show, do not rise to a level of unimpeachable criminality but rather are the sort of specious slander unbefitting the majesty of a Roman court. I'm confident I
can identify the culprit who has invented these charges, too, the
identity of the author behind this farce, the writer of the drama
that has ensnared us all.

There's nothing wrong with needing money, which my client did, so he borrowed it from this woman, without difficulty.
It speaks loudly to my client's innocence that he never anticipated he would need a witness to corroborate the circumstances of the loan. Being on familiar terms with her, he seems
never to have suspected that such financial or legal safeguards
would be necessary. Would you? Yet what does the prosecution assert but that the whole plot to kill her originated at that
one exchange of gold: the who, the what, the when, the how,
all of it connected to my client's receipt of the money. To hear
the prosecutors' version of it, my client used his windfall to
procure the murder weapon, the poison. He bribed her servants, concocted a deadly draft, and chose the time and the
place to administer it. Make no mistake about it, friends. Anger
has been motivating these wild claims. A woman of insatiable
anger has been orchestrating this sordid affair, a woman well-
known, perhaps too well-known: Clodia of Rome. But I'm not

going to let myself be distracted by what's irrelevant or immaterial to the facts of this case. . . .

But how should I address a distinguished *materfamilias*, a well-born woman who has the gift, shall we say, of being on amicable terms with every man in Rome? Should I adopt the harsh tone of bygone days, chastising her the way previous generations from the dustier world of our republic's marble busts and wax masks spoke to each other? Or does this situation call for a lighter, a more playful, more humorous touch? Let's start by imagining [Cicero says, answering his own question] what this woman's ancestor Appius Claudius Caecus might have said if he were able to join us, shall we? He should be able to tell her everything I wish I could say but which the propriety of our own age dissuades me from doing, that is, if I want to avoid angering her. Besides, we know the sight of her in court would not cause him any grief, don't we?

Cicero's last point sought a cheap laugh from the well-known fact that Clodia's fourth-great-grandfather Appius's *cognomen* Caecus meant "the Blind." At that point in the trial, Cicero theatrically took on Appius's persona, imitating the grumbling, grouchy style of a bygone age. Cicero startled listeners by beginning with a crude Latin word for "woman," *mulier*, where decorum would have required a more deferential term, *femina*:

"Woman! By what measure or under what circumstance was it ever appropriate for a woman of our family to have relations with a gentleman who has shown himself capable of such childish behavior? How did you become so intimate with this louse that you loaned him money? How have you become so despised that you supposedly feared for your life? Have you forgotten with what frequency a member of our own storied family—your father, your uncle, your grandfather, great-grandfather, second-great-grandfather, third-great-grandfather—has been elected to the consulship? . . .

"Was your marriage with Metellus, one of the bravest, most outstanding and most patriotic men of our time, meaningless? Whenever he left the atrium of his house, he surpassed every Roman around him on the street with his family's impressive list of accomplishments, his courage, and his character. Two eminent Roman households, joined in storied matrimony—and you choose this Rufus, a man possessing neither name nor connections, all on account of your reckless libido! . . .

"If the masks of your family's valiant men have not changed your ways, maybe the story of [one of] our family's leading women might still convince you? Have you forgotten your great-relation Claudia Quinta, that paragon of domestic virtue who, during our city's war with Hannibal when she stepped into the harbor at Ostia, released the skiff with the statue of the Great Mother goddess from the marshy banks and famously saved the republic? Without her singular act of heroism, none of us might have had a city to celebrate today. . . .

"Yet with so many patriotic men and women distinguishing every generation of your family's historic line, you have let your brother's vices become your moral compass. There were countless other examples for you to follow. . . .

"While I myself was negotiating treaties with one of the republic's most ruthless enemies, King Pyrrhus, you were making disgraceful pacts with a young lover. While I was building one of the republic's recognizable roads, you were trafficking in sordid adventures. Was it to improve the quality of life for every resident of Rome that I built such an impressive new aqueduct, just so that, centuries later, you could draw a satisfied lover's bath?"

Cicero then dropped the theatrical posturing and resumed his legal rebuttal.

Now, the prosecutors have alleged that my client is the one who indulged in a lurid lifestyle. You've heard how they used their arguments to paint a disreputable impression of my client's social circle. Talk of sexual encounters and love affairs, the resort at Baiae has come up, beach trips, dinner engagements, concerts and shows, boat trips around the Crater, after-hours parties: All that was meant to prejudice you against him. Well, since—for whatever reckless reason—the prosecution has undertaken this case, I believe it is past time, gentlemen of the jury, that we hear from their star witness what she thinks of these accusations. Either Clodia corroborates every word of the prosecutors' narrative or, if she is unwilling to address the litany of these preposterous claims, then you should feel free to conclude the obvious. Neither her testimony nor the charges have any basis in fact.

"What would her own brother say?" Cicero pondered aloud, preparing the jurors like a well-rehearsed showman for yet another impersonation, this time, in the more colloquial language of Clodius's generation. Mimicry and voice acting was a common feature of Roman public speaking, but Cicero's virtuoso display of multiple personas in one speech would have garnered significant admiration.

"Why cause a courtroom fuss, my dear sister? Why not just drop the whole matter? I understand perfectly well. You laid your eyes on a good-looking gent in the neighborhood, a beau who set your heart aflutter. Accidental run-ins at the park, casual meetups around the city: The level of your infatuation was obvious. You don't need to explain love to me. But what do the comedians say? *So much fuss about nothing!* You have to admit, looking at the matter from the outside, this whole fiasco has the appearance of a clumsy, contrived drama, an artificial plot plucked straight from the theater. I can hear the advertisements for the show myself: *Wealthy, high-society woman captures the heart of a handsome, provincial young man until* ——. Everyone in Rome can predict the disastrous outcome for this story. It even has a role for Rufus's father as the miserly, overbearing parent. . . .

"But this plot didn't follow the formula, did it, my dear sister? The docile lover and sympathetic leading man whom audiences are accustomed to admiring onstage broke character, played against the adoring sweetheart, and rejected your advances. . . .

"You were insulted, weren't you, when he refused to acknowledge your generosity, when he showed contempt for your properties, your estates, your manicured gardens next to the river, where every man in Rome these days seems to enjoy a swim. It's high time to hook another gentleman with whom you can while away your idle hours. This one's not worth your harassment."

At this point Cicero resumed his own voice and, like a concerned father, addressed his client. Quoting verses from two Latin comedies, he offered a breezy reflection about the high expectations that every Roman man set for his son. The spirited vignettes lightened the mood and refocused the jurors' attention.

Let me end this playacting, gentlemen, and put my client's case in the simplest terms. Do you honestly believe Rufus wasn't smart enough to protect himself in such a dangerous situation with this woman? Members of the jury, I'm not criticizing her, mind you. But if, I say, there were someone like her, a widow, who teased men's desires, who always appeared at social occasions escorted by different men, whose houses and villas saw a steady flow of visitors, who funded men's ventures and supplemented young lovers' games with her fortune, if there were such a widow living so unconventionally, so extravagantly in Rome, a wanton widow living in the manner of a common prostitute, then, gentlemen, should we not exonerate this young man for having shown the moral clarity on his own to stand up and, in one brave act, separate from her?

As Rufus had amply demonstrated with his actions, learning to be a responsible member of society did not require fancy lessons in philosophy or adherence to formal schools of thought. The Epicureans taught their adherents to "do everything for the sake of pleasure," Cicero explained, in the affable tone of a beloved lecturer. The Academics instructed their followers "to find a happy partnership between virtue and desire," he went on. Stoics advocated "a path to personal satisfaction by maintaining a strong work ethic." But this sort of overly intellectual thinking posed its own set of dangers.

Can you imagine a Roman boy who never confessed an inclination to peek at beauty, who never expressed a desire for the intoxicating delight of a touch, a taste, or an aroma, who shut his ears to another's charm? The more traditionally minded, like me, might think that the gods had done this young man a favor by providing him with an exceptional gift, to live a life untroubled by such vices. But you and I both know, when it comes to today's customs, that we find ourselves holding a minority opinion. To most, a young man's life is empty without the enjoyments of his youth. So let's allow our boys to have a little fun, and grant the younger generation some allowance to make mistakes. It's unreasonable to expect a young man to reach adulthood without succumbing to the occasional temptation. A boy's strongest desires might not always respond to the strict rules of reason. . . .

That is why it's so crucial to govern one's actions by following a few basic moral principles, which is exactly what we teach them. Respect the importance of modesty for yourself and others, we say. Don't take another's wife. Don't squander your inheritance. Don't fall into debt. Don't disrupt another's house and home. Don't corrupt the wholesome, don't stain the pure. Don't bring disrepute to those morally upright and good. Don't engage in public acts of violence. Don't fall prey to seditious conspiracies. Be free from all accusations of crime.

Rufus may have erred by starting a relationship with a woman of Clodia's level of wealth and privilege, Cicero said. But when it mattered most, he had done as any good Roman should do. Subscribing to the simplest moral maxims, he had shown common sense and parted from her wicked ways. In doing so, Rufus offered the strongest testimony to his own decency.

> Besides, do you not detect the foul odor of disgrace emanating from Palatine Hill, the one that has polluted the otherwise pleasant airs around the Bay of Naples? I will not stoop to name the person responsible for it, but it is not, I can assure you, my client. . . .
>
> If a certain unmarried woman throws open the doors of her mansion to any desirous suitor, hosts dinners for strange men, and embraces such a meretricious lifestyle; if she acts this way in the city, in the parks and gardens, among the crowds around the Crater; if she comports herself this same way in the streets, in her preference for how she dresses, and her choice of the company she keeps—with her bedroom eyes and her salty demeanor; her constant need for affection, treks to the beach, excursions around the bay, elaborate meals; dare I say it, with her kisses—so that she not only looks the part of a prostitute but acts the part of one, shamelessly and impertinently—I say, if a young man were to encounter this hypothetical woman, I would like to ask our dear friends, the prosecutors, which of the following two scenarios they think better would suit the facts of this case: that the young Rufus was some sort of prof-

ligate lover on the warpath out to steal a lady's virtue or that he was an understandable romantic, hoping to satisfy an older woman's wants?

The Latin implies that Cicero spoke directly to Clodia at this point in the speech in an aggressively *ad feminam* manner:

If you're not the woman we have been led to suppose, then why are the prosecutors dragging my client's good name through the mud? But if you are the one behind this case, should the defense not be troubled by your participation if, as it appears, the litany of these unsavory stories fails to disturb you in the least? . . . Maybe Appius's great-granddaughter will educate us all by showing us the road out of this dilemma. For, either her own scruples should compel her to testify resoundingly about my client's innocence or the obviousness of her own brazen behavior will aid our defense. . . .

I should think at this stage we've sailed past the reefs and rounded the peninsula, gentlemen. It's clear sailing from here. . . . What more are you hoping for, members of the jury? That the facts and truth of what happened will cry out in plain, unequivocal language as if some miraculously sent omen? There's no need for divine intervention when it's clear as day this entire affair stems from a hostile, disreputable, tactless, crime-ridden, sex-driven house. . . .

Who among us is unable to admit it: that in such a home where the mistress's family motto is "What happens inside the walls stays inside the walls," in which there have arisen unusual liaisons, shows of gross levels of extravagance, and reports of unheard-of vices, where so-called slaves did their mistress's bidding—some of whom were entrusted with highly sensitive matters, many of whom were implicated in the house's lurid

comings and goings, and all of whom benefited from their mistress's largesse—who does not see that the *materfamilias* of this
home in no way qualifies to hold the title of respectable lady? . . .

Unfortunately, my friends, what usually happens in life is
that, when presented with an obvious pattern of behavior, no one
connects the dots until it's too late, isn't that so? I remember, I
myself saw—admittedly, during a regrettable chapter in my past,
I confess—what happened when Metellus, a patriot born and
bred to serve our republic, only three days after he had addressed
the Senate, after everyone had witnessed him in vigorous health
discoursing energetically from the speaker's platform in the
Forum, how suddenly, tragically, and unexpectedly he had suc-
cumbed to illness. Metellus had tried to warn me, then, stricken
on his deathbed, about the coming political tempest. Delirious
and despondent, or so I was told, Metellus had banged his bedroom wall and cried out to a neighbor, a former magistrate who
had already, sadly, predeceased him. If only those bedroom walls
could tell us what they saw and heard that dreadful night!

The real crime was that Metellus had been taken too soon—eliminated,
Cicero implied, by his treacherous wife, Clodia. He then returned to the
details of the present case.

Why plan the ambush at such a venerable bathhouse unless
Clodia was conspiring with the spa attendant? They say she's
earned quite a discount over the years as a loyal customer. . . .

Does the prosecution's story really hold up under scrutiny, I
ask? Even from a veteran writer of countless dramas, the whole
production lacks coherence, strains credulity, and as we will
now see, falls apart during the last act. . . .

Look what happened. The accomplices escaped. Music plays!
Curtain! Everything about this one-woman drama from start to
finish has played out like a farce. . . .

How did Madame Emperor, our republic's first glorified *imperatrix*, allow a lineup of such essential witnesses to elude capture? Neat and tidy resolutions may not be expected in a comedy. But enough is enough. . . .

Gentlemen, I would like to offer by way of conclusion a reminder that the task of reaching a responsible verdict falls solely to you. I would also like to remind you that we are here because my client faces a series of charges related to public violence, a grave matter pertaining to the safety of our homeland that calls for the most thoughtful reflection. Our republic's laws on this subject are unequivocal, given the events of the last twenty years when the very existence of the republic has increasingly looked to be in danger. The legislative foresight of Quintus Catulus ensured that we would have a law to punish violent uprisings. That was the law of the land when I held the consulship. That was the law I enforced, the law with which I extinguished the stubborn fires of deadly insurrection. Under that same solemn law, prosecutors have charged my young client, Rufus, not to punish him for any crime against the republic but to fulfill one woman's lustful whim. . . .

As you ponder why Rufus has been hauled before this court, gentlemen, know this. I, too, wish Rufus's ambition had led him at the outset of his career to make a different set of personal choices. But in the end, he did what was necessary. In the Forum, in his business dealings, in his earliest cases before the court, he surpassed everyone's expectations. All the qualities that men learn after years of hard work and effort—attention to detail, a serious demeanor, grit—he quickly learned. . . .

As both his lawyer and his friend, I'll be the first to admit his reputation staggered a bit as he rounded that first turning post in our republic's race for honors. But let's be honest. Much of his misfortune has been due to circumstances beyond his control: a regrettable choice of landlords, the temptations of finer living, and of course, one woman's insatiable need for celebrity. But those chapters of his life—or perhaps, I should more accurately say, the *rumors* of them, since none of his behavior ever truly reached the depths of depravity that you have heard alleged in this courtroom—you should consign to the history books. Whatever it was that really happened in recent months, this boy has emerged from it. His decency told him to extricate himself from it. He would have successfully escaped it, too, had not the forces of enmity and resentment, awakened by his ill-conceived relationship with that woman, chased him into court. . . .

Let's not ruin the life of a well-educated young man from a respectable home over this. A vote to acquit would be a welcome display of gratitude to Rufus's father for his tireless encouragement of the civic dreams of his son, as well as a strong investment in the future of Rufus and the republic. No ancestral line, not even a shoot, deserves to be so cruelly axed before its time. Decency demands we not uproot the scion of such a promising Roman family.

As soon as Cicero finished his remarks, which in the Roman system of justice counted as both opening and closing argument, the court went into recess. The case lay in the hands of the jurors.

The entertainer, raconteur, and intellectual Cleobulina, born on the island of Rhodes sometime in the sixth century B.C., excelled at keeping her audiences in suspense. A friend of Greek philosophers, a poet, and a performer, she authored a collection of mind-bending riddles that tested her listeners' ability to transcend the literal meanings of words. Her artistry inspired countless imitators after her death. Two now lost comedies from antiquity, both titled *The Cleobulinas*, are said to have featured a chorus of sharp-witted, clever women modeled after her. From her once voluminous material, three riddles, all in verse, survive.

Cleobulina's riddling technique depended on metaphor. "I saw one man weld bronze to a second / so seamlessly he united their blood. Can you tell me what I saw?" The answer was "a physician," because with the help of bronze cups, gently warmed and placed against the skin, doctors were known to correct an ailing body's imbalanced humors, alleviating their patients' discomforts, or so it was believed, by drawing blood to the surface of the skin.*

The trick to solving one of Cleobulina's enigmas was to discern how she manipulated language to transform an otherwise commonplace scenario into a disorienting or unusual depiction of the world—"for this," said Aristotle, "is the nature of a riddle, to attach impossibilities to a description of real things." After she died, people of the Mediterranean continued to play her games. Revelers posed riddles during nightlong drinking parties, generating hours of entertainment. "I was hit by a donkey shank's horned bones. Can you explain what happened to me?" Answer: You heard a musician play the Phrygian flute, a wind instrument that achieved its distinctly sonorous depth from a donkey's sturdy tibia. The last of Cleobulina's known puzzles earned a reputation as her most diabolical.

"I saw a figure use great force to steal / and deceive, a practice most brilliantly done. What did I witness?" Carelessness and snap judgment led some hasty audiences to misinterpret the question, assuming it referred to a criminal act. But as one authority in antiquity explained in an anonymous treatise titled *On the Nature of Right and Wrong, or What Is Justice and Injustice?*, a literal solution occluded appreciation for a more penetrating truth: "In writing, just as in the visual arts, the one who takes home the prize is the artist whose depiction of the truth deceives audiences the best."

The thief in Cleobulina's riddle—the shadowy figure using "great force to steal / and deceive"—referred, in short, to a storyteller, and deception was that magical moment when an accomplished actor, performer,

---

* The technique, known as cupping, is used today, for example, in alternative medicine.

or writer seduced their audience. In Roman times audiences and critics alike praised poets, playwrights, and writers for mastering this technique, which they called *illusio*. A vivid, engaging style of communicating, at times to inspire, at other times to swindle, it was unafraid to set aside the literal constraints of words in favor of more figurative or imaginative artistry. A powerful substitute for reality, the practice of *illusio* connected the dots where none existed in a fragmented narrative and filled in the gaps of a historical account where firm ground had been eroded. It invited audiences through careful scene-building and complex characterization to imagine themselves as a story's protagonist, identify with a character's dilemmas, or encourage them to find profit in seeing the world from another's surprising point of view. At its most insidious, it built alternate, elaborate, inaccurate versions of the truth. At its most destructive and self-serving, it preyed on an audience's fears and confirmed their long-held biases.

On April 4, 56 B.C., Cicero's illusions, his fictions, convinced the all-male jury to acquit his client. Cicero sold them a story they were eager to hear: that boys could be absolved from the most egregious behavior provided they professed to become respected citizens. Rufus's crime, in Cicero's telling, was an innocent "vice" of allowing himself to be taken as the boy-toy of a wealthy older woman though, in fact, he stood accused of murder. In the unabridged speech, Cicero never addresses the details of Dio's death; scholars deduce that the task of refuting that charge must have fallen to another member of the defense team. Nor does Cicero refute the intricacies of the conspiracy from which Rufus hoped to profit—he simply blames the Egyptian plot on Ptolemy, who by then had left Rome.

Cicero's primary gambit, that a man's word would weigh more than a woman's, echoed a culture in which ignoring, condoning, and excusing men's poor judgments was axiomatic, particularly if a man hailed from a family of wealth and power. In ancient Rome, a husband could always bring a charge of adultery against his wife. The law never allowed a wife to pursue charges against her philandering husband.

Decades after the trial, between 18 B.C. and A.D. 9, senators instituted an additional series of misogynistic laws: the *Leges Juliae* and the *Lex Papia Poppaea*. Each was named for its sponsors, the former after Augustus, the adopted heir of Julius Caesar, and the latter after two legislators, Marcus Papius and Quintus Poppaeus. This new legislation specifically prevented a woman from inheriting most of her husband's fortune, exercising discretion over her own savings, or liberating her slaves. Under the rhetoric of restoring Roman morality, the laws required marriage for all Roman men between twenty-five and sixty years old and for all Roman women between twenty and fifty years of age. Tying a woman's legal identity to the responsibilities of Roman motherhood, the laws prohibited a widow from claiming more than one-tenth of her deceased husband's estate and from claiming her own rightful inheritance at all unless she had carried a minimum of three of her husband's children to term. Cicero's lurid but rhetorically masterful characterization of Clodia's behavior continued to resonate in the Fathers' memory: The young women of Clodia's daughter's generation would face even more legal restraints than their mothers had known.

That women like Metella entered the first century A.D. stigmatized by the law as "weak" and "infirm" is not because history was naturally headed in that perilous direction—Clodia's life story confirms the opposite—but because the Fathers dreaded the thought of future generations enjoying the liberties that Clodia and other pioneering Roman women had claimed for themselves. Clodia might have envisioned for her daughter a Rome where an informed, if disenfranchised, woman could still make valuable contributions to the welfare of the republic. After Clodia that promise abruptly dimmed.

When, nonetheless, Roman women in successive generations rose to speak in public forums or offered their views in private deliberations, mockery and ridicule followed. By the time the New Testament was compiled, Christian authors regularly drew inspiration from ancient Rome's values to secure their own paternalistic authority, preaching that Christian wives must obey their husbands' authority in all matters, as in multiple scriptural passages attributed to St. Paul. Over time, Christian men used these biases to monopolize leadership throughout the early church, then codified the rules to limit women's participation in the increasingly powerful religious institutions of the Middle Ages.

On the thinnest of unfounded assertions, Cicero's speech introduced Clodia to generations of readers as the Roman republic's most notorious *meretrix*, or "whore," her city's most "promiscuous noblewoman." His virtuoso speech mesmerized generations of men with one condescending trope after the next: that an outspoken woman with authority was a dangerously sexualized one, that impugning her character with unfounded charges of prostitution was enough to dismiss any woman's argument, that name-calling and caricature could find applause among the masses as a substitute for intellectually rigorous debate.

Cicero's portrayal of opinionated women as scheming murderesses spawned more irrational fears about women in Rome's imperial palace. When, three decades after the trial, Rome first had a female leader—the Empress Livia, born to a neighboring family on Palatine Hill during the last year of Clodia's marriage to Metellus—male critics whispered that she had poisoned her husband to secure the throne for Tiberius, her son by a previous marriage. Livia may have been one of Clodia's distant cousins. The accusations against her were entirely unsubstantiated, but Cicero's fictions had furnished a lasting blueprint for traditional Roman men to retain their iron grip on power.

CHAPTER TWELVE

Clodia's Verdict

What once we loved is already ashes.

—ERINNA, *THE YARN*

After Rufus's acquittal, Cicero quickly left Rome. His house at Cumae called him to the idyllic surroundings of the Bay of Naples, where he was scheduled to throw a party for his daughter's second engagement. The departure marked a shameless moment of hypocrisy for the attorney who had turned the Crater's reputation for luxury into a mark against Clodia's credibility. Construction had not yet finished on his new Palatine Hill townhouse; the site was littered with builders' detritus: rocks, rubble, and partially sawed wooden beams. After the trial, residents of the elite enclave stood on edge, as if expecting the hurling of stones to follow the outbreak of grievances between its houses.

Vindicated by his return to public life, Cicero basked in the glow of his performance. Emboldened by the trial's outcome, he marched to the Capitoline Hill's legislative wall of fame, a panel of bronze plaques on which the republic commemorated a politician's accomplishments in office and pried the records of Clodius's year as tribune off the wall. Contemporaries remarked upon this brazen act of partisan vandalism. It went unpunished.

In coming weeks, electioneering signs and slogans were painted on the façades of the houses on Palatine Hill—where, as in all Roman neighborhoods, homeowners and businesses confronted the perennial appearance of that year's campaign advertisements on their walls.

Rising food prices, delayed paths to citizenship, and suppressed voting rights remained key issues in the upcoming elections. In Clodia's neighborhood, political hostilities simmered. Rufus's trial had done nothing to bridge Rome's intractable partisan policy divides.

Over the next twelve months, as Romans consigned Cicero's defense and Clodia's testimony to history, workers spruced up the city to celebrate the opening of a dazzling cultural attraction, a stunning popular entertainment complex six years in the making. Rising from the flat plains on the northwest side of the city's walled perimeter, crafted from the best brick masonry, the building's surprising height of nearly 45 meters rivaled a small Roman hill, which in a city surrounded by fourteen of them was no accident of architectural planning. On September 28, 55 B.C., Pompey's Theater, the first permanent playhouse in the city of Rome, opened to wondrous acclaim. The days-long celebration featured an unparalleled display of looted artifacts and stolen wealth—what the Romans termed the spoils of war—won during its benefactor's eastern conquests, including that of Mithridates's Black Sea kingdom.

An instant landmark, Pompey's Theater, with its sculpture museum, gardens, meeting rooms, and public stage, put Rome, once a backwater, on a par with Athens in Greece, Syracuse in Sicily, and the other grand cities of the time. Lovers strolled beside its manicured hedges. Extravagant theatrical shows with high production values drew Romans to enjoy the performances. For two of the inaugural season's debuts— Accius's Latin version of Aeschylus's murderous homecoming classic *Clytemnestra* and *The Trojan Horse*, based on a story by one of Rome's first tragedians, Livius Andronicus or Naevius—critics counted upward of 600 animal extras and some 3,000 bronze props deployed on the stage. An untold number of extras joined hundreds of stagehands and costume designers in spectacular stagings of these plays, what Roman dramaturges called *fabulae praetextae*, over-the-top "costume dramas" that transposed stories from distant history, like the Trojan War, to contemporary times, with actors clothed in Roman dress.

Pompey's eastern conquests, although eight years in the past, had boosted the Roman treasury with 85 million sesterces of tax revenue, so no expense was spared for the theater's opening. The actor Aesop (unrelated to the fabulist) came out of retirement to participate in the once-in-a-lifetime event. The actress Gaia Copiola, who debuted on stages during Clodia's youth and who won hearts with her charming dances, also performed. Audiences cheered the reappearance of the onetime child actress, now in her forties. Pompey's Theater introduced her to a new generation of Roman fans. She gave her last performance, says Pliny, at the age of 104.

Among the most popular features of the theater's grounds were its colorful, exotic plantings. The general's landscape architects had artfully arranged a botanical marvel in the pathways behind the theater. Balsam trees from Judaea, prized for the piney perfume of their resin, stood alongside date palms from Arabia and majestic plane trees, which were esteemed by Persian monarchs. Designers dubbed the area the Portico of Nations, for the plants and artworks it showcased—a veritable world's fair of curiosities from places whose locations, if not their names, still remained mysterious to ordinary Romans: Pontus, Armenia, Cappadocia, Paphlagonia, Media, Colchis, Iberia, Albania, Syria, Cilicia, Mesopotamia, Phoenicia, Palestine, Judaea, and Arabia. For the first time in its history, the Roman republic could celebrate its subjugation of peoples across three continents. Artists created a living tableau of these defeated peoples for display in the portico where, as custom dictated, the nations were personified as mournful enslaved women.

Nor were these personifications the only women to decorate the space. Gracing a series of plinths, enhancing the theater's prestige, were statues of the goddess of creation, Venus, and the famous Muses of myth—and, in a nod to the Muses' abiding power of inspiration, row upon row of women writers and poets from across classical antiquity. The celebrated Greek poet Erinna was there, praised and memorialized for her absorbing work *The Yarn*. So, too, was Praxilla, who entertained her listeners with bawdy songs, and Nossis, Corinna, and Anyte, the experimental forerunners of the Hellenistic avant-garde. The whole collection, visitors remarked, commemorated "the god-voiced women whom Mount Helicon nurtured," whose sophisticated, entertaining, insightful poetry remained "undying." Chief among the statues in Pompey's portico stood the beloved "female Homer," Sappho, whose archaic Greek verses had given first expression to romance, friendship, and family life from a woman's perspective. Erected in an age when women on pedestals were a rare sight, the statues taught generations of young girls to search for role models in the bookstalls of a marketplace and on the shelves of a library.

Yet, as the course of history advanced, nearly every statue of a woman writer in Pompey's Portico of Nations gradually disappeared—toppled, smashed, or repurposed for the manufacturing of lime, an ingredient of cement. Given the entrenched ideology of the premodern day, the entire display was doomed, just like the literary masterpieces with which these women had won their fame. As the statues vanished, so, too, were collections of the women's work discarded, overlooked, and lost. Even Sappho's work has survived only in fragments.

In the very year Pompey's Theater opened to applause, 55 B.C., a bloodbath deluged the palace halls of Egypt, as the rogue Roman general Gabinius, a puppet of Pompey's, restored the once-exiled Ptolemy the Twelfth to his palace. Stationed at the Euphrates River, where he had been preparing Roman troops to engage the Parthians of Mesopotamia, Gabinius had agreed to change missions after receiving a letter from Pompey, hand-delivered to his camp by the Alexandrian king. It came with the exiled king's verbal promise of more than 10,000 talents for logistical reimbursement—the equivalent of millions of sesterces in military aid.

Though senators had repeatedly and expressly forbidden military action, fearing that any windfall from Egypt's treasury would alter the balance of political power in Rome, Gabinius's aide-de-camp, an enterprising Marc Antony, accepted the king's offer. As everyone in

Rome well knew, thanks to the unspoken lesson of Rufus's acquittal and the fact that the murderer of the Egyptian ambassador had never been brought to justice, Egypt lay free for the taking—or, at least, was worth the risk of flouting the Senate. With more men seeking office to avoid prosecution for their crimes and the electoral framework depressing the voices of ordinary Romans, senators showed little appetite for reform. They continued to refuse citizenship to the residents of the North Po. Representative government was in crisis. Greed and influence mattered more than the pursuit of a long-term, stable republic. Accountability, which Clodia had bravely championed, ceased to matter.

With the help of Jewish guards stationed on Egypt's eastern border, men loyal to Gabinius and Antony, Roman commanders marshaled their forces to strike at the Nile delta's easternmost city, Pelusium. The capital of Alexandria fell by the spring. Queen Berenice, the estranged daughter of the exiled king, was executed on her father's orders, as was her con-

Among her six siblings, only Clodia's elder brother, Appius Junior, has plausibly been identified in the surviving portraits known from classical antiquity. Now in Copenhagen, this portrait's sober, wizened look was characteristic of many Romans' faces by the end of the first century B.C.

This stoic marble portrait depicts an unknown woman of mature years and is known to have been sculpted at the end of the first century B.C., when Clodia vanishes from the historical record.

sort king, to clear the throne. The Roman army restored law and order to the streets around Alexandria's palace quarter, and a Roman banker was installed at the head of Egypt's treasury. His mandate was to study the balance sheets of the royal monopolies—the kingdom reaped handsome profits from linen and glass manufacturing, as well as the production of papyrus, in high demand for tax receipts, bureaucratic documents, and personal letters—and skim off the amounts that might be appropriate for repaying Rome's creditors.

Among the fifty-one-year-old Ptolemy's first orders of business was the drafting of his last will and testament, in which he bequeathed his realm to the joint care of his son, Ptolemy the Thirteenth, and his dearest daughter who, if not always at his side during those difficult three and a half years of exile, had endured its trials with him. She was fourteen years old when her father reclaimed his throne. The events of 55 B.C. secured young Cleopatra's inheritance.

⅏

Clodia turned forty that year. Roman portrait artists, working in stone, depicted mature men and women with crow's feet, puffy jowls, baggy eyes, and deeply furrowed brows. Age in the first century B.C. communicated experience. It was prized, warts and all.

In antiquity, those who survived childhood illness and disease and reached the age of ten might live four more decades. Statistically, men and women who reached their fifties might live fifteen more years.

How did Clodia's daughter regard her mother in these years? Metella's marriage to Lentulus Spinther was fast approaching. If scholars' surmises are correct, neither woman welcomed the occasion. Before dying, Metellus had signed papers that betrothed Metella to the son of an archconservative family, who had become one of Clodius's fiercest partisan opponents. Clodia, for all her decades of creative maneuvering behind the scenes of public life, was powerless to break the contract.

Amid the entertainments and distractions at Pompey's Theater, partisan tempers still flared. Establishment politicians ignored calls for reform. On the streets, rioting increased in frequency and intensity. The elections for consul in 54 B.C. were postponed. By the time voters cast their ballots, the victors, Pompey and Crassus, the men with perhaps the greatest name recognition, would serve less than a full term in office, furthering the republic's breakdown. Says the later Roman historian Cassius Dio: "Murders occurred practically every day." But the deteriorating civic morale did not deter Clodius, who announced another run for office, a judgeship. Alongside a nobility of spirit and a playful irreverence, a high level of self-regard had always been a feature of the Appius family tree. (Romans in these years coined a word for the family's arrogance: *appietas*. The appellation, which played off the Romans' reverence for *pietas*, or selfless devotion, implied that Clodia's family characteristically lacked it.)

During the next two years, the issues that had propelled Clodia's involvement in her brother's 59 B.C. campaign—enfranchising new citizens, enfranchising freed slaves, and ameliorating economic inequality—remained important. Sources depict Clodius as the family's stalwart progressive voice. At the same time, there are clues that Cicero's grandstanding and vanity had diminished his reputation, a development Clodia undoubtedly cheered.

Three unusual Latin writers offer an eye-opening look inside these years. The first, known by his proper name, Asconius, lived closest to Clodia's time. His writings offer a quasi-journalistic reporting of events in the 50s and 40s B.C. The second, anonymous, source was found in the library of the remote northern Italian monastery of Bobbio, where, sometime between the end of antiquity and the Middle Ages, a scribe used the monastery's extensive collection of texts to write a commentary on Cicero's speeches, incorporating ancient testimony that otherwise no longer survives. By far the most fascinating, most enigmatic of the three sources, however, is the anonymous author of an early imperial invective, most likely written as a classroom exercise in a Roman rhetorical school, and subsequently included in medieval manuscripts containing texts attributed to Clodia's contemporary Sallust. Its short Latin title, *In Ciceronem*, can be translated as "The Case Against Cicero."

Asconius lived in the first century A.D. A father with great expectations for his son, he was disappointed by the shortcomings of the rhetorical instruction in his son's classical grammar school. As his children's self-appointed schoolmaster, he dedicated years to compiling notebooks of idiosyncratic reflections and homespun observations on Rome's intellectual life and political culture to supplement their education. During those years, the beginnings of the Roman Empire, teachers often demanded little more than rote memorization of the gender and cases of Latin and Greek nouns. When asked by students to repeat basic concepts or explain definitions, haughty professors left the classroom in a huff, as Asconius related to his two sons:

I inquired at Rome of a certain grammar teacher who had the highest repute, not for the sake of testing his patience but from an earnest desire for knowledge, about the origin and meaning of the Latin word *obnoxius*. And he, looking at me askance and ridiculing what he considered to be my puerile question, said, "I can't possibly take the time to answer such a question. Do you have an endless supply of sleepless nights?"

To make one's name as a respected academic in the empire meant one had to "ferret out everything that had ever been said on a subject, even by the most worthless writers," contemporaries explained. As researchers endlessly prattled on about their obscure interests, well-meaning students abandoned their education, dejected. Outrageous egos impeded the joys of learning. "The commentaries of the classical teachers are full of such encumbrances to learning," the textbook writer Quintilian explained. These were the *obnoxius* ones, the men "guilty" of civic negligence. As an antidote to the growing pedantry of the classical classroom, Asconius assembled his own extensively researched commentaries on Cicero's collected works.

One generation after Clodia, educators had enshrined the orator at the center of a canon of writers who were assigned in the study of rhetoric, to promote excellence in writing and oration. Even as the pall of Augustus's single-family monarchy upended many of Rome's older republican ideals, modeling a speech on one of Cicero's or writing commentaries on his orations still led to success in the most important careers for Roman men.

Asconius, aspiring to enliven the history of the end of the Roman Republic for his sons, availed himself of every possible scrap of documentation about Cicero's texts to compile a handy guide that would augment their study. Notes to former prosecutors' speeches, surviving trial records, pieces of Cicero's corpus of personal correspondence, excerpts from scholars of Clodia's generation like the lost histories of the Roman writer Fenestella, transcripts of the Senate's daily deliberations from the first century B.C., even Cicero's own research materials, which Cicero's slave Tiro had made public after his death—all of this Asconius collected, reviewed, and synthesized for his sons. He socialized with Rome's leading men and jotted down notes from conversations. His writing reveals an impressive knowledge of the streets and alleyways of the first-century city. Transcriptions of texts authored by Cicero that time might otherwise have stolen from bookshelves miraculously found their way into Asconius's papers, ensuring their survival. Four centuries after Asconius, what began as a quirky family project remained in circulation. Medieval writers copied and preserved Asconius's notes for their own sons.

With remarkable prescience and sympathy, Asconius furnished reliable, detailed reporting of the events that shaped Clodia's weeks, months, and years after the trial. While Clodius vacillated about declaring his candidacy for a judgeship, for example, he advocated for a set of consequential reforms to address the inequity of Rome's "vermiculated" voting districts. The system continued to disenfranchise Rome's freed slaves who, noted Asconius, "voted in no more than four Roman urban voting districts" regardless of where they lived on the Italian peninsula. With unusual insight, Asconius explained to his sons how the republic manipulated the outcome of its elections by mathematically distorting voters' preferences. For, Asconius said, the Fathers' resistance to the principles of shared representation in the assemblies "reserved the balance of these thirty-one rural districts for freeborn citizens alone."

On Clodius's initiative, Asconius reports, a bill was again proposed in these years to distribute the freed slaves more equitably among those thirty-one districts. The issue that had led to the murder of a reformist politician in Clodia's childhood neighborhood and had occupied Clodia in 59 B.C. was still her younger brother's fervent cause.

From the shelves of the fifteenth-century library in the remote monastery of Bobbio comes a second voice whose testimony shapes history's account of the final years of Clodia's life. Situated at the northwestern base of the Apennine Mountains, Bobbio was home to a community of

diligent monks who, during the instability that settled upon the peninsula after Rome's fall, collected, copied, and thereby protected scores of
classical texts from destruction. When new texts arrived, works of Arabic pharmacology or Persian metallurgy from Mediterranean traders,
for example, clean vellum was purchased to make a copy for the scripto-
rium's shelves; when no fresh supply was available, monks used a rough-
edged pumice stone to scrape the writing surface of an older piece of
vellum clean. In this way, hundreds of thousands of old, unneeded
words were wiped away, consigned to oblivion, so that the page could
hold a new layer of ink for a text deemed more relevant. Palimpsests—
recycled manuscripts that bore the faint traces of the original, erased
texts—became common.

In 1814, in one such Bobbio palimpsest, the expert linguist, future
cardinal, and onetime Jesuit priest Angelo Mai discovered a previously
unknown Latin text haunting the vellum underneath a later ecclesiasti-
cal treatise. It would irrevocably change the way historians write the last
years of the Roman Republic. As Mai deciphered the spectral forms of
individual words, strings of coherent sentences materialized. One of the
abiding challenges of working with handwritten Latin manuscripts is that
they lack punctuation marks or spaces between words; without these aids
to comprehension, every attempt to read a medieval text requires something akin to the trained eye of a decoder. A long-lost ancient Roman commentary on twelve of Cicero's published speeches had come to light—a
treasure trove of information from the end of Clodia's lifetime.

The text's author—known by the affectionate moniker Bobbio—
crystallizes the enmity between Cicero and Clodia's family after the
trial, explaining "how much Cicero hated Clodius" and how Clodia's
brother gleefully antagonized his family's nemesis. Bobbio reports that
Clodius, outside his own Palatine Hill house, erected a monument that
advertised the impressive list of his legislative accomplishments as tribune. Cicero was required to pass it daily on his walks to the Forum.
Bobbio also confirms Clodia's brother's unflagging commitment to electoral reform. "Clodius proposed a law that would give voting rights to

Rome's freed slaves," Bobbio says, "so that their enfranchisement would be equal to that of other Roman voters." One ignominious courtroom speech would not derail Clodia's family's campaign to guarantee greater electoral representation.

To these wisps of Rome in the 50s B.C. can be adduced "The Case Against Cicero." References in this scathing monologue to the Roman invasion of Egypt in 55 B.C. confirm that it was written after that event, although scholarship suggests a slightly later composition, in the first century A.D. It might have been performed for a crowd in the Forum, distributed as a political pamphlet, or, more likely, submitted as a homework assignment in response to a teacher's creative prompt to encourage original thinking. The message it delivered is a refreshing antidote to Cicero's bombastic presence at the center of public life, as amusing as it is unsparing in its critique of the orator's moral bankruptcy. It called Cicero "a self-appointed resident of Mount Olympus" and blamed him for the ugly tone that consumed Roman civic society after his return from exile.

In a series of forceful accusations, the anonymous author claimed that Rome's civil discourse had suffered because of Cicero's shamelessly self-serving behavior.

> Rome might have been able to endure the endless barrage of your unjust verbal abuses, Cicero, if there were any indication that your impudence was born from an occasional lack of judgment, not from the sickness of your mind. But I see there's neither measure nor restraint in anything you offer our republic. So let me take this opportunity to respond in kind and address my counter-remarks to you and these "Chosen Fathers." Men who take such pleasure in such unrestrained speech should, every once in a while, endure it themselves.

Unmasking Cicero as a huckster, a hypocrite, and a charlatan, the speaker launches a salvo against his unrepentantly egocentric behavior, the moral collapse of the establishment that his return has precipitated, and the dereliction of the many ruling Fathers who condoned Cicero's personal greed. So fragmented has Rome's once united republic become, the anonymous author says, that "ignoble men now grab for personal profit at every turn, without any concern for the commonwealth." In a society where corruption has become commonplace, "it is you, Fathers, whose abject shamelessness and moral turpitude have made a laughing-stock of our republic."

The author excoriates Cicero for using delays, distractions, and obstructions to falsely claim the mantle of the republic's most patri-otic champion: "a rank amateur, this man, a curse from the moment he arrived on Rome's political scene." It casts his crusade to exact retribu-tion from his political enemies, upon his return from exile, as the ulti-mate betrayal of his commitment to the republic's principles. The man was a political menace, a threat to the very state he feigned to protect. In a moment of innuendo that surely raised a bemused smile from sym-pathetic readers or listeners, the author accuses Cicero's wife, Terentia, of sexual impropriety.

"The Case Against Cicero" provides a counterbalance to the glowing views of the establishment on Cicero's career. Cicero's illegality, in the end, knew no bounds: He was "unreliable, deferential to his enemies, and abusive to his friends. At one moment he supports one side, at the next the other. He has been loyal to nobody and a thoroughly undependable senator." In the author's final summation, every part of Cicero's body elicits a loathsome response from those who interacted with him. "The man's tongue trafficked in conceit, his hands took whatever their owner wanted, the volume of his insufferable voice engulfed every conversa-tion. In the shiftiness of his feet were the obvious symptoms of duplicity and deceit. He dares remind us Rome was blessed with his leadership?"

With his relentless sermonizing that played on Romans' fears, Cicero brought nothing but an end to the innate goodness of society. "Of your personal grudges and constant abuses, our republic, our collective ears have heard enough." Twenty-one centuries later, the jury is still

out on the question of the authorship of the text known as "The Case
Against Cicero."

⟩☜

In 53 B.C., for the second time in a decade, the republic postponed its
elections. The decision may have delayed Clodius's path to the judgeship. Mobs terrorized the streets. Cicero, Appian, Plutarch, and Cassius Dio all recorded the outbreak of violence, which culminated in the
tragic events of January 18, 52 B.C.

"It was around four o'clock in the afternoon," Asconius began, "when
Clodius, on his way back to the capital from the hills of Ariccia, was
accosted on the road just outside the highway stop at Bovillae, near the
local shrine of Bona Dea." He had made the trip to the small municipality to address a group of distinguished men and influential citizens. His
entourage, consisting of about thirty slaves, was, just like the leader of the
cavalcade, traveling on horseback when they encountered a hostile party
coming toward them from the direction of Rome. Cicero's confederate,
Milo, led the opposing pack; he was joined by his wife (who was Sulla's
daughter), Marcus Fufius, some other friends, and a pair of burly gladiators, the latter of whom dismounted and instigated an altercation with
Clodius's slaves. A swordfight and fistfight erupted beneath the stone
pines on the wintry country road. One of Milo's men advanced toward
Clodius and with his sharp Thracian sword lashed him in the side.

Clodius was hurried to a tavern, where his wounds were tended.
Milo, panicked at the thought that a partisan opponent, in a fit of judicial revenge, might ruin his career by hauling him into court on charges
of assault, ruthlessly ordered his henchmen to raid the tavern, find the
injured Clodius, and eliminate him. They dragged Clodius into the dark
street, beat him, and left his battered body by the side of the inn. A passing senator saw the bloodied body and ordered it lifted onto his carriage.
By the time the men returned to the gates of the city, Clodius was dead.

"The time was just before 6 p.m. that day," in Asconius's version of the
events, "when Clodius's body, on the senator's sedan, arrived back in the

city." The body was delivered to his home, and as word of the tragedy spread, a sizable crowd of commoners and slaves poured into the streets to mourn the murder of one of their generation's most revered populist leaders. That evening, Fulvia allowed her husband's mangled corpse to remain on display in the entry hall of their Palatine Hill townhouse.

Respect for the dead, bonds of sisterhood, and shared sorrow all would place Clodia at the scene, at her sister-in-law's side. By dawn, an even more impressive group of sympathizers, this time including many eminent Roman families, gathered at Fulvia's home to convey their respects to the grieving family. The mourners raised her husband's body on their shoulders—still bloody, still laid out on the sedan, lacking the usual pall—and carried him down to the speaker's platform in the Forum, where the horror would be visible for every citizen to see. One of Clodius's speechwriters, whose craft no doubt influenced his perception of the moment's symbolism, proposed that they place Clodius's body in the Senate House. Eulogies were regularly held in the Forum, but the laying out of a recently murdered citizen was a provocative act.

Mourners demolished the senators' wooden benches, dismantled the Senate's wooden tribunal, and heaped wooden desk upon desk to construct a makeshift pyre. Every combustible piece of material the crowd could lay its hands on, including the Senate's parchments and scrolls, they used for kindling. A torch was touched to the heap. Flames shot up from beneath the bier, enveloped Clodius's corpse, and reached higher and wider inside the Senate House until there was no stopping the uncontrollable blaze. As plumes of smoke smudged the skies, citizens scattered.

As Bobbio explained in his unadorned account of that day, "The Roman people had derived so many benefits from Clodius's career" that from Clodius's murder "they drew an equal rage." With both the Senate House and an adjacent courthouse engulfed in fire, the Fathers called an emergency meeting on Palatine Hill. Wary of dictatorship but faced with few viable options for regaining control of the city, they appointed Pompey sole consul of the republic.

By late afternoon, Asconius says, the Senate House's timber roof and brick walls "collapsed on themselves in a fiery conflagration." By nightfall, the once hallowed, mighty symbol of Rome's republican government lay in a heap of "still smoldering" embers.

❧

One year after Clodius's murder, the reigning king of Egypt, Ptolemy the Twelfth, died at sixty-six of natural causes. The king was survived by two sons and two daughters. In accordance with their father's wishes Ptolemy the Thirteenth, eleven, and Cleopatra the Seventh, eighteen, inherited responsibility for governing the kingdom's 3 million people. The inauguration would mark the first great event in Cleopatra's celebrated life. In coming years every sexist jeer and paternalistic trope practiced in classical antiquity by Cicero and others would be sharpened, refined, and redeployed against the young queen.

Clodia withdrew. No trace of her remains: no rousing curtain call, no glamorous exit walk across history's stage. She removed herself from the final act of her life and disappeared from the historical record. Apart from a brief mention of her in a piece of correspondence involving the sale of one of her houses, in the 40s B.C., the only answer she marshaled to her society's worsening ills was, as far as we know, silence.

AUTHOR'S NOTE

In October 2023, I was strolling through Rome's botanical gardens where, nearly two millennia ago, Clodia had her country house and near where Caesar, too, had a sprawling estate. Elite Romans loved their suburban villas, with their outdoor dining rooms, sumptuous displays of marble, and shaded walkways, amenities perfect for entertaining and impressing exclusive sets of guests. Cleopatra lived on the grounds of Caesar's villa when he invited her to Rome in 46 B.C.

Beneath soaring Mexican sequoias and beside Japanese yews, brushing up against the waxy, fingerlike leaves of the hill's ancient oaks, I pictured a garden party at which Caesar would introduce the visiting twenty-three-year-old queen to his forty-nine-year-old Roman neighbor, Clodia of Metellus. In this quiet corner of the ancient capital, two overlapping histories would at last intersect. One woman would pass the sum of her generation's experiences—the torch of history—to the next.

The poet Sappho once wrote, "I am confident someone out there, / a second person, will remember us." I never found any evidence that Clodia and Cleopatra ever met. But if they had—or even if, in the chatter of the small social circles at the heart of the Roman Republic, Cleopatra did hear Clodia's story—the thought stayed with me: Surely she would remember her.

ACKNOWLEDGMENTS

Had it not been for certain men's preoccupations with her character, precious little of Clodia's story would have survived antiquity, hardly enough to shape into a biography. Honoring her family of rhetoricians and road-builders, however, I listened to the sources' every word and turned every paving stone until I had assembled a fair record with which to write her life.

In Rome, visits to the Museo Nazionale Romano, the Forum and Palatine Hill, the Capitoline Museums, and the archaeological park of Ostia Antica provided rich context for Clodia's life, as did study visits to the Museo Archeologico dei Campi Flegrei at Baia, to the archaeological sites at Cuma and Santa Maria Capua Vetere around the Bay of Naples, and to the Museo Archeologico Nazionale di Napoli. In Denmark, my gratitude goes to Dr. Rune Frederiksen, Head of Collections at the Ny Carlsberg Glyptotek, who passed away before this project was finished, and to Jennie Gunnarsen, the Glyptotek's librarian, for opening their collection's doors to me. Three trips funded by Stolle faculty development awards through Saint Louis University's College of Arts and Sciences ensured my access to the library of the American Academy at Rome. For the opportunity to join the Academy community as a Visiting Scholar in Rome during the fall of 2023, a position that allowed me to complete this manuscript, I owe my thanks to the Academy's director, Dr. Aliza Wong, to the residents who welcomed me, and to Saint Louis University's Office of Vice President for Research.

Over the years I have been afforded the opportunity to learn from a wonderful set of scholars. Andrew Riggsby and Penelope Davies in Texas guided me through the Roman Republic's history, art, architecture, and literature. Lesley Dean-Jones introduced me to ancient medicine. Barbara Weiden Boyd at the Intercollege Center for Classical Studies was among those who introduced me to the Roman Bay of Naples. Before I knew that ancient history was a viable career, Alex Sens in Washington, DC, sang the praises to me of the Hellenistic poets. My own students at the University of Texas at Austin and Georgetown University read Cicero with me in the original. It is David Mathers's Latin classroom at Loyola Academy, though, where I first encountered Clodia's story some thirty years ago, that will always hold a dear place at this story's center, as does Donald Sprague's mentorship, which continues to endure.

At Saint Louis University, the Dean of the College of Arts and Sciences, Dr. Donna LaVoie, and two History Department chairs, Tom Finan and Mark Ruff, facilitated my research. Colleagues in the U.S. and abroad have been the source of delightful conversation: Lorri Glover, Jen Popiel, Silvana Siddali, Claire Gilbert, Fabien Monchert, Enrique Dávila, Filippo Marsili, Hal Parker, Tom Keeline, Luis Salas, Tim Joseph, Letizia Ceccarelli, and Jessica Hughes. To Mary Boatwright, my gratitude for the support she lent in the writing process; to Darius Arya in Italy, for his friendship and logistical help. Thanks, as well, to Jamie Emery in our libraries and to research assistance provided by Tom Morin and Brian Merlo. Undergraduates offered invaluable insights. Feedback on early drafts from Julia Harvey, Bridget Evarts, and Kristy Sorensen was confidence-building. Later drafts benefited from the expertise of Kit Morrell, Eric Orlin, and Mary Jane Cuyler. YJ Wang, Mo Crist, and Allegra Huston pushed me toward greater clarity. I'm grateful for their input. Any errors are mine.

Clodia's story would have looked noticeably different had it not been for the welcome insights and critiques of Alane Mason, whose editorial guidance shaped this book. My sincerest thanks to her and to the team at W. W. Norton, as well as to Ayesha Pande for her continued support and to Gardiner, my husband.

NOTES

To recover the singularity of Clodia's life meant working in two ancient languages and three modern ones, excluding my own. The evidence pulled me in just as many directions. Her brother-in-law Lucullus's villa sits underneath an Angevin castle on a seaside promontory in Naples. A portrait of older brother Appius has been plausibly identified among a gallery of Romans in Copenhagen. Clodius built a set of city walls at Ostia, a pleasant trip from Rome. The notes offer a snapshot of where I looked and what I found, to my surprise and my disappointment. It seemed appropriate to let . Cicero, a figure whose voice could range from sophisticated to crude, speak through as many translators as needed until the climactic moment when he cleared his throat in court. That translation, as well as his correspondence with Atticus in 59 B.C., are mine.

Abbreviations

Loeb   Loeb Classical Library (Harvard University Press).

Ancient Sources

Appian   *C*: *Civil War* in *Roman History, Volume III: The Civil Wars, Books 1–3.26*, translated by H. White (Loeb, 1913); and *Roman History, Volume IV: Civil Wars, Books 1–2*, translated by B. McGing (Loeb, 2020). *M*: *The Mithridatic War*, in *Roman History, Volume III*, translated by B. McGing (Loeb, 2019).

Asconius   Edited by A. Clark and published as *Orationum Ciceronis Quinque Enarratio* (Clarendon Press, 1907).

Bobbio   Text discovered at the monastery of Bobbio, Italy, by an anonymous medieval commentator who used the monastery's ancient manuscripts to fill in the gaps of Cicero's writing. Those sources are now lost. The Latin text is given in *Ciceronis Orationum Scholiastae*, edited by T. Stangl (G. Olms, 1964).

Case   "The Case Against Cicero": In A. Novokhatko, *The Invectives of Sallust and Cicero: Critical Edition with Introduction, Translation, and Commentary* (De Gruyter, 2009), 150–63.

Catullus   *Catullus: The Complete Poems*, translated by G. Lee (Oxford University Press, 1990).

Cicero   *A*: Letters to his friend Atticus, in *Letters to Atticus, Volume III*, translated by D. Shackleton Bailey (Loeb, 1999); and E. Shuckburgh, *The Letters of Cicero, Volume 1* (George Bell and Sons, 1899).

Archias: *In Defense of Archias* in *Cicero: Defense Speeches*, translated by D. Berry (Oxford University Press, 2000), 107–21.

B: Letters to his brother Quintus, in *Letters to Quintus and Brutus. Letter Fragments. Letter to Octavian. Invectives. Handbook of Electioneering*, translated by D. Shackleton Bailey (Loeb, 2002).

Brutus: In *Brutus. Orator*, translated by G. Hendrickson and H. Hubbell (Loeb, 1971).

F&F: Letters to friends and family, including Terentia, in *Letters to Friends, Volume I: Letters 1–113*, translated by D. Shackleton Bailey (Loeb, 2001).

H: "An Appeal for the Return of My House," in *Pro Archia. Post Reditum in Senatu. Post Reditum ad Quirites. De Domo Sua. De Haruspicum Responsis. Pro Plancio*, edited by N. Watts (Loeb, 1923).

K: *On Rome's Relationship with the Alexandrian King*, fragments of the speech preserved in the Bobbio palimpsest. The Latin text is given in *Ciceronis Orationum Scholiastae*, edited by T. Stangl (G. Olms, 1964), 91–93.

M: *In Defense of Lucius Murena* in *Cicero: Defense Speeches*, translated by D. Berry (Oxford University Press, 2000), 67–106; and *In Catilinam 1–4. Pro Murena. Pro Sulla. Pro Flacco*, translated by C. Macdonald (Loeb, 1976).

O: *On the Orator: Books 1–2*, translated by E. Sutton and H. Rackham (Loeb, 1942).

R: *In Defense of Marcus Caelius Rufus* in *M. Tulli Ciceronis Pro M. Caelio Oratio*, edited by R. Austin, 3rd ed. (Clarendon Press, 1988). Citations are given as §, section numbers in the Latin, and "p.," page numbers of the English commentary.

Roscius: *In Defense of the Client from Ameria, Roscius*, in *Cicero: Pro Quinctio. Pro Roscio Amerino. Pro Roscio Comoedo. On the Agrarian Law*, translated by J. Freese (Loeb, 1930); and in *Cicero: Defense Speeches*, translated by D. Berry (Oxford University Press, 2000), 3–58.

V: *The Prosecution of Verres* in *The Verrine Orations, Volume II: Against Verres, Part 2, Books 3–5*, translated by L. Greenwood (Loeb, 1935).

Cleobulina	Riddles in *Elegy and Iambus, Volume I,* edited by J. Edmonds (Loeb, 1964), 164–65.
D	Dio Cassius in *Roman History, Volume III: Books 36–40,* translated by E. Cary and H. Foster (Loeb, 1914).
EH	*An Election Handbook* in Cicero, *Letters to Quintus and Brutus, Letter Fragments, Letter to Octavian, Invectives, Handbook of Electioneering,* translated by D. Shackleton Bailey (Loeb, 2002).
Erinna	Excerpts from *The Yarn,* printed as *The Distaff* in *Select Papyri, Volume III: Poetry,* translated by D. Page (Loeb, 1941), 486–87; and I. Plant, *Women Writers of Ancient Greece and Rome* (University of Oklahoma Press, 2004), 48–49.
L	Lucretius, *On the Nature of Things,* edited by W. Rouse, revised by M. Smith (Loeb, 1924); and *De Rerum Natura,* translated by W. Leonard (E. P. Dutton, 1916).
Livy	*History of Rome, Volume I: Books 1–2,* edited by B. Foster (Loeb, 1919); *History of Rome, Volume IX: Books 31–34,* edited by J. Yardley (Loeb, 2017); *History of Rome, Volume XIII: Books 43–45,* edited by A. Schlesinger (Loeb, 1951).
Pliny	*Natural History, Volume I: Books 1–2,* translated by H. Rackham (Loeb, 1938); *Natural History, Volume II: Books 3–7,* translated by H. Rackham (Loeb, 1942); *Natural History, Volume IV: Books 12–16,* translated by H. Rackham (Loeb, 1945); *Natural History, Volume VII: Books 24–27,* translated by W. Jones and A. Andrews (Loeb, 1956); *Natural History, Volume VIII: Books 28–32,* translated by W. H. S. Jones (Loeb, 1953); *Natural History, Volume IX: Books 33–35,* edited by H. Rackham (Loeb, 1952) .
Plutarch	***Advice***: "Advice to a Bride and Groom," in *Moralia, Volume II,* translated by F. Babbitt (Loeb, 1928), 297–343.
	Antony: In *Lives, Volume IX: Demetrius and Antony. Pyrrhus and Gaius Marius,* translated by B. Perrin (Loeb, 1920).
	Caesar: In *Lives, Volume VII: Demosthenes and Cicero. Alexander and Caesar,* translated by B. Perrin (Loeb, 1919).
	Cicero: In *Lives, Volume VII: Demosthenes and Cicero. Alexander and Caesar,* translated by B. Perrin (Loeb, 1919); and in *Fall of the Roman Republic: Six Lives by Plutarch,* translated by R. Warner with an introduction and notes by R. Seager (Penguin, 1972).
	Lucullus: In *Lives, Volume II: Themistocles and Camillus. Aristides and Cato Major. Cimon and Lucullus,* translated by B. Perrin (Loeb, 1914).
	Pericles: In *Lives, Volume III: Pericles and Fabius Maximus. Nicias and Crassus,* translated by B. Perrin (Loeb, 1916).

Pompey: In *Lives, Volume V: Agesilaus and Pompey. Pelopidas and Marcellus*, translated by B. Perrin (Loeb, 1917).

Sulla: In *Lives, Volume IV: Alcibiades and Coriolanus. Lysander and Sulla*, translated by B. Perrin (Loeb, 1916); and in *Fall of the Roman Republic: Six Lives by Plutarch*, translated by R. Warner with an introduction and notes by R. Seager (Penguin, 1972).

Q   *A Speaker's Education* in *The Institutio Oratoria of Quintilian*, translated by H. Butler (Loeb, 1920).

S   Sulpicia, *Elegies* in *Catullus. Tibullus. Pervigilium Veneris*, translated by F. Cornish, J. Postgate, and J. Mackail, and revised by G. Goold (Loeb, 1913).

Sappho   Fragments in *Greek Lyric, Volume I: Sappho and Alcaeus*, edited by D. Campbell (Loeb, 1982).

Strabo   *The Geography of Strabo*, translated by H. Hamilton and W. Falconer (G. Bell and Sons, 1903); *Geography, Volume I: Books 1–2*, edited and translated by H. Jones (Loeb, 1917); *Geography, Volume VIII: Book 17*, edited and translated by H. Jones (Loeb, 1932).

V   Valerius Maximus, *Memorable Doings and Sayings, Volume II: Books 6–9*, translated by D. Shackleton Bailey (Loeb, 2000).

Preface

xi   **Twenty meters beneath Rome's hills:** E. Sassi, "Metro C, acquedotto di 2.300 anni scoperto sotto piazza Celimontana," *Corriere della Sera*, April 4, 2017.

xi   **"Everyone crafts his own future":** *Sallust II: Fragments of the Histories. Letters to Caesar*, edited by J. Ramsey (Loeb, 2015), 478, my translation.

xi   **lengthier nasal intonation:** W. Allen, "Claudius or Clodius?" *Classical Journal* 33 (1937): 107–10, clarification by A. Riggsby, "Clodius/Claudius," *Historia* 51 (2002): 117–23, at 120.

xii   **"the right to possess what money [she] earned":** Virginia Woolf, *A Room of One's Own* (Harcourt, 1929), 22.

xii   **tribunes, or Protectors of the People:** For the translation, I followed novelist Robert Graves's *I, Claudius* (Vintage, 1989), 16, whose flair makes both the office and the history more intelligible.

xiii   **Clodia's "penetrating eyes":** Cicero *R* §49.

xiii   **"mouse to millionaire":** *The Satyricon of Petronius*, translated by W. Arrowsmith (University of Michigan Press, 1959), 78.

xiv   **"originators and inheritors":** Woolf, *A Room of One's Own*, 109.

Chapter One: Clodia's Moment

3 **"The woman you're reading about":** National Museum of Roman Antiquities, Rome, inventory number 58694, my translation. For the text, *Terme di Diocleziano: La collezione epigrafica*, edited by R. Friggeri, M. Cecere, and G. Gregory (Electa, 2013), 545.

3 **a young Roman girl named Cloelia:** Pliny *Natural History* 34.13–14, in *Natural History, Volume IX*.

3 **For ten centuries:** M. Roller, *Models from the Past in Roman Culture* (Cambridge University Press, 2018), 66–94.

3 **"unconventional spirit":** Livy 2.13, my translation.

4 **census office; census records:** S. Hin, *The Demography of Roman Italy: Population Dynamics in an Ancient Conquest Society, 201 BCE–14 CE* (Cambridge University Press, 2013), 351–53.

4 **"As long as our republic lasts":** Cicero *Roscius*, translated by Berry, 37, slightly modified.

5 **"shouting", lazy riders:** Plutarch *Cicero* 5.6, my translation. Nicely illustrative are C. Rosillo-López, "The Common (*Mediocris*) Orator of the Late Roman Republic: The Scribonii Curiones," and J. Wisse, "The Bad Orator: Between Clumsy Delivery and Political Danger," both in *Community and Communication: Oratory and Politics in Republican Rome*, edited by C. Steel and H. van der Blom (Oxford University Press, 2013), 292 and 169.

5 **the leisurely life of a poet:** *The Satyricon of Petronius*, 118.

6 **worst speakers in the Forum:** Cicero *Brutus* 217.

6 **"I desire, and I endeavor":** Translated by I. Plant, in *Women Writers of Ancient Greece and Rome* (University of Oklahoma Press, 2004), 15.

6 **"I worked with my hands":** Translated by M. Lefkowitz and M. Fant, in *Women's Life in Greece and Rome*, 4th ed. (Bloomsbury, 2016), 287.

6 **the Jewish writer Maria:** Plant 2004, 130.

7 **"It does women credit to keep quiet":** Sophocles, *Ajax*, line 293, in *Sophocles: Ajax. Electra. Oedipus Tyrannus*, edited by H. Lloyd-Jones (Loeb, 1994), my translation.

7 **arguments about women's inferiority:** E. Cantarella, *Pandora's Daughters: The Role and Status of Women in Greek and Roman Antiquity*, translated by M. Fant (Johns Hopkins University Press, 1987), 58–61.

7 **"Except [for] the bear and the leopard":** Aristotle, *History of Animals, Volume III: Books 7–10*, edited and translated by D. M. Balme (Loeb, 1991), 217–19.

7 **"least talked about by men":** Thucydides 2.24.2, quoted in S. Pomeroy, *Goddesses, Whores, Wives, and Slaves: Women in Classical Antiquity* (Schocken, reissued 1995), 74.

7 **Aspasia:** Cantarella 1987, 53–54.

7   **kissed Aspasia goodbye:** Plutarch *Pericles* 34.6 .

8   **a similar prudish patriarchy:** Starting points include J. Grubbs, *Women and the Law in the Roman Empire* (Routledge, 2002) and J. Gardner, *Women in Roman Law and Society* (Indiana University Press, 1986).

8   *pater ... to control:* J. Hallett, *Fathers and Daughters in Roman Society* (Princeton University Press, 1984), 67.

8   **subject to divorce:** V 6.3.9–12.

8   **"while their daughter was watching":** From Plutarch's *Life of Cato the Elder* 17.7, my translation; text in Plutarch *Lucullus*.

9   **"Nobody gets a better return from his land than you":** Martial, *Epigrams* 10.43, line 2, in *Epigrams, Volume II: Books 6–10*, edited and translated by D. Shackleton Bailey (Loeb, 1993), 356–57, slightly adapted.

10 **intentionally unflattering:** Very helpful is A. Corbeill, *Controlling Laughter: Political Humor in the Late Roman Republic* (Princeton University Press, 1996), 57–60, 83–84.

10 **70 percent:** Statistics and analysis at K.-J. Hölkeskamp, *Reconstructing the Roman Republic: An Ancient Political Culture and Modern Research,* translated by H. Heitmann-Gordon (Princeton University Press, 2010), 89–102.

10 **Gaia Caecilia:** S. Rutledge, *Ancient Rome as a Museum: Power, Identity, and the Culture of Collecting* (Oxford University Press, 2012), 174.

10 **"domestic tranquility ... good housekeeping":** Plutarch, *Moralia* 30 in *Moralia, Volume IV,* edited by F. Babbitt (Loeb, 1936), 52–53, my translation.

11 **Oppius's Law:** R. Bauman, *Women and Politics in Ancient Rome* (Routledge, 1992), 25–26.

11 **"blockaded every street":** Livy 34.1, my translation.

11 **"female fury", "womanly rebellion":** Livy 34.2, translated by Lefkowitz and Fant 2016, 173–74.

12 **"Our ancestors, who required":** Livy 34.2, my translation, slightly abridged.

13 **"My heart turns to and fro":** Quoted in Margaret Busby, ed., *Daughters of Africa: An International Anthology of Words and Writings by Women of African Descent* (Ballantine, 1992), 13.

13 **seven generations of women:** J. Haynes and M. Santini-Ritt, "Women in Ancient Nubia," in *Ancient Nubia: African Kingdoms on the Nile*, edited by M. Fisher, P. Lacovara, S. Ikram, and S. D'Auria (American University in Cairo Press, 2012), 172.

13 **In Macedonia, young women:** Indispensable is S. Pomeroy, *Women in Hellenistic Egypt: From Alexander to Cleopatra* (Wayne State University Press, 1990), 9–12.

13 **In Greek-speaking Egypt:** Pomeroy 1990, 14–23, 152–72, 168–69. Queen Arsinoe, wife of Ptolemy II, owned the shipping line; Berenice, wife of Ptolemy III, the horses.

15 **"For Hercules's sake"**: Juvenal, *Satires* 6, lines 450–51, in *Juvenal and Persius*, edited by S. Braund (Loeb, 2004), my translation.

15 **"good *female* scholars"**: Juvenal, *Satires* 6, lines 451–52, 445, my translation.

15 **Maesia**: A. Marshall, "Roman Ladies on Trial: The Case of Maesia of Sentinum," *Phoenix* 44 (1990): 46–59; A. Marshall, "Ladies at Law: The Role of Women in the Roman Civil Courts," in *Studies in Latin Literature and Roman History*, edited by C. Deroux (Latomus, 1989), 35–54.

15 **"the great concourse of people"**: V 8.3.1, translated by Shackleton Bailey.

15 **"a woman could possess"**: V 8.3.1, my translation.

16 **"Will I never be allowed to speak?"**: *Iurisperta*, or *The Lady Lawyer*, fragment 1 in *Fabula togata: Titinio e Atta* by T. Guardí (Editoriale Jaca, 1984), 50, my translation.

Chapter Two: Clodia's Roots

17 **"How tender her look"**: From Nossis 6.353, in *The Greek Anthology, Volume I: Books 1–6*, edited by W. Paton (Loeb, 1916), 486–87, lines 2–3, my translation.

17 **well-heeled families**: J. Tatum, *The Patrician Tribune: Publius Clodius Pulcher* (University of North Carolina Press, 1999), 161–62.

17 **A single square meter**: Adduced in A. Carandini, "Domus e insulae sulla pendice settentrionale del Palatino," *Bullettino della Commissione Archeologica Comunale di Roma* 91 (1986): 263–78, at 264 n. 24.

18 **Rosters of specialized laborers**: K. Bradley, *Slavery and Society at Rome* (Cambridge University Press, 1994), 57–84, with the Palatine Hill household at 62–63.

18 **the murder of Livius Drusus**: Appian *C* 1.34–37.

18 **"Whatever I do"**: Velleius Paterculus 2.14 in *Compendium of Roman History. Res Gestae Divi Augusti*, translated by F. Shipley (Loeb, 1924).

19 **bill to extend Roman citizenship**: L. R. Taylor, *The Voting Districts of the Roman Republic* (American Academy in Rome, 1960), 101–2.

19 **A shoemaker's knife**: Appian *C* 1.36.

20 **The epicenter of the uprising**: Appian *C* 1.39; Velleius Paterculus 2.15.

20 **An estimated 300,000**: Velleius Paterculus 2.15.

20 **In 88 B.C. . . . a truce**: Taylor 1960, 101–7, 118–31.

20 **resembled a tree**: Pliny *Natural History* 35.2–6, in *Natural History, Volume IX*. Essential is H. Flower, *Ancestor Masks and Aristocratic Power in Roman Culture* (Clarendon Press, 1996), 211–12.

20 **Attius Clausus**: Livy 2.16. Nicely summarizing the history is Hölkeskamp 2010, 96–97, 116. T. Wiseman, in *Catullus and His World: A Reappraisal* (Cambridge University Press, 1985), 16–17, attempts one version of the family's tree; alternate possibilities can be found in Tatum 1999, 34–35, whose reconstruction of full siblings I have followed.

23 **a series of democratic changes:** H. Flower, *Roman Republics* (Princeton University Press, 2010).

23 **Pride, self-interest, and a delightful irreverence for authority:** Excellent is G. Fiske, "The Politics of the Patrician Claudii," *Harvard Studies in Classical Philology* 13 (1902): 1–59, at 51–54.

23 **Appius Claudius Caecus:** Roller 2018, 95–133. For Appius's words, *Fragmentary Republican Latin, Volume III: Oratory, Part 1,* edited and translated by G. Manuwald (Loeb, 2019), 1–11.

23 **"a corpse's smile":** Recounted in Martianus Capella, *De Nuptiis Philologiae et Murcurii (The Wedding of Philology to the Imagination)*, edited by J. Willis (Teubner, 1983), 3.261, with discussion of syllables at 264, my translations.

24 **new monument, the Aqua Appia:** S. Platner and T. Ashby, *A Topographical Dictionary of Ancient Rome* (Oxford University Press, 1929), 21.

25 **No second-rate Macedonian monarch:** For the speech, see *Fragmentary Republican Latin*, vol. III, 9. A second version appears in Appian's treatment of foreign wars at *Roman History, Volume I,* edited and translated by B. McGing (Loeb, 2019), 3.10.

26 **"Minds that once did stand":** Ennius, quoted in Cicero's *On Old Age*, in *On Old Age. On Friendship. On Divination*, translated by W. Falconer (Loeb, 1923), 24–25, translation adapted.

26 **vast new highway ... Via Appia:** G. Sartorio, "Origins and Historic Events," in *The Appian Way: From Its Foundation to the Middle Ages*, edited by I. Della Portella, G. Sartorio, and F. Ventre (J. Paul Getty Museum, 2004), 14–39.

27 **Roman law barred incumbents:** A. Yakobsen, *Elections and Electioneering in Rome* (Franz Steiner Verlag, 1999), 49; and R. Feig, *Roman Elections in the Age of Cicero* (Routledge, 2012).

27 **electoral college:** Essential, if technical, is Taylor 1960, 132–49. Connecting the road to the reforms is P. Davies, *Architecture and Politics in Republican Rome* (Cambridge University Press, 2017), 68.

29 **Voting blocs ... "tribes":** Taylor 1960, 3–9, 12, 14–15.

29 **vermiculated mosaic floor:** Lucilius, *Satires* 2.84–86, in *Remains of Old Latin, Volume III: Lucilius. The Twelve Tables*, edited by E. Warmington (Loeb, 1938), 28–29.

31 **"If a census director":** Livy 45.15, my translation.

Chapter Three: Clodia's Education

33 **"Into the deep wave":** Erinna, lines 1–3, translation by Page adapted incorporating Plant.

33 **"To be sold at public auction"!:** Cicero *Roscius* 126, my translation.

34 **"knew her letters":** The phrase is idiomatic in Latin; outstanding is E. Hemel-

rijk, *Matrona Docta: Educated Women in the Roman Elite from Cornelia to Julia Domna* (Routledge, 1999), 70–79.

34 **Musonius Rufus:** L. Caldwell, *Roman Girlhood and the Fashioning of Femininity* (Cambridge University Press, 2015), 19–27.

35 **"if we are finally to move beyond":** Text in C. Lutz, "Musonius Rufus: The Roman Socrates," *Yale Classical Studies* 10 (1947): 3–147, at 45.

35 **"never be intimidated":** In Lutz 1947, 43.

36 **"of literature and extensive learning":** Macrobius 2.5.2 in *Saturnalia, Volume I: Books 1–2*, translated by R. Kaster (Loeb, 2011).

36 **recitation from Homer's *Iliad*:** Hemelrijk 1999, 22.

36 **changing trends in women's education:** Hemelrijk 1999, 21, 70–79; Caldwell 2015, 15–45, 128. The story of the "mischievous boys" and the tally of private schools is at D. Metz, *Daily Life of the Ancient Romans* (Hackett, 2002), 5–9.

36 **a dead-end investment:** Caldwell 2015, 128.

36 **"musical voices", "higher vocal pitch":** Q 1.8.2, my translation. A welcome addition to the scholarship is T. Sapsford, *Performing the "Kinaidos": Unmanly Men in Ancient Mediterranean Cultures* (Oxford University Press, 2022).

37 **"If you're auditioning for musical theater":** Q 1.8.2, my translation.

37 **"When a young man should breathe":** Q 1.8.1, my translation.

37 **"dignity and charm":** Q 1.8.2.

37 **Women's experiences were not only omitted:** Cantarella 1987, 34–46. Excellent is C. Rosillo-López, *Political Conversations in Late Republican Rome* (Oxford University Press, 2022), 84–126.

37 **Homer's *Odyssey*:** Aptly observed by M. Beard, *Women and Power: A Manifesto* (Liveright, 2017), 3–6.

38 **"Go to your chamber":** Homer, *Odyssey* 1.357–59, translated by E. Wilson (W. W. Norton, 2017).

38 **"bitch's mind and thieving heart":** Hesiod, *Works and Days*, quoted in Cantarella 1987, 34.

38 **the "Tenth Muse":** A phrase wrongly attributed to Plato, as explained by A. Gosetti-Murrayjohn, "Sappho as the Tenth Muse in Hellenistic Epigram," *Arethusa* 39 (2006): 21–45, at 32.

38 **fifty-five Greek and Latin women authors:** Plant 2004, 1.

38 **the Praxilleion:** Plant 2004, 38.

39 **"Rest here, my murderous spear":** Anyte poem 1, in Plant 2004, 57.

39 **"No longer exulting in the swimming sea":** Anyte poem 12, in Plant 2004, 58.

39 **the popular game of Tortoise:** J. Snyder, *The Woman and the Lyre: Women Writers in Classical Greece and Rome* (Southern Illinois University Press, 1991), 94–95; Pomeroy 1995, 137–39.

39 **"When you were Tortoise":** Erinna lines 3–4, translated by Page.

40 **"towards dawn your / Mother":** Erinna lines 9–11, translated by Page.

40 **"the monster Mormo", "massive ears":** Erinna lines 12–13, translated by Plant.

40 **"We clung to our dolls":** Erinna lines 8–9, translated by Page.

40 **"Aphrodite filled your thoughts":** Erinna lines 17, translated by Plant.

41 **"a man of exceptional moral disposition":** Plutarch *Sulla* 6.7. The earlier synthesis is A. Keaveney, *Sulla: The Last Republican* (Croom Helm, 1982).

41 **a fixed number of cycles:** J.-R. Jannot, *Religion in Ancient Etruria*, translated by J. Whitehead (University of Wisconsin Press, 2005), 13–16.

41 **"whenever the circuit":** Plutarch *Sulla* 7.4, my translation.

41 **After losing his father:** S. Mueller, "The Disadvantages and Advantages of Being Fatherless: The Case of Sulla," in *Growing Up Fatherless in Antiquity*, edited by S. Hübner and D. Ratzan (Cambridge University Press, 2009), 195–216.

42 **invented his own origin story:** Mueller 2009, 197–201.

42 **"actors and buffoons":** Plutarch *Sulla* 2.2, translated by Perrin.

42 **"as her own son":** Plutarch *Sulla* 2.4, translated by Perrin.

42 **"Stingy Umbrians":** Catullus 39, lines 11–12, my translation.

43 **opposed an equitable distribution of the voters:** Details in Appian *C* 1.55–64, with Taylor 1960, 109, 118–31, 144; Keaveney 1982, 45–47; and Flower 2010, 91–93.

44 **Colline Gate:** Vivid on the battle is M. Duncan, *The Storm Before the Storm* (PublicAffairs, 2017), 225–45.

45 **"Rest is impossible":** Marius the Elder, from a fragment of Posidonius, quoted in M. Crawford, *The Roman Republic*, 2nd ed. (Harvard University Press, 1992), 147, translation slightly modified.

45 **eighty men were declared public outlaws:** Plutarch *Sulla* 31.3; Keaveney 1982, 148–68.

45 **banned from ever holding office:** A. Rosenblitt, "The Turning Tide: The Politics of the Year 79 B.C.E.," *Transactions of the American Philological Association* 144 (2014): 415–44.

45 **find his name "proscribed":** Plutarch *Sulla* 31.6.

45 **"were receiving correction":** Plutarch *Sulla* 30.3, translated by Warner.

45 **"the size of a man's house":** Plutarch *Sulla* 31.5, my translation.

45 **"ill-omened Romulus":** Rosenblitt 2014, 436, quoting from Sallust's *Histories*.

45 **"unrestrained atrocities":** F. Vervaet, "The *Lex Valeria* and Sulla's Empowerment as Dictator (82–79 B.C.E.)," *Cahiers du Centre Gustave Glotz* 15 (2004): 37–84, at 75.

46 **"No legislative question":** Appian *C* 1.59, translation adapted from White.

46 **His daughter, who purchased an elegant mansion:** Keaveney 1982, 148–49.

47 **Sulla spent the next months:** Keaveney 1982, 204–13.

47 **"disgraced his years":** Plutarch *Sulla* 2, translated by Perrin.

47 **six thousand sympathizers:** Flower 1996, 100.

Chapter Four: Clodia's Path

48 **"Love the brave":** Praxilla 749, in Snyder 1991, 55, translation adapted.

49 **imbalanced humors:** Caldwell 2015, 79–89. Foundational are R. Flemming, *Medicine and the Making of Roman Women* (Oxford University Press, 2000) and L. Dean-Jones, *Women's Bodies in Classical Greek Science* (Clarendon Press, 1994).

49 **dissection of human cadavers:** Flemming 2000, 95; Caldwell 2015, 82.

50 **Told to extract natural medicines:** H. King, *Hippocrates' Women: Reading the Female Body in Ancient* Greece (Routledge, 1998), 37.

50 **"feebleness of the mind", *imbecillitas*:** S. Dixon, "*Infirmitas sexus*: Womanly Weakness in Roman Law," *Tijdschrift voor Rechtsgeschiedenis* 52 (1984): 343–71.

50 **"double the health benefit":** Rufus, *Regimen for Young Girls*, text in Caldwell 2015, 90–91, my translation.

50 **"while there is a demonstrated value":** Rufus, *Regimen for Young Girls*, my translation.

51 **six celibate priestesses:** M. DiLuzio, *A Place at the Altar: Priestesses in Republican Rome* (Princeton University Press, 2016), 119–239; Gardner 1986, 5–25.

52 **Pomponia:** Cicero *A* 5.1.

52 **elephants:** Flower 1996, 138–39, 354–55.

53 **"[Be] a first-class warrior":** *Fragmentary Republican Latin*, vol. III, 33, my translation.

53 **wives as trifling "annoyances":** *Fragmentary Republican Latin*, vol. III, 75.

54 **Appius's funds were tight:** The assumption, however, is undermined by J. Tatum in "The Poverty of the Claudii Pulchri: Varro, *De Re Rustica* 3.16.1–2," *Classical Quarterly* 42 (1992): 190–200, whose analysis I have followed.

54 **payment plan for dowries:** J. Balsdon, *Roman Women: Their History and Habits* (Harper & Row, 1962), 187.

54 **wedding planning settled on June:** Balsdon 1962, 180–81; details about the bride and ceremony at 183.

54 **investment property on Palatine Hill:** Wiseman 1985, 25.

55 **Ancient marriage contracts:** R. Saller, *Patriarchy, Property and Death in the Roman Family* (Cambridge University Press, 1994), 204–24.

55 **These waxen masks:** Flower 1996, 91–127, 185–95.

55 ***vividus*:** Flower 1996, 34, quoting Martial.

56 **"to impose the customs of peace":** Virgil's quip at *Aeneid* 6.852, though slightly later, evokes the reigning sentiment.

56 **"still dripping with blood":** Orosius, *The Seven Books of History Against the Pagans* 5.23.18, translated by I. Raymond (Columbia University Press, 1936).

56 **Thracian warrior, Spartacus:** Narrative at B. Strauss, *The Spartacus War*

(Simon & Schuster, 2009); analysis at A. Schiavone, *Spartacus*, translated by J. Carden (Harvard University Press, 2013).

56   **the cause of death was disease:** Eutropius 6.2 in *Eutropius: Breviarium*, edited and translated by H. Bird (Liverpool University Press, 1993); and Orosius 5.23.19 in *Orosius: Seven Books of History Against the Pagans*, edited and translated by A. Fear (Liverpool University Press, 2010).

57   **"By sharing memories":** Polybius 6.54 in *The Histories, Volume III: Books 5–8*, edited by W. Paton, revised by F. Walbank and C. Habicht (Loeb, 2011), translation modified.

57   **"death-white bones":** Horace, *Satires* 1.8, lines 14–16, in *Satires. Epistles. The Art of Poetry*, edited by H. Rushton Fairclough (Loeb, 1926), my translation.

57   **Troupes of actors:** Flower 1996, 92.

58   **"expert storyteller", "author of compelling dramas":** Cicero *R* §64.

58   **The relief that Appius Junior:** Tatum 1992, 200.

58   **"What is the point of all these family trees":** Juvenal, *Satires* 8, lines 22–23, my translation.

58   **"What can such precious relics":** "In Praise of Piso," in Flower 1996, 296–97, lines 8–10, 12–13, my translation.

59   **eradication of infectious disease:** For the imagery, Cicero *V* 2.5.7. Good analysis also in B. Shaw, *Spartacus and the Slave Wars* (St. Martin's Press, 2001), 126–27.

59   **to sell at auction:** Bradley 1994, 31–56.

59   **an estimated 20,000 Carthaginians:** Statistics in Bradley 1994, 33.

59   **"cretaceous earth":** Pliny *Natural History*, 35.58, translated by Rackham.

60   **"Bluish welts":** Apuleius in *Metamorphoses, Volume II: Books 7–11*, edited by J. Hanson (Loeb 1989), my translation.

60   **"Capua to Rhegium":** Quoted and translated by Shaw 2001, 61.

61   **"kitchen knives and cooking skewers":** Plutarch, *Life of Crassus*, in Shaw 2001, 131–33.

61   **between two and four million people:** Numbers estimated in K. Harper and W. Scheidel, "Roman Slavery and the Idea of a 'Slave Society,'" in *What Is a Slave Society? The Practice of Slavery in Global Perspective*, edited by N. Lenski and C. Cameron with J. Fincher (Cambridge University Press, 2018), 86–105, at 97.

61   **the findings of dream interpreters:** Bradley 1994, 154, citing Artimedorus.

61   **"After being elected to a judgeship":** Quoted and translated in Shaw 2001, 61.

62   **return to his native land:** Views summarized at Schiavone 2013, 93.

63   **swift public execution:** Schiavone 2013, 48.

63   **every thirty-five yards:** Estimated in Shaw 2001, 144.

63   **Spartacus's body . . . never found:** Appian *C* 1.120.

Chapter Five: Clodia's Sisters

64 **"Our problems are more difficult"**: Euripides, *Andromache*, translated by M. Lefkowitz and M. Fant in *Women's Life in Greece and Rome*, 4th ed. (Bloomsbury, 2016), 17.

64 **anatomical votives:** Outstanding is J. Hughes, *Votive Body Parts in Ancient Greek and Roman Religion* (Cambridge University Press, 2017). Also insightful for Italy is E.-J. Graham, "The Making of Infants in Hellenistic and Early Roman Italy: A Votive Perspective," *World Archaeology* 45 (2013): 215–31.

64 **"dazzling foot on the worn sill"**: Catullus 68b, lines 71–72, translated by Lee.

65 **"known to have spoken twenty-two languages"**: Pliny *Natural History* 25.3, in *Natural History, Volume VII*.

66 **Three hundred warships:** Appian *M* 13.

66 **pouring molten gold:** The story, related by Appian *M*, analyzed in A. Mayor, *The Poison King* (Princeton University Press, 2010), 169–70. Also helpful is D. Roller, *Empire of the Black Sea* (Oxford University Press, 2020).

66 **80,000 Roman citizens ... slaughtered:** Mayor 2010, 19; Appian *M* 22.

66 **microdose of toxins; blood of Black Sea ducks:** Pliny *Natural History* 25.3, in *Natural History, Volume VII*.

66 **Lucius Licinius Lucullus:** A. Keaveney, *Lucullus* (Routledge, 1992), 72. The excellent contribution by A.-C. Harders, *Suavissima Soror: Untersuchungen zu den Bruder-Schwester-Beziehungen in der römischen Republik* (C. H. Beck, 2008), 219–28, recognizes the history of the wives.

66 **Praecia:** Keaveney 1992, 70–71.

66 **"associates and companions"**: Plutarch *Lucullus* 6.2.

67 **unusually high number of shipwrecks:** A. Wallace-Hadrill, *Rome's Cultural Revolution* (Cambridge University Press, 2008), 356–78.

68 **Lucullus's none-too-obedient lieutenant:** Outstanding is Tatum 1999, 45–52. Plutarch *Lucullus* has the material, as does D 36.17.

68 **diplomatic envoy to Armenia:** Tatum 1999, 44–48.

68 **"would obstruct the business", "transform every military march"**: Tacitus, *Annals* 3.33, in *Histories: Books 4–5. Annals: Books 1–3,* translated by C. Moore and J. Jackson (Loeb, 1931), my translation.

68 **"at beck and call"**: Tacitus, *Annals* 3.33.

69 **"from all sides like rain"**: Ennius, *Annals* 391, translated by O. Skutsch, in M. Leigh, "Primitivism and Power: The Beginnings of Latin Literature," in *Literature in the Roman World*, edited by O. Taplin (Oxford University Press, 2001), 11.

69 **"eminent men"**: Sallust, *War with Jugurtha* 4, translated by J. Rolfe in C. Kraus, "Forging a National Identity: Prose Literature down to the Time of Augustus," in Taplin 2001, 46.

69 **"to try their luck as sea merchants"**: A. Feltovich, "The Many Shapes of Sis-

terhood in Roman Comedy," in *Women in Roman Republican Drama*, edited by D. Dutsch, S. James, and D. Konstan (University of Wisconsin Press, 2015), 128–54, quoted at 131.

69 **"on the very day he was scheduled":** Cicero *F&F* 92, my translation; see also S. Treggiari, *Terentia, Tullia, and Publilia: The Women of Cicero's Family* (Routledge, 2007), 77.

69 **wives who visited the bankers:** Treggiari 2007, 112, 121–22.

70 **Latin translation by Accius:** *Remains of Old Latin, Volume II: Livius Andronicus. Naevius. Pacuvius. Accius*, translated by E. Warmington (Loeb, 1936), 542–43.

70 **fragments of Sophocles's original script:** L. Coo, "A Tale of Two Sisters: Studies in Sophocles' *Tereus*," *Transactions of the American Philological Association* 143 (2013): 349–84.

70 **"Nothing is what I've become":** Sophocles, *Fragments*, edited by H. Lloyd-Jones (Loeb, 1996), 292–95, my translation.

71 **Seated at her sister's loom:** Explained in A. Kiso, *The Lost Sophocles* (Vantage Press, 1984), 128–32.

71 **learns her sister's terrible fate:** Coo 2013, 361–63, 366.

71 **"Humanity belongs to a single":** Sophocles, *Fragments*, 298–99, my translation following Coo 2013, 376–81.

72 **like a demagogue, would then wield:** Excellent on the politics of public works construction is Davies 2017, 239.

72 **death of King Mithridates:** Appian *M* 113–17.

73 **informative hand-painted placards:** Appian *M* 117.

73 **rhinoceros, tigers, and serpents:** Rutledge 2012, 208–9.

74 **Apelles and Lysippus:** Rutledge 2012, 22–61.

74 **cherry tree, red-veined black marble:** Davies 2017, 227; Keaveney 1992, 144–45.

74 ***contaminatio*:** G. Traina, "Lycoris the Mime," in *Roman Women*, edited by A. Fraschetti, translated by L. Lappin (University of Chicago Press, 2001), 85.

75 **"Every day's a holiday":** Theocritus, *Idyll* 15, line 26, in *Theocritus, Moschus, Bion*, translated by N. Hopkinson (Loeb, 2015).

75 **"He loved Galatea":** Quoted in Cantarella 1987, 95.

75 **"temperate, impassioned":** Sallust, *The War with Catiline* 25, edited by J. Rolfe (Loeb, 1931), my translation.

75 **"verses, crack jokes":** Sallust, *The War with Catiline* 25, translation adapted.

75 **The poet Cinna ... the poet Calvus:** A. Hollis, *Fragments of Roman Poetry, c.60 BC–AD 20* (Oxford University Press, 2009).

76 **Cinna mocked the nine years:** Hollis 2009, 14.

76 **"as befitting recital by a monkey":** Hollis 2009, 50.

76 **"wrapping for mackerel":** Hollis 2009, 14.

76 **"first-hand insight":** *Fragmenta Historicorum Graecorum* (*Fragments of the Greek Historians*), edited by C. Müller, vol. 3 (Didot, 1949, available in a digital edition), 520, my translation. Other fragments at Plant 2004, 127–29.

77 **the widening gap in wealth ... portended a revolution:** Plutarch *Cicero* 10.

78 **"A Clean Slate":** Clear and straightforward on the events is S. Shapiro, *O Tempora, O Mores: Cicero's Catilinarian Orations* (University of Oklahoma Press, 2005), 174–89.

78 **Quintus Curius, "gifts of the mountains and the seas":** Sallust, *The War with Catiline* 23, my translation.

79 **"gloom", nightwatchmen:** Sallust, *The War with Catiline*, 30.

79 **December 3, 63 B.C.:** Shapiro 2005, 159–204.

80 **pursued the remaining outlaws:** Cicero *F&F* 1–2. Excellent here is C. Brennan, *The Praetorship in the Roman Republic*, vol. 2 (Oxford University Press, 2000), 581–83.

80 **Nepos, who had voted against Cicero's victory lap:** Cicero *F&F* 2.

80 **"People grew tired of hearing him":** Plutarch *Cicero* 24.1.

81 **Roman widow Julia:** Plutarch *Caesar* 5.1–4; Suetonius *Caesar* 6.1.

81 **lionize her as a stateswoman:** Caesar displayed Marius's masks, for which see Flower 1996, 124.

Chapter Six: Clodia's Fortunes

82 **"The moon has set":** Sappho fragment 168b, my translation.

82 **red flag ... atop the Janiculan Hill:** D 37.27–28. Terrific for a reconstruction of an election day is C. Nicolet in *The World of the Citizen in Republican Rome*, translated by P. Falla (University of California Press, 1980), 207–315.

82 **"to take the oath and participate":** The text is recorded on a public inscription from Málaga, Spain (Nicolet 1980, 276), translation slightly adapted.

83 **no organized party system:** H. Mouritsen, *Politics in the Roman Republic* (Cambridge University Press, 2017), 126–36; Tatum 1999, 1–31.

83 **a *petitio*, a "request":** EH 1.

84 **"companion of solitude", "submissiveness to injury":** Plutarch, *Life of Coriolanus* 15.4, in Plutarch *Sulla*.

84 **"Always be seen traveling in large groups":** EH 35.

84 **"Every day when you descend", "Consider what you're seeking":** EH 2, translation by Shackleton Bailey, slightly modified.

85 **"gossip that most poisons":** EH 17, my translation.

85 **"lover of all things new and novel":** D 36.14, my translation.

85 **name came to the public's attention:** Tatum 1999, 62–86.

85 **neighborhood associations:** Excellent are E. Hemelrijk, *Hidden Lives, Public Personae: Women and Civic Life in the Roman West* (Oxford University Press,

2015), 37–109; C. Shultz, *Women's Religious Activity in the Roman Republic* (University of North Carolina Press, 2006), 43–44; and DiLuzio 2016, 85–98.

86 **"hated the eyes of males":** DiLuzio 2016, 93, citing Ovid.

86 **"elsewhere" on the evening in question:** Tatum 1999, 81.

87 **"Among the many features":** Cicero *H* 1, my translation.

88 **the married priests of Jupiter:** DiLuzio 2016, 17–48, has the details.

89 **dormant for two decades:** Balsdon 1952, 180.

89 **"Foul a clear well":** From *The Eumenides* in *The Oresteia*, translated by R. Fagles (Penguin, 1984), 262.

89 **a bribery scandal:** E. Watts, *Mortal Republic* (Basic Books, 2018), 182.

90 **an inexcusable fifteen years:** Taylor 1960, 119–20; Davies 2017, 215–26.

90 **a new law that guaranteed voting rights:** Discussion in Watts 2018, 171.

91 **speech impediment:** EH 3.

91 ***perfectissimus . . . mediocris:*** C. Rosillo-López, "The Common (*Mediocris*) Orator of the Late Roman Republic: The Scribonii Curiones," in *Community and Communication: Oratory and Politics in Republican Rome,* edited by C. Steel and H. van der Blom (Oxford University Press, 2013), 287–98.

91 **"He seems to be speaking from the deck":** Cicero *Brutus* 216, my translation.

91 **"that he had aroused the audience's pity":** Cicero *O* 2.69, translation modified.

92 **"Always be counting":** EH 35, my translation.

92 **"Make a demographic canvass":** EH 30–31, translation slightly modified.

92 **"Commit the electoral map to memory":** EH 30–31, my translation.

92 **"merest whisper of a rumor":** Cicero *M* 35.

93 **"Their stupidity is often on full display":** Horace, *Satires* 1.6, lines 15–17, in *Satires. Epistles. The Art of Poetry,* edited by H. Fairclough (Loeb, 1926), my translation.

93 **the appallingly low rate of 2 percent:** R. MacMullen, "How Many Romans Voted?," *Athenaeum* 58 (1980): 454–57.

93 **"Nothing is more dispiriting":** Cicero *M* 35, my translation.

93 **"I can't stand the confident airs":** Cicero *A* 21, my translation.

93 **A bare-bones entry in an ancient Roman almanac:** In Livy, *Julius Obsequens: History of Rome, Volume XIV: Summaries. Fragments. Julius Obsequens,* translated by A. Schlesinger (Loeb, 1959), 303–5.

94 **"the other guy":** Cicero *A* 19, my translation.

94 **"people were thrown into the Tiber":** In Livy, *Julius Obsequens,* 303–5.

94 **benefits for veterans:** D 37.49. Helpful on the politics of the moment is F. Drogula's study of Pompey and Metellus's contemporary, *Cato the Younger: Life and Death at the End of the Roman Republic* (Oxford University Press, 2019), 102–56.

94 **"in spite of having had children with her":** D 37.49.

95 **barricaded Metellus inside:** D 37.50; Everitt 2003, 128–29.

95 **Clodia and Metellus's stormiest marital rows:** Cicero *A* 21.

95 **vetoed the idea:** D 37.51.

96 **letter of June 3, 60 B.C.:** Cicero *A* 21, sections 4–5, my translation.

97 **only an estimated 10 percent drafted a will:** E. Champlin, *Final Judgments: Duty and Emotion in Roman Wills, 200 B.C.–A.D. 250* (University of California Press, 1991), 42–43.

98 **Formal invitations were sent:** Champlin 1991, 76.

98 **freed slave . . . successful businessman:** Champlin 1991, 52.

98 **"Weasels", "chirping brood", "vultures":** Champlin 1991, 93–97, quoting Lucan and Seneca, respectively.

98 **That permissive arrangement ended:** Insightful are Treggiari 1991, 365–66; Gardner 1986, 171–74; and Hallett 1984, 93–97.

99 **"I wish to be immortal":** Champlin 1991, 168, quoting Phaenia Aromation.

99 **"No one should dare":** K. Harter-Uibopuu, "The Trust Fund of Phaenia Aromation (IG V,1 1208) and Imperial Gytheion," *Studia Humaniora Tartuenses* 5 (2004): 1–17, at 7, translation slightly adapted.

99 **"advantages . . . bestowed upon men":** Gardner 1986, 173–74, quoting Cicero.

100 **One strategy . . . reclaim it:** Gardner 1986, 173; Champlin 1991, 45.

Chapter Seven: Clodia's Second Start

103 **"On a windswept seaside cliff":** Funerary epitaph, translated by M. Lefkowitz and M. Fant in *Women's Life in Greece and Rome*, 4th ed. (Bloomsbury 2016), 235, translation slightly modified.

104 **Solonium:** F. Corelli, "Solonium," *Mélanges de l'École française de Rome: Antiquité* 2018 (130): 283–87.

104 **required to remarry after ten months:** Treggiari 1991, 493.

105 *vilica:* Sources include Columella, *On Agriculture, Volume I: Books 1–4*, translated by H. Ash (Loeb, 1941), 1.1; Columella, *On Agriculture, Volume III: Books 10–12*, translated by E. Forster and E. Heffner (Loeb, 1955), 12.7–10; and Cato, *On Agriculture*, translated by W. Hooper and H. Ash (Loeb, 1934), 1.143.

106 **aspiration to become a tribune:** Tatum 1999, 87–113.

107 **overhaul of the filibuster technique:** Tatum 1999, 125–33.

107 **the passage of land distribution:** Plutarch *Pompey* 48.4.

108 **"do-nothing Bibulus", "Caesar will do":** Suetonius, *Julius Caesar* 20.1–2, in *Lives of the Caesars*, vol. 1, translated by J. Rolfe (Loeb, 1914), my translations.

108 **"at the ninth hour":** Suetonius, *Julius Caesar* 20.5.

108 **embassy to Armenia:** M. Skinner, *Clodia Metelli* (Oxford University Press, 2011), 64–65; discussion at Tatum 1999, 169–70.

108 **Fulvia:** C. Schultz, *Fulvia: Playing for Power at the End of the Roman Republic* (Oxford University Press, 2021).

109 **"Neither weaving nor women's usual domestic chores":** Plutarch *Antony* 10.3, my translation.

109 **"sounded the charge":** Cicero *A* 30, following Wiseman 1985, 42.

109 **letter of April 19, 59 B.C.:** Cicero *A* 30, my translation.

110 **the epithet "cow-eyed":** D. Griffith, "The Eyes of Clodia Metelli," *Latomus* 55 (1996): 381–83. My thanks to M. J. Cuyler, whose correspondence helped me find the nuances here.

111 **Clodius . . . first legislative priority:** Tatum 1999, 118–48.

111 **last attempt to hold a census:** Watts 2018, 175.

112 **letter of April 26, 59 B.C.:** Cicero *A* 34, my translation.

113 **"Bibulus's action in":** Cicero *A* 35, translated by D. R. Shackleton Bailey, 175.

113 **a quarter of the correspondence:** The most relevant are at J. Hejduk, *Clodia* (University of Oklahoma Press, 2008), 31–62.

113 **Atticus:** A. Byrne, *Titus Pomponius Atticus: Chapters of a Biography* (Bryn Mawr University Press, 1920), 1–27.

115 **sweet-scented apples and myrtle berries:** Pliny *Natural History* 15.15, 15.36, in *Natural History, Volume IV*.

115 **Partisans styled themselves Clodiani:** Tatum 1999, 115–16.

115 **"anticipated each other's every move":** Bobbio 135–36.

115 **"With scarcely any noise":** Cicero *A* 41, translation modified from Shuckburgh.

116 **letter of late July 59 B.C.:** Cicero *A* 42, my translation.

117 **"There's going to be an eruption soon":** Cicero *A* 42.6, my translation.

117 **"a widespread contempt":** Cicero *A* 42.6, my translation.

117 **letter of August 59 B.C.:** Cicero *A* 43, my translation.

117 **"I've done my part", "captain of the ship of state":** Cicero *A* 36, translated by Shuckburgh.

118 **On December 10, the patrician-turned-plebeian:** Tatum 1999, 114.

118 **"three-headed monster":** C. Rosillo-López, *Public Opinion and Politics in the Late Roman Republic* (Cambridge University Press, 2017), 124–25, discussing the quotation from Varro.

119 **"divinely seductive perfume":** S. Butler, "Making Scents of Poetry," in *Smell and the Ancient Senses*, edited by M. Bradley (Routledge, 2015), 74–89, at 84.

119 **Ancients regarded the island's salt:** Pliny *Natural History* 33.41, in *Natural History, Volume IX*.

119 **appointed . . . Cato the Younger:** E. Hussein, *Revaluing Roman Cyprus* (Oxford University Press, 2021), 23–56.

119 **lifetime appointment, priest of Aphrodite:** Hussein 2021, 26.

120 **6,000 talents:** Suetonius, *Julius Caesar* 54.3.

120 **"sailors, as they approach their destination":** Eratosthenes, as preserved in Strabo 1.20, translated by Hamilton and Falconer.

Chapter Eight: Clodia's Romance

122 **"Journeys, my kinsman, are oft ill-timed":** From S 3.14, line 6.

122 **"For immediate availability":** E. D'Ambra, "Real Estate for Profit: Julia Felix's Property and the Forum Frieze," in *Women's Lives, Women's Voices: Roman Material Culture and Female Agency in the Bay of Naples*, edited by B. Longfellow and M. Swetnam-Burland (University of Texas Press, 2001), 85–105, translation at 88–89, slightly modified.

123 **Born in the 80s B.C.:** Wiseman 1985, 65; Cicero *R*, p. 144–46.

123 **Cleitarchus of Colophon:** Cicero *F&F* 86.

123 **trekked hundreds of miles:** Appian *M* 20.

123 **took up a post as adjutant:** Brennan 2000, 2.546–47.

124 **Rufus's father's investment portfolio:** Cicero *R* §72.

124 **filed a corruption lawsuit:** Wiseman 1985, 41–42.

124 **Rufus ... elected to his first public office:** Cicero *R* §5, p. 49.

125 **monthly rent, 10,000 sesterces:** Cicero *R* §§17–18.

125 **"Play as you please":** Catullus 61, lines 204–5, translated by Lee, 69.

125 **"Lesbia whom alone":** Catullus 58, lines 2–3, translated by Lee, 51.

125 **"no sooner ... / Do I look":** Catullus 51, lines 6–7, translated by Lee, 55.

125 **"at every street corner and back alley":** Catullus 58, line 4, translation from Hejduk 2008, 134.

126 **researchers at Oxford:** G. Hutchinson, "Booking Lovers: Desire and Design in Catullus," in *Catullus: Poems, Books, Readers*, edited by I. Du Quesnay and T. Woodman (Cambridge University Press, 2012), 48–78, at 56 n. 16.

126 **best-loved comedies:** Cantarella 1987, 94–97.

126 **beach town of Lanuvium:** C. Shultz, "Juno Sospita and Roman Insecurity in the Social War," in *Religion in Republican Italy*, edited by C. Schultz and P. Harvey (Cambridge University Press, 2006), 207–27.

127 **"a serpentine tongue":** Schultz 2006, 219–20, quoting Propertius.

127 **Sulpicia:** Pomeroy 1995, 173; Plant 2004, 106–11.

127 **coifs her hair:** S 3.8.

127 **"Let Love in a thousand ways devise":** S 3.12, lines 11–12, my translation.

127 **"Love, if you are just":** S 3.11, lines 13–14, my translation.

127 **"Our masks removed"; "May the joys that others lack":** S 3.13, lines 9–10, my translation.

128 **expressions of affection ... a disease:** R. Caston, "Love as Illness: Poets and Philosophers on Romantic Love," *Classical Journal* 101 (2006): 271–98. Important for reclaiming ancient women's romantic lives is A. Richlin, *Arguments with Silence: Writing the History of Roman Women* (University of Michigan Press, 2014), 123.

128 **"shamelessly deserted [their] wailing children":** Juvenal 6, lines 85–86, in *Juvenal and Persius,* translated by S. Braund (Loeb, 2004).

128 **"No one, / she knew":** Apollonius of Rhodes, *Jason and the Argonauts*, in *Argonautica*, edited by W. Race (Loeb, 2009), 3.451–58, my translation.

128 **To those who followed Stoic philosophy:** Caston 2006, 273–74.

128 **Even the Epicureans:** Caston 2006, 274. Helpful is M. Nussbaum, *The Therapy of Desire: Theory and Practice in Hellenistic Ethics* (Princeton University Press, 1994), 150–54.

128 **Politically, the spring of 58 B.C.:** Tatum 1999, 150–58.

129 **annual Great Goddess holiday:** M. Salzman, "Cicero, the *Megalenses,* and the Defense of Caelius," *American Journal of Philology* 103 (1982): 299–304.

130 **"thunderous" expressions of "maddened minds":** L 2, lines 618–23, translations adapted from Leonard.

130 **The goddess's most ardent followers:** Essential is J. Latham, "Roman Rhetoric, Metroac Representation: Texts, Artifacts, and the Cult of Magna Mater in Rome and Ostia," *Memoirs of the American Academy in Rome* 59/60 (2014–15): 51–80.

130 **"smoother than Aphrodite's own":** Martial 2.47 in *Epigrams, Volume I: Spectacles, Books 1–5,* edited by D. Shackleton Bailey (Loeb, 1993), translation adapted.

130 **third gender:** Latham 2014–15, 60–61.

131 **restricted women . . . from leaving the Italian peninsula:** A. Marshall, "Roman Woman and the Provinces," *Ancient Society* 6 (1975): 109–27.

131 **the Crater:** J. D'Arms, *Romans on the Bay of Naples* (Harvard University Press, 1970), vii, citing Strabo.

132 **swallowed entire towns:** Pliny *Natural History* 2.89, in *Natural History, Volume I.*

132 **the world of the first Greeks:** D'Arms 1970, 3–9.

133 **"to build," *aedificare*:** D'Arms 1970, 40.

133 **a "continuous city":** Strabo 5.4, my translation.

133 **Sulla's grandson had a house:** D'Arms 1970, 122.

134 **"There are so many people here":** Cicero *A* 5.2, my translation.

134 **"contentment of the soul and of the mind":** D'Arms 1970, 13, quoting Cicero.

134 **"As they do it in Baiae":** D'Arms 1970, 41–42, quoting Pliny the Younger.

135 **"working vacation":** *peregrinationis opera,* Cicero *A* 15.13, my translation.

135 **three now-fragmentary farces:** D'Arms 1970, 60.

137 **the journey took three days:** D'Arms 1970, 134.

Chapter Nine: Clodia's Cross-Examiner

138 **"Under every stone, my friend":** Praxilla fragment 750, in *Greek Lyric, Volume IV: Bacchylides, Corinna, and Others,* edited by D. Campbell (Loeb, 1992), 378–79, my translation.

138 **the family's "shared calamity":** Cicero *B* 3.3, my translation.

138   **real estate . . . Formiae and Frascati, and in Rome:** Treggiari 2007, 60.

138   **new community center:** Davies 2017, 223–24; Tatum 1999, 159–66.

139   **Terentia was summoned:** Cicero *F&F* 7.

139   **nearly 400,000 sesterces:** Treggiari 2007, 31–32.

140   **smitten by Clodia's intellect:** Treggiari 2007, 50, citing Plutarch.

140   **circumstances that led to the couple's divorce:** J.-M. Claassen, "Documents of a Crumbling Marriage: The Case of Cicero and Terentia," *Phoenix* (1996): 208–32.

140   **She was "ambitious":** Treggiari 2007, 38, quoting Plutarch.

140   **"My beloved, my heart's longing":** Cicero *F&F* 7.2, my translation, adapting Shackleton Bailey.

140   **loyal friends, rich friends:** Cicero *F&F* 8.5.

141   **"I'm to blame for everything":** Cicero *F&F* 9.1, my translation.

141   **"I'm ashamed":** Cicero *F&F* 9.2, my translation.

141   **"the most comprehensive and detailed accounts":** Cicero *F&F* 9.5.

141   **"I have thanked":** Cicero *F&F* 9.3, translation in Treggiari 2007, 31.

141   **verb that Cicero uses:** *defatigari*, Cicero *F&F* 8.1.

142   **"From every piece of correspondence":** Cicero *F&F* 8.1, my translation.

142   **his dream of retiring to the ranch:** Treggiari 2007, 33–34.

142   **"All our ranch needs":** Cicero *A* 24.5–6, my translation.

142   **before Cicero's ship docked:** Treggiari 2007, 71.

143   **In late September 57 B.C.:** Tatum 1999, 190.

144   **ability to retain strangers' names:** Plutarch *Cicero* 7.2.

144   **"cruel jokes", "propensity to attack":** Plutarch *Cicero* 27.1–4, translated by Warner.

144   **"aroused a good deal of ill-feeling":** Plutarch *Cicero* 6.5, translated by Warner.

144   **"Apollo clearly never meant for him to beget":** Plutarch *Cicero* 27.1–4, translated by Warner.

144   **Lawyers were assumed . . . "Law puts bread on the table":** Petronius, *Satyricon* 46, in *Satyricon. Apocolocyntosis*, translated by G. Schmeling (Loeb, 2020).

145   **"As soon as our prosecutor found":** Cicero *Roscius* 59, my translation.

146   **"Who could be so unprincipled":** Cicero *Roscius* 32, translated by Berry.

146   **"It's your responsibility":** Cicero *Roscius* 35, my translation.

146   **"Every hour":** Cicero *Roscius* 154, my translation.

146   **"I argued rather vehemently":** Cicero, *In Defense of Caecinia* 97, in *The Orations of Marcus Tullius Cicero*, translated by C. Yonge (H. G. Bohn, 1856).

146   **"model for others"; "When everyone else had given up":** Cicero *Roscius* 27, translation adapted from Berry.

146   **"a *femina* beyond compare":** Cicero *Roscius* 147, my translation.

146   **"Now everything you're hearing":** Cicero *M* 26, my translation.

146 **"twisted and perverted":** Cicero *M* 27, translated by Berry.

147 **"they still haven't managed to tell us":** Cicero *M* 27, my translation.

147 **"I think poets and writers invent stories":** Cicero *Roscius* 48, my translation.

148 **"an enemy of the gods":** Cicero *H* 3, my translation.

149 **"If money has truly so consumed":** Cicero *K* fragment 2, my translation.

149 **"These people have accused me":** Cicero *H* 34, my translation.

149 **incest:** Outstanding is S. Ager, "Familiarity Breeds: Incest and the Ptolemaic Dynasty," *Journal of Hellenic Studies* 125 (2005): 1–34; additional context at M. Skinner, "Clodia Metelli," *Transactions of the American Philological Association* 113 (1983): 273–87, at 276. For the source of Cicero's language in Rome's alleyways, see A. Richlin, *The Garden of Priapus: Sexuality and Aggression in Roman Humor*, rev. ed. (Oxford University Press, 1992), 96–104.

149 **Sycophantic court poets:** Ager 2005, 7, quoting Theocritus.

150 **3.5-million-sesterce mansion:** Cicero *F&F* 4.

150 **outraged Romans flooded the streets:** Tatum 1999, 192–93.

Chapter Ten: Clodia's Resolve

151 **"If the two compounds do not bind":** Maria the Alchemist 3.28.9, text in M. Berthelot, *Collection des Anciens Alchimistes Grecs* (Steinheil, 1888), 196–97, my translation.

151 **Evergreen holm oaks:** The species are known thanks to scientific efforts at Rome's botanical gardens, for which see F. Bruno, *Roma e il suo orto botanico*, 2nd ed. (Università La Sapienza, 2014).

151 **Word games and puzzles:** In *Athenaeus: The Deipnosophists, Volume IV, Books 8–10*, translated by C. Gulick (Loeb, 1930), 577–81.

151 **"Shall I say the sweat from the Bromiad spring?":** *Athenaeus*, 537.

152 **"to enjoy reciprocal affection":** Athenaeus, *The Learned Banqueters, Volume V: Books 10.420e–11*, edited by S. Olson (Loeb, 2009), 194–95, my translation.

152 **Plutarch tells the story:** Plutarch *Advice* 48.

152 **"to hold another person's money":** Wiseman 1985, 79–80.

153 **threatened to file a series of lawsuits:** Tatum 1999, 192–96.

153 **Clodius's long-standing political enemies:** Bobbio 85–89.

154 **bust of Venus:** Cicero *R* §52.

154 ***pigmentarius*, the cosmetics dealer:** Wonderful is K. Olson, "Cosmetics in Roman Antiquity: Substance, Remedy, Poison," *Classical World* 102 (2009): 291–310.

154 **"thousands of colors":** Olson 2009, 297, citing Ovid.

154 **Tears of Helen:** Olson 2009, 300.

154 **crocodile dung ... "odoriferous flowers":** Pliny *Natural History* 28.28, in *Natural History, Volume VIII*.

155 **Corsican honey or a generous smear of tallow:** Pliny *Natural History* 30.10, in *Natural History, Volume VIII.*

155 **Kings in Asia Minor:** Mayor 2010, 58.

155 **"if they recklessly hand over to anyone hemlock":** Olson 2009, 306, quoting Roman law.

155 **Scythian women . . . birds' nests:** Mayor 2010, 70, 101–2.

155 **tasteless, odorless *zamikh,* arsenic:** Mayor 2010, 71.

156 **Crateuas of Pergamon:** Mayor 2010, 101–2, 254.

156 **Pompey's enslaved Greek secretary:** Mayor 2010, 240, 357–59, 394.

156 **"No great accomplishment ever":** Pliny *Natural History* 35.77, in *Natural History, Volume IX,* my translation.

156 **garlic or anise or rhubarb:** Mayor 2010, 240.

157 **"islands in the open sea":** Strabo 17.1–5, translated by Jones. The "delta" was so called, Strabo explained, because it was shaped like the Greek letter, and the wealthy Ptolemaic city stood at "the vertex of a triangle formed by the streams that split in either direction."

158 **Its leader, Dio:** Strabo 17.1.11; Cicero, *Academics* 2.4, in *On the Nature of the Gods. Academics,* translated by H. Rackham (Loeb, 1933), 481; Cicero *R,* p. 152.

158 **the Academic school:** As characterized in Cicero, *Academics* 2.4, 477–83.

158 **mansion of a certain Coponius:** Cicero *R* §§51–55.

158 **Publius Asicius was arrested:** Plutarch *Pompey,* D, and Cicero *B* have the evidence for this brief window of time. See also Berry 2000, 124–25; Tatum 1999, 196–11; Wiseman 1985, 54–91; Cicero *R* §23 and p. 153.

159 **"If the king of Egypt comes requesting any aid":** D 39.15.2.

159 **withdrew their support for the exiled king:** Cicero *B* 6.

159 **Temple of the Nymphs:** A. Claridge, *Rome: An Oxford Archaeological Guide,* 2nd ed. (Oxford University Press, 2010), 246–47.

159 **won election on January 20:** Tatum 1999, 198.

159 **February 7, 56 B.C.:** Cicero *B* 7.

160 **"Who is starving the Roman people?":** Cicero *B* 7.2.

160 **By three o'clock:** Cicero *B* 7.3.

160 **"a rabble of the lewdest and most arrogant ruffians":** Plutarch *Pompey* 48.6–7.

160 **descending into civic madness:** D 39.15–19.

160 **"intertwined":** Plutarch *Advice* 20.

161 **a contested inheritance dispute:** Bradley 1994, 165–66.

161 ***crematio:*** K. Bradley, *Slaves and Masters in the Roman Empire* (Oxford University Press, 1987), 131–32, 165–67.

161 **manumitted status excluded them:** Bradley 1987, 81–112, with important additions by N. Lenski, "Ancient Slaveries and Modern Ideology," in Lenski and Cameron with Fincher 2018, 105–50.

161 **too "cerebral" an exercise:** Bradley 1994, 137.

161 **"after eight years":** Bradley 1994, 163.

162 **"to carry the lantern":** V 6.8.1.

162 **Publius Licinius . . . bathhouse:** Cicero *R* §§56–69.

162 **three litigators:** Cicero *R*, pp. 154–57.

163 **five counts of criminal behavior:** Cicero *R*, pp. 152–53; Berry 2000, 125.

163 **"after receiving the input of her brothers":** Cicero *R* §68.

Chapter Eleven: Clodia's Testimony

164 **"I saw a figure use great force":** Cleobulina, my translation.

164 **Gnaeus Domitius:** Brennan 2000, 422.

165 **seven broad categories:** Elucidated by D. Cloud, "The Constitution and Public Criminal Law," in *The Cambridge Ancient History, Volume IX: The Last Age of the Roman Republic, 146–43 B.C.*, edited by J. Crook, A. Lintott, and E. Rawson, 2nd ed. (Cambridge University Press, 1994), at 505–26; also helpful is A. Riggsby, *Crime and Community in Ciceronian Rome* (University of Texas Press, 1999), ix–xii, 150–71.

165 **sat fifty-one:** E. Badian and A. Lintott, "quaestiones," in *The Oxford Classical Dictionary*, 4th ed., ed. S. Hornblower and A. Spawforth (Oxford University Press, 2012).

166 **"necklaces and pearls":** Q 11.1.3, translation adapted.

166 **"knockoff Clytemnestra", "honorary member":** Q 8.6.52–53, my translation.

166 **"frequent metaphors, antique words":** Q 11.1.49, translation adapted.

166 **Lucidity:** Q 11.1.50–51.

167 **libraries across Europe . . . their own editions:** Cicero *R*, p. xvii.

167 **challenge even an educated copyist's ability:** *Cicero R*, pp. 14–15.

167 **abridged in my own translation:** Based on R. G. Austin's third edition of the Latin text, *Pro M. Caelio Oratio*, with introduction and commentary (Clarendon Press, 1960).

167 **"Gentlemen of the jury":** Cicero *R* §§1, 18, 28, 30–31, 33.

171 **"Woman!":** Cicero *R* §34.

173 **"Now, the prosecutors have alleged":** Cicero *R* §35.

173 **"What would her own brother say?":** Cicero *R* §36.

173 **"Why cause a courtroom fuss":** Cicero *R* §36.

174 **"Let me end this playacting":** Cicero *R* §38.

175 **"do everything . . . strong work ethic":** Cicero *R* §41.

175 **"Can you imagine a Roman boy":** Cicero *R* §42.

176 **"Besides, do you not detect":** Cicero *R* §§47, 49.

177 **"If you're not the woman we have been led to suppose":** Cicero *R* §§50, 55, 57, 59.

178 **"Why plan the ambush":** Cicero *R* §§62, 64, 65, 67, 70, 74–75, 80.

180 **Cleobulina:** Plant 2004, 29–32.

181 **"I saw one man weld bronze to a second":** Cleobulina, my translation.

181 **"for this . . . is the nature of a riddle":** Aristotle *Poetics*, 1458a, lines 26–27, in *Aristotle, Longinus, Demetrius: Poetics. Longinus: On the Sublime. Demetrius: On Style*, translated by S. Halliwell, W. Fyfe, D. Innes, and W. Roberts, and revised by D. Russell (Loeb, 1995).

181 **"I was hit by a donkey":** Cleobulina, my translation.

181 **Carelessness and snap judgment:** Proposed by Plant 2004, 31, and Cleobulina 164.

181 **"in writing, just as in the visual arts":** *Die Fragmente der Vorsokratiker (Fragments of the Pre-Socratic Philosophers)*, edited by H. Diels, revised by W. Kranz, 6th ed. (Weidmann, 1952), 580–87, at 584, my translation.

182 *illusio:* Q 8.6.54.

182 **a charge of adultery against his wife:** Grubbs 2002, 187, and Treggiari 1991, 441–46.

183 **series of misogynistic laws:** Treggiari 1991, 60–80; Grubbs 2002, 83–87; and L. McClure, *Women in Classical Antiquity* (Wiley, 2020), 176–77.

183 **one-tenth of her deceased husband's estate:** Gardner 1986, 178–79.

183 **stigmatized by the law as "weak" and "infirm":** Grubbs 2002, 51–55.

183 **wives must obey their husbands' authority:** D. Boin, *A Social and Cultural History of Late Antiquity* (Wiley, 2017), 205.

184 **monopolize leadership throughout the early church:** Nicely countered by K. Cooper, *Band of Angels: The Forgotten World of Early Christian Women* (Overlook Press, 2013).

184 **"promiscuous noblewoman":** Everett 2003, 102, 119.

184 **an outspoken woman . . . sexualized one:** S. Dixon, *Reading Roman Women: Sources, Genres and Real Life* (Duckworth, 2001), 143–44.

Chapter Twelve: Clodia's Verdict

185 **"What once we loved is already ashes":** Erinna line 7, my translation adapting Plant 2004, 50.

185 **his daughter's second engagement:** Treggiari 2007, 76.

185 **pried the records . . . off the wall:** Tatum 1999, 220.

186 **hostilities simmered:** Bobbio 171.

186 **rivaled a small Roman hill:** As observed by Davies 2017, 233.

186 **On September 28, 55 B.C.:** M. Erasmo, "The Theater of Pompey: Staging the Self Through Roman Architecture," *Memoirs of the American Academy in Rome* 65 (2020): 43–69; Davies 2017, 233–45.

186 **For two of the inaugural season's debuts:** Erasmo 2020, 45–49.

187   **85 million sesterces:** Plutarch *Pompey* 45.3.

187   **The actor Aesop:** Erasmo 2020, 44.

187   **The actress Gaia Copiola:** Pliny 7.49.

187   **Balsam trees from Judaea:** A. Kuttner, "Culture and History at Pompey's Museum," *Transactions of the American Philological Association* 129 (1999): 343–73.

187   **Pontus, Armenia, Cappadocia:** Plutarch *Pompey* 45.2.

187   **row upon row of women writers and poets:** Kuttner 1999, 346–48.

188   **"the god-voiced women", "female Homer":** Kuttner 1999, 349, quoting Antipater of Thessaloniki.

188   **Gabinius, a puppet of Pompey's:** E. Sanford, "The Career of Aulus Gabinius," *Transactions and Proceedings of the American Philological Association* 70 (1939): 64–92, has the evidence, drawn from D and Plutarch *Pompey*.

188   **letter from Pompey, hand-delivered:** Sanford 1939, 84–85.

188   **Gabinius's aide-de-camp:** Sanford 1939, 86–87.

189   **With the help of Jewish guards:** R. Williams, "Gabinius' Defense of His Restoration of Ptolemy Auletes," *Classical Journal* 81 (1985): 25–38, discussing Josephus.

190   **Ptolemy's . . . last will and testament:** As the king's obituary, M. Siani-Davis, "Ptolemy XII Auletes and the Romans," *Historia* 46 (1994): 306–40, is unparalleled.

191   **Statistically, men and women who reached their fifties:** M. Beard, *SPQR: A History of Ancient Rome* (Liveright, 2015), 316.

191   **powerless to break the contract:** Skinner 2011, 89–90.

191   **elections for consul in 54 B.C. were postponed:** Tatum 1999, 233.

191   **"Murders occurred practically every day":** D 40.48.1.

191   *appietas:* Cicero *F&F* 71.

192   **Asconius:** A. Marshall, *A Historical Commentary on Asconius* (University of Missouri Press, 1985), 26–27, 37–45, 53–54, 60–62.

192   **rote memorization of the gender and cases:** Gellius 4.1 in *Attic Nights, Volume I: Books 1–5* and *Volume II: Books 6–13*, translated by J. Rolfe (Loeb, 1927).

193   **"I inquired at Rome":** Gellius 6.17 in *Attic Nights, Volume I.*

193   **"ferret out everything . . . encumbrances to learning":** Q 1.8.18–19.

194   **Four centuries after Asconius:** Marshall 1985, 37–40.

194   **"voted in no more than . . . freeborn citizens alone":** Asconius 52, my translation.

195   **In 1814:** G. La Bua, *Cicero and Roman Education: The Reception of the Speeches and Ancient Scholarship* (Cambridge University Press, 2019), 78–85.

195   **"how much Cicero hated Clodius":** Bobbio 169.

195   **"Clodius proposed a law":** Bobbio 173; see Tatum 1999, 236–37.

196   **"The Case Against Cicero":** My title and translation of the text. Useful also

is F. Santangelo, "Authoritative Forgeries: Late Republican History Re-Told in Pseudo-Sallust," *Histos* 6 (2012): 27–51.

196   **"a self-appointed resident":** *Case* 3, my translation.

196   **"Rome might have been":** *Case* 1, my translation.

197   **"ignoble men . . . political scene":** *Case* 1, my translation.

197   **"unreliable, deferential to his enemies":** *Case* 5, translated by Novokhatko.

197   **"The man's tongue trafficked":** *Case* 5, my translation.

197   **"Of your personal grudges":** *Case* 6, my translation.

198   **In 53 B.C., for the second time:** Tatum 1999, 222.

198   **tragic events of January 18, 52 B.C.:** Following Tatum 1999, 239 n. 136.

198   **"It was around four o'clock":** Asconius 31–33, my translation.

199   **"The Roman people had derived":** Bobbio 111–12, my translation, with elaboration by G. Sami, "Power and Ritual: The Crowd at Clodius's Funeral," *Historia* 46 (1997): 80–102.

199   **an emergency meeting:** D 40.49.5.

200   **"collapsed on themselves":** Asconius 33, my translation.

200   **"still smoldering":** D 40.49.3.

Author's Note

201   **"I am confident someone":** Sappho fragment 147, my translation.

WORKS CITED AND FURTHER READING

Bauman, R. 1992. *Women and Politics in Ancient Rome*. Routledge.

Beard, M. 2017. *Women & Power: A Manifesto*. Liveright.

Boatwright, M. 2021. *Imperial Women of Rome: Power, Gender, Context*. Oxford University Press.

Caldwell, L. 2015. *Roman Girlhood and the Fashioning of Femininity*. Cambridge University Press.

Cantarella, E. 1987. *Pandora's Daughters: The Role and Status of Women in Greek and Roman Antiquity*. Translated by M. Fant. Johns Hopkins University Press.

D'Ambra, E. 2007. *Roman Women*. Cambridge University Press.

Davies, P. 2017. *Architecture and Politics in Republican Rome*. Cambridge University Press.

DiLuzio, M. 2016. *A Place at the Altar: Priestesses in Republican Rome*. Princeton University Press.

Dixon, S. 2001. *Reading Roman Women: Sources, Genres and Real Life*. Duckworth.

——. 1988. *The Roman Mother*. University of Oklahoma Press.

Duncan, M. 2017. *The Storm Before the Storm: The Beginning of the End of the Roman Republic*. PublicAffairs.

Fantham, E., H. Foley, N. Kampen, S. Pomeroy, and H. Shapiro (eds.). 1994. *Women in the Classical World: Image and Text*. Oxford University Press.

Flower, H. 2010. *Roman Republics*. Princeton University Press.

Fraschetti, A. 1999. *Roman Women*. Translated by L. Lappin. University of Chicago Press.

Gardner, J. 1986. *Women in Roman Law and Society*. Indiana University Press.

Gruen, E. 1995. *The Last Generation of the Roman Republic*. University of California Press.

Hallett, J. 1984. *Fathers and Daughters in Roman Society*. Princeton University Press.

Hejduk, J. 2008. *Clodia: A Sourcebook*. University of Oklahoma Press.

Hemelrijk, E. 2015. *Hidden Lives, Public Personae: Women and Civic Life in the Roman West*. Oxford University Press.

———. 1999. *Matrona Docta: Educated Women in the Roman Elite from Cornelia to Julia Domna*. Routledge.

Hölkeskamp, K.-J. 2010. *Reconstructing the Roman Republic: An Ancient Political Culture and Modern Research*. Translated by H. Heitmann-Gordon. Princeton University Press.

James, S., and S. Dillon (eds.). 2015. *A Companion to Women in the Ancient World*. Wiley.

Kampen, N. 1981. *Image and Status: Roman Working Women in Ostia*. Mann.

Kleiner, D., and S. Matheson (eds.). 1996. *I, Claudia: Women in Ancient Rome*. Yale University Press.

Liebs, D. 2012. *Summoned to the Roman Courts: Famous Trials from Antiquity*. Translated by R. Garber and C. Cuerten. University of California Press.

Longfellow, B., and M. Swetnam-Burland (eds.). 2021. *Women's Lives, Women's Voices: Roman Material Culture and Female Agency in the Bay of Naples*. University of Texas Press.

McClure, L. 2020. *Women in Classical Antiquity: From Birth to Death*. Wiley.

Morell, K. 2017. *Pompey, Cato, and the Governance of the Roman Empire*. Oxford University Press.

Morstein-Marx, R. 2021. *Julius Caesar and the Roman People*. Cambridge University Press.

Mouritsen, H. 2017. *Politics in the Roman Republic*. Cambridge University Press.

Olson, K. 2008. *Dress and the Roman Woman: Self-Presentation and Society*. Routledge.

Osgood, J. 2025. *Lawless Republic: The Rise of Cicero and the Decline of Rome*. Basic Books.

———. 2014. *Turia: A Roman Woman's Civil War*. Oxford University Press.

Plant, I. 2004. *Women Writers of Ancient Greece and Rome: An Anthology*. University of Oklahoma Press.

Pomeroy, S. 1995. *Goddesses, Whores, Wives, and Slaves: Women in Classical Antiquity*. Reissue. Schocken.

Rantala, J. (ed.). 2019. *Gender, Memory, and Identity in the Roman World*. Amsterdam University Press.

Richlin, A. 2014. *Arguments with Silence: Writing the History of Roman Women*. University of Michigan Press.

Riggsby, A. 1999. *Crime and Community in Ciceronian Rome*. University of Texas Press.

Rosillo-López, C. 2022. *Political Conversations in Late Republican Rome*. Oxford University Press.

———. 2017. *Public Opinion and Politics in the Late Roman Republic*. Cambridge University Press.

Rosillo-López, C., and S. Lacorte (eds.). 2024. *Cives Romanae: Roman Women as Citi-*

zens During the Republic. Prensas de la Universidad de Zaragoza y Editorial Universidad de Sevilla.

Schultz, C. 2006. *Women's Religious Activity in the Roman Republic*. University of North Carolina Press.

Skinner, M. 2012. *Clodia Metelli: The Tribune's Sister*. Oxford University Press.

Snyder, J. 1991. *The Woman and the Lyre: Women Writers in Classical Greece and Rome*. Southern Illinois University Press.

Southon, E. 2021. *A Fatal Thing Happened on the Way to the Forum: Murder in Ancient Rome*. Abrams.

Steel, C., and H. van der Blom (eds.). 2013. *Community and Communication: Oratory and Politics in Republican Rome*. Oxford.

Tatum, J. 1999. *The Patrician Tribune: Publius Clodius Pulcher*. University of North Carolina Press.

Treggiari, S. 2007. *Terentia, Tullia, and Publilia: The Women of Cicero's Family*. Routledge.

———. 1991. *Roman Marriage*. Clarendon Press.

Wallach Scott, J. 1988. *Gender and the Politics of History*. Columbia University Press.

Watts, E. 2018. *Mortal Republic*. Basic Books.

Wiseman, T. 1985. *Catullus and His World: A Reappraisal*. Cambridge University Press.

ILLUSTRATION CREDITS

INDEX

Page numbers in *italics* refer to illustrations.